China's Great Transformation

CHINA'S GREAT TRANSFORMATION

Selected Essays on Confucianism, Modernization, and Democracy

Ambrose Yeo-chi King

THE CHINESE UNIVERSITY PRESS

China's Great Transformation:
Selected Essays on Confucianism, Modernization, and Democracy
  By Ambrose Yeo-chi King

© The Chinese University of Hong Kong 2018

ISBN: 978-988-237-015-9

The Chinese University Press
The Chinese University of Hong Kong
Sha Tin, N.T., Hong Kong
Fax: +852 2603 7355
Email: cup@cuhk.edu.hk
Website: www.chineseupress.com

Printed in Hong Kong

Contents

Introduction

I took Ambrose King's "Chinese Society" course when I was a freshman at The Chinese University of Hong Kong in 1971. His course is so interesting and stimulating that it unlocked my intellectual curiosity, making me determined not only to major in sociology, but also to specialize in the fields of modernization and development when I took my PhD qualifying exams at UCLA in 1978.

Therefore, I felt deeply honored that Ambrose King asked me to write an introduction for the present volume. This is because King is not only my former teacher, but he also is an esteem sociologist, a cherished public intellectual, and a superb university administrator. King was one of the founding fathers of the sociology discipline in Hong Kong, a Fellow of Academia Sinica in Taiwan, and the Vice-Chancellor of The Chinese University of Hong Kong. Like many intellectuals of his generation, King is concerned about the new developments in Chinese nation as it sloughed off the old society and the subsequent course that Chinese culture might take.

Titled as *China's Great Transformation: Selected Essays on Confucianism, Modernization, and Democracy,* the present volume is a collection of King's twelve papers published between 1975 and 1997. These two decades are turning points for China as we observed the following dramatic historical trends: the shift from revolutionary Maoism to Four Modernizations in mainland China; the unexpected democratic transition in Taiwan; and the rise of four little dragons (Hong Kong, Taiwan, South Korea, and Singapore) in East Asia. Focusing on the cultural dimension, King's papers in this volume are aimed to understand, to interpret, or to explain all these new developments from a historical, comparative framework.

The twelve chapters in this volume centered on the following three themes: (1) Confucianism, (2) modernization, and (3) democracy.

There are four chapters on Confucianism. Chapter 1 articulates an innovative *"relational perspective"* to examine the organic linkages between the individual and society. King argues that Western literature has wrongly presented an "over-Confucianized view of Chinese society" because the individual's action is wrongly interpreted as the result of a complete internalization of Confucian norms and values.

King argues that complete Confucianization is impossible because there are inconsistent values and norms with the Confucian ethics. In addition, the very ambiguity or elasticity of the family group would give individual ample room for maneuver in constructing his social networks. The boundaries of both the family and other groups are thus very much dependent upon the decision of the individual. Thus, King argues for *"self-centered voluntarism"* in Confucian ethic, i.e., the individual's freedom of action in constructing a personal relational network.

Although an individual has considerable social and psychological space for constructing a personal network, the emphasis, however, is placed on the particular relations between oneself and other concrete individuals. Thus, *the individual interacts with others always on a particular relationship basis*. As a result, when the individual faces an amorphous entity called group (or society), he finds himself no longer structurally situated in a relation-based social web. In this group setting, the Confucian values and norms would seem to him not morally abiding and relevant. The Chinese common saying ("if one does not think of his own interest, neither heaven nor earth will save him"), by no means a socially embarrassing statement, only becomes thinkable and understandable in a relation-free context. Using a relational perspective, King is thus able to explain the puzzle why the Chinese individual often ceases to be a "social being" in the true Confucian sense in relation to the amorphous group (or society). According to King, this is because the Confucian paradigm has not provided a "viable linkage" between the individual and the group, and it only focuses on *particular relations between oneself and other concrete individuals*. For example, a Chinese is happy to donate a large sum of money to a charity organization because many of his friends and relatives are members and leaders in the charity organization, but he is not willing to donate a single penny to the same organization if he knows nobody there.

Chapter 2 follows up this line of argument by examining the concepts of face (*mian*) and shame (*chi*) in Chinese culture. Chapter 2 demonstrates that the concepts of face and shame have often been interpreted too rigidly by students of Chinese culture. The tendency has been to speak of Chinese culture one-dimensionally as a face-conscious one in purely the social sense and a shame-conscious one on the behavioral level.

King argues that Ruth Benedict's single dichotomy between the Chinese *face-shame* complex and the Western *sin-guilt*, one fails to do justice to the complexities of the Chinese understanding of the key terms utilized in posing such a dichotomy. King explains that face and shame are not merely external sanctions lacking potentiality of internalization: the long tradition of intrinsic Confucianism testifies not only to the possibility of their being internalized as individual moral guidelines but insists that internalization is a moral necessity. Thus, King concludes that examining face-shame in a purely *social* sense (a social face) in traditional Chinese society is incomplete. The concept of face-shame also involves a *moral* component (a moral face) which does not require the judgment of others to be lost (audience is not necessary) because it is internalized in the conscience or superego.

Chapter 3 further develops these ideas into the Confucian paradigm of man. The literature depicts Confucianism as a social force that tends to mold the Chinese into group-oriented, or more specifically, family-oriented and socially dependent beings. King, however, challenges this Western presentation of Confucianism because it grasps only a part of total complexity. Chapter 3 attempts to show that the Confucian paradigm of man has a built-in structural imperative to develop a person into a *relation-oriented individual* who is not only socially responsive and dependent but also capable of asserting a self-directed role in constructing a social world.

In Confucian paradigm of man, man is socially situated, defined, and shaped in a relational context. In brief, man is a relational being. King emphasizes that the individual is more than a role-player mechanically performing the role-related behavior prescribed by the social structure. The individual has an active self that is capable of shaping the role-relationship he enters.

The self-oriented precepts became vital for the individual when he was caught in a dilemma resulting from divided loyalties. Confucian scholar-bureaucrats were often under cross pressures coming from the family group (for which the ethical principles were particular) and from bureaucratic organizations (for which the ethical principles were universalistic), the resolution of such conflicting demands required active struggle and individual choice.

Western analysts tend to stress that Chinese people have a strong sense of belonging to a group. Compared with the individualistic culture of the West, this statement can hardly be debated. However, King insightfully points out that in comparison with the Japanese, the Chinese is less group-centered. For example, while in Japan, family ethics are always based on the collective group (i.e., member of a House or a Company), not on the relationship between individuals. In China, family ethics are always based on relationship between particular individuals (such as father and son, brothers and sisters, parents and child, husband and wife). King remarks that perhaps the source of difference between Chinese and Japanese culture is the consideration given within Confucianism to the individual.

The Confucian version of individualism has, however, a relational emphasis. Confucian "individualism" means the fullest development by the individual of his creative potentialities, not however for the sake of self-expression but because he can thus best fulfill that particular role which is his within his social nexus.

This is because the Chinese individual was also locked into a hierarchical and cohesive family structure. The structural restraints of the Chinese family have produced a tendency to subordinate the individual to the wishes of superiors as well as to those of the group (family). Since the early twentieth century, however, the Chinese family system has been eroded by urbanization and the increasing influence of Western individualistic values. As a result, individual's life space has been extended more and more from this primary group into secondary group. The Chinese individual is no longer tightly locked in a family structure, but finds himself in a quite a new social situation where the individual is given a much broader scope for self-expression.

King also observes that once outside the rigid role requirements of the immediate family structure, the individual self has considerable freedom in constructing the relational network. What cannot be overemphasized is that the boundary of the Chinese relational network is highly elastic in the sense that it can be expanded or contracted according to the decisions of the self. Family is in fact an elastic entity. It can mean only the members of a nuclear family, or it may also mean all members of a lineage or a clan. This ambiguity or elasticity of the family gives the individual ample room for maneuver in kin-relation network construction. It is this vortex of voluntary network building that the Chinese have demonstrated impressive and sophisticated skills, and Chinese culture has developed interpersonal relationships to the level of an exquisite and superb art.

King observes that this culture of network building has not only survived in socialist China but has become increasing rampant. Indeed, the phenomenon is so widespread that a new term, *guanxi xue* (relationology), has been coined for it. King further remarks that this phenomenon is no monopoly of the mainland Chinese, but is quite widespread in all Chinese communities in the world.

To a certain extent, Chapter 4 builds upon the discussion in the previous chapter to further develop the concept of *guanxi*. Chapter 4 begins with the premises that *guanxi* (personal relationship) is a key sociocultural concept to understand the Chinese social structure and has played a significant role in shaping the social behavior of the Chinese people.

Chinese *guanxi* building is based on shared "attributes" such as kinship, locality, surname, dialects, schooling, and so on, which are the building blocks the individual employs to establish "pluralistic" identifications with multiple individuals and groups. Indeed, network building is used (consciously or unconsciously) by Chinese adults as a cultural strategy to mobilize social resources for goal attainment in various spheres of social life. To a significant degree, the cultural dynamics of *guanxi* building is a source of vitality in Chinese society.

However, for a long time, *guanxi* has been perceived as undesirable or dysfunctional for Chinese modernization and development. *Guanxi*, for example, is deplored by Chinese modernists, Communists or not, who believe *guanxi* is a private and particularistic morality and what China needs is a universalistic morality. However, King points out that, with the Chinese cultural system, there are mechanisms to neutralize or to freeze the practice of *guanxi* (like the employment of an official in his native place was prohibited in the Qing dynasty) in order to carve out room for the universalistic rationality that is necessary for the management of economic and bureaucratic conduct in Imperial China.

King further observes there is no sign that *guanxi* building is disappearing in modernizing Chinese societies, like Taiwan and Hong Kong. In the modernizing societies where market rationality and law are becoming the predominant values, the scope of *guanxi* practices has been narrowed and circumscribed and its strategy subtly transformed.

What is interesting to note is that the devious practice of *guanxi* for personal or organizational purposes in Communist China has reached an unprecedented level. The widespread phenomenon of "going through the back door" (to get things done through *guanxi*) has indeed become a social epidemic in Communist China since 1978. King explains that a drastic change has occurred in socioeconomic life in post-Communist China. The market is being partially reinstituted and civil society is being revived. The often-criticized traditional behavioral norms are now officially sanctioned in privatized, interpersonal relations. During this rapid transition period, when the socialist universalistic values are cast into doubt, and the market is not yet fully operational, *guanxi* blossoms to play a new instrument which enables people to achieve what has usually denied them through normal channels. King concludes that the widely cursed phenomenon of "going through the back door" will not go away easily, not until the day when market rationality is fully operational, and law becomes the rules of everyday political life.

The chapters on Confucianism are followed by chapters on modernization and development in Great China (mainland China, Taiwan, and Hong Kong). Chapter 6 critically examines the concepts of modernization and modernity in its discussion of the construction of a modern Chinese civilization order.

King starts with the premise that any consideration of China's cultural modernity must begin with a rethinking of traditional Chinese civilization in its orientation and the problem it takes that it has to face in the modern age. King characterizes ancient China as a "*civilizational state*," with a peculiar cultural order and made up a world of its own. In the mid-nineteenth century, the Chinese civilizational order was faced with an unprecedented challenge from the West in the forms of imperialism and colonialism, and China responded with the modernization project, the renewal and further development of traditional Chinese civilization.

The first wave of China's modernization was the "*Yangwu Yundong*" (Westernization movement). The early reformers merely saw the material and technological sides of modern Western civilization, putting their efforts on mining and building ships and guns, but they at the same time advocated the preservation of traditional Chinese values. Their slogan is "Chinese studies as essence, Western learning for practical use." Since the New Culture Movements of 1919, however, the urge to develop a powerful and prosperous nation was so strong that even Chinese "essence" was abandoned. New applications and new essences were sought from the West in a modern Chinese civilization. Intentionally China did want to imitate Western modernization, but historically China's modernization did not and could not simply follow the Western route in the twentieth century.

King argues that as a latecomer, China's experience of modernization was radically from that of the West, with regard to the foundation on which the processes began, the agents of the processes, the strategies of development, different intensities of the pressure of time in the course of development, and the cultural conditions. Even within different Chinese societies, namely Taiwan, Hong Kong, and mainland China, their experiences of modernization were very different. The divergent experience of Chinese modernization would lead researchers calling for a rethinking of the problem of modernization and modernity. Thus, King raises the following intriguing questions: Did the modernization of China follow exactly the same route as that of the West? Is the modernity pursued by or appeared in China a replica of the West? More importantly, can China develop a form of modernity different from that of the West?

Drawing upon the Chinese experience of modernization, King questions the universality of Western modernity as a model. This is because the dominant theoretical view of the literature of modernization wrongly assumes that all societies travel along the same path in modernization, resulting that all modernized societies will become similar. Modernization researchers generally see modernity as the growth of reason, secularization and the development of instrumental rationality, and they define modernity in terms of changes in social processes, such as industrialization and urbanization. In the a-cultural theory of modernity, all culture must inevitably go through this social transformation and any culture will change along the way like the secularization of religions and erosion of the ultimate values by instrumental reason.

However, King remarks that the form of Western modernity takes is not necessarily universal in application. There is "universality" in modernity, but it does not follow that all forms of the modern cultural order are "homogeneous." For example, capitalism and individualism are inseparable in Western experience. But what one finds in East Asia is a "non-individualistic version of capitalist

modernity." In addition, King remarks that though China is condemned to modernize, her "modern turn" is as much "destined"
as is a matter of choice. The objective of China's modernization is
to construct a new civilizational order and it is not possible that
Western modernity has played no role there. Yet, Chinese modernization does not need to subscribe to the whole Western modernity
package. Instead, the Chinese should draw upon the cultural tradition of China, and self-consciously adjust and broaden their vision
of modernity. King concludes that building a new modern Chinese
civilizational order involves not only a process of deconstructing
the cultural tradition but also a process of reconstructing it. The
new Chinese civilization, after all, needs to be both "modern" and
"Chinese."

Chapter 10 further develops the above idea in studying
the modernization of Hong Kong. By the 1990s, Hong Kong has
become a modern city and a newly industrializing economy, yet Confucian familial values still played an important role in Hong Kong
society. For example, it was a common practice that Hong Kong
factory owners hired their children and relatives in their factory.

King argues that the Chinese in Hong Kong no longer live
uncritically under the traditional Confucian familistic persuasion,
though they remain modern Chinese in the sense that they still, ideologically and behaviorally, attach importance to some Confucian
values. But they do not necessarily deem such values intrinsically
good in the economic sphere of life. Instead, they have adopted a
rational, instrumental attitude toward familistic values (e.g., their
children and relatives are hired in the factory because they are seen
as cheap and trustworthy workers), thus turning them into a cultural resource to achieve other instrumental purpose like making

profit. Therefore, though a continuous process of cognitive selection, the Hong Kong Chinese have transformed Confucianism into a kind of *"rationalistic traditionalism."* This cultural transformation, King believes, is an important contributing factor in making Hong Kong one of the most successful newly industrializing societies.

Chapter 7 studies how Hong Kong political system has coped with the problem of stability and, especially, the way it has been coping with the crisis of political integration resulting from rapid industrialization in Hong Kong's march to modernization.

King argues that Hong Kong's political stability in the last hundred years could be accounted for primarily by the successful process of *"administrative absorption of politics."* It is a process through which the British governing elites co-opt or assimilate the non-British socioeconomic elites (mostly Hong Kong Chinese businessmen) into the political-administrative decision-making bodies, thus attaining elite integration on one hand, and a legitimacy of political authority on the other. However, once Hong Kong undergoes rapid industrialization, urbanization, and social mobilization whereby the apolitical strata are politicized, it is not elite integration but elite–mass integration which becomes necessary for a stable political system. Hong Kong in the 1960s and 1970s has undergone the process of social mobilization. King laments that Hong Kong in the 1970s is no longer just an economic city but also a political city, because more people, especially the young generation, demands ever-increasing participation in the political decision-making process. The basic problem of legitimacy in Hong Kong in the 1970s lies not in the lack of elite consensus, but in the elite–mass gap, as exemplified by the riots of 1966 and 1967.

The Hong Kong Government's response to the political crises was not more democracy, but the creation of the City District Officer (CDO) Scheme. Although the CDO Scheme is effective in bridging the information gap which result from misunderstanding of goals (or interests) between the rulers and the ruled, King argues that it is too much to expect it to reconcile the conflict arising from incompatibility of goals (or interests) between the governors and the governed. Therefore, it cannot be very useful as an administrative absorber of community politics as such; and this will become more evident when community life becomes progressively politicized in scale with rapid urbanization and the rising young generation entering the political strata. King remarks that how Hong Kong can maintain a viable political system poses a question of the first order to the students of the science of governing.

Aside from Hong Kong, Taiwan is another Chinese society which is undergoing the process of modernization. Chapter 8 focuses on the democratic transition of Taiwan because the relationship between modernization and democracy has long been one of the central interests for students of modernization and development.

King remarks that in the earlier phase of modernization, roughly up to the mid-1970s, the development-oriented, authoritarian power of the Guomindang (GMD) regime in Taiwan did not face any serious society-wide or structurally-based political protests and challenges. Its legitimacy was, in a large measure, justified by its capability in producing a very successful and equitable economy.

However, in the later phase the very success of economic development produced a number of structural forces, including especially a growing middle class, which began to affect Taiwan's liberalization and democratization. As a result of industrialization, a new political culture that is more congenial to democracy has been evolving since the 1970s. Thus, Taiwan seems to be the working example of the Lipset's democracy theory that economic progress should bring in its wake democratic inclinations and a healthy surge of pluralism, which in time will undercut the foundations of the authoritarian rule common in developing countries.

Nevertheless, King argues that Taiwan's transition to democracy would not be likely without the democratic engineering from above (particularly that of the charismatic leader of President Chiang Ching-kuo). In addition, Taiwan's half century–long history of holding elections at local and provincial levels had institutionalized the values and "rule of the game" of democratic participation and competition. King concludes that Taiwan democratization—which took place in a unique social-historical context—had no paradigm to follow. Taiwan was a heroic, non-paradigmatic search for democracy, and her case is not likely to be made a paradigm of democratic transition.

Chapter 9 studies the same topic (the democratic transition of Taiwan) but examining it from the angle of the transformation of state Confucianism and the restructuring of state–society relation in Taiwan. In other words, Chapter 9 aims to analyze the transformation of Taiwan's state system, which shows a marked discontinuity with the state Confucianism of Imperial China. The focus is on the state–society relationship and changes in it.

King points out that from the Han dynasty onwards, Confucianism became what can be called "*institutional Confucianism*" (IC) as the result of the mutual penetration of the cultural system and the political system.

IC refers to an institutional cultural complex. It refers to political institutions, including imperial authority as the keystone of the state system, the imposing bureaucracy as an instrument of the imperial state, the literati and gentry as a status group linking the state with society. All these institutions were intermingled with Confucian cultural values.

As the keystone of the state system, imperial authority was embodied in the concept of a cosmically based universal kingship. The legitimacy of the universal king was based on the "Mandate of Heaven." Under the vast heaven, the universal king had all-encompassing jurisdictional claims over the sociopolitical life of the people. Since imperial power was a religiously consecrated structure, it precluded the possibility of the development of a powerful priesthood or independent religious force. Since the universal king had all-encompassing jurisdictional claims, no independent or resisting forces were allowed to exist in Imperial China.

In addition, since state institutions (kingship and bureaucracy) were permeated by Confucian ethical values, to say the state has an all-encompassing jurisdictional claim on the sociopolitical life of the people is tantamount to saying that the state has a comprehensive responsibility to provide for, to enrich, and to educate the people. Whether from the viewpoint of power or duty, the state had an interventionist or transformative stance toward society. King labels this cultural ethos of the imperial state as "*state Confucianism*" to highlight its interventionist or transformative stance toward society.

Although the state in Imperial China has the right and the duty to intervene in the socioeconomic activities of society, in reality the generalized power of the state was rather limited. The state's penetration into society reached at most to the county level. Below that level, informal government, which is represented by traditional elite groups (such as the gentry) and a variety of social institutions (e.g., the clan), tended to dominate the local scene.

King points out that the modernization which has taken place in Taiwan in the 1950s led to the fundamental transformation of state Confucianism. A civil society has emerged owing to the development of a market economy and political pluralism. A new state–society relation has come into existence. In the process of transformation, the GMD state played a dominant and guiding role in developing strategies for the economy. The Taiwan state's people-oriented developmental and transformative strategies toward the economy and society were reminiscent of the Confucian tradition, but Confucianism was no longer the state ideology in modern Taiwan.

Thus, King acknowledges that "institutional Confucianism" as existed in Imperial China has been fundamentally restructured in Taiwan in the process of modernization. Institutional Confucianism has now become what may be called *"intellectual Confucianism,"* which means nothing more than a philosophical-cultural system (like liberalism, Hegelism, and so on). King points out the story of state Confucianism and its transformation is still an unfolding process. It is part of the great drama of China's search for political modernity.

The last chapter (Chapter 12) discusses all the three themes—Confucianism, modernity, and democracy—in this volume. It starts with a critical assessment of *"liberal democracy"* and asks the question: Is liberal democracy universalizable?

King argues that "liberal democracy" is paradoxical because the relationship between liberalism and democracy has been a deeply ambiguous one. Liberalism has provided not only the necessary foundation for, but also a significant constraint upon democracy in the modern world.

King said that there are actually two different types of democracy in history, namely, *Athenian democracy* and *liberal democracy*. While democracy first made its first appearance in the Athenian city-state, liberal democracy did not emerge in Europe until the seventeenth century. Athenian democracy, which manifested itself in the universal device of having the people manage their own affairs, was grounded in a sense of community. It was a form of collective existence—a community ruling itself. Athenian democracy's legacy to posterity is the concept of "rule by the people," which has indeed become the ground of legitimacy for any kind of government called a democracy. In contrast, liberal democracy was grounded on the individual and the existence of basic individual human rights superior to those of the state and community. Liberalism affirms the basic worth of individuals as the ultimate and irreducible unit of society. In other words, the individual is conceptually prior to the society. Individual rights are cherished and respected, but those rights are not defined in "social" or "communal" terms.

King argues that the liberal idea derived from the West is culturally and historically specific. And a democracy based upon such a culturally specific principle can hardly claim to be intrinsically universal in nature. Therefore, while non-Western societies have no difficulty in accepting democratic values, they are very uneasy with, if not downright hostile, to liberal values because liberalism breaks up the community, undermines the shared body of ideas and values, and places the isolated individual above the community.

Students of East Asia modernization believe that the economic success of East Asia is linked to its distinctive social and cultural feature, which include a very strong achievement-oriented work ethic, a highly developed sense of collective solidarity, and the enormous prestige of education. East Asian societies, following the success of economic development, have made a fundamental shift in their political orientation. Some of their authoritarian systems have undergone a basic transformation toward democracy.

King argues that although institutional Confucianism is long dead, Confucian ethics and values are still a living cultural force. For East Asia, if democracy is going to be fully developed, it has to come to terms with Confucianism.

Thus, King argues that East Asian democracy does not necessarily follow the Western model of liberal democracy. Indeed, East Asian countries are consciously or unconsciously searching for an alternative to Western liberal democracy. East Asian democracy may meet the "formal requisite of democracy" but differ significantly from the Western democratic systems. For example, an East Asian type of political system may offer democracy without turnover, and it may represent an adoption of Western practice to serve not Western values of competition and change, but Asian values of consensus, collective solidarity and stability.

The adherence to values of consensus and collective solidarity may strike the Western observer as very different from his accustomed democratic values and conduct. Could it be that East Asia has successfully generated a non-individualistic version of capitalist modernity or capitalist democracy? If so, the linkage between modern capitalism, democracy, and individualism have not been inevitable or intrinsic; rather, it would have to be interpreted as the outcome of contingent historical circumstances.

King concludes that Asian democracy, by which he means a "democratically Confucian" political system, is still in its early stages of developing and unfolding. But King predicts that if there is to be a viable alternative to liberal democracy provided by the non-Western world, it will take the form of "Asian democracy."

All in all, the twelve chapters in this volume are very well written. It is indeed a pleasure to go through the chapters because I find them interesting to read and full of insightful ideas. King is a sophisticated researcher. He always provides a comprehensive analysis and presents a balanced review of controversial issues. King obviously is a culturalist and a scholar in the modernization camp, but he at the same time voices many sharp criticisms on the modernization theory and offers a fresh reinterpretation of Confucian culture. For example, King questions the universalistic assumption of the modernization school and contends that it is wrong to assume all countries will move along the same path to adopt the Western model of modernization. Even though King is a culturalist and emphasizes the role of culture in societal transformation, he never takes culture for granted but examines it as a dynamic historical process always subject to change and embedded in political economy and social institutions (like institutional Confucianism).

As a result, King asks thoughtful research questions, offers original interpretation, and opens up new frontiers for researchers in the fields of Confucianism, modernization, and democracy. For instance, King articulates an innovative *"relational perspective"* to understand Confucianism. The Chinese individual is not so fully oriented to group as the Japanese do. Instead, the Chinese individual is committed to group only when he develops a particular relationship with other individuals in that group. I think King is one of the first researchers to discuss the ambiguity and contradiction of liberal democracy. His formulation of "Asian democracy" (a political system with democratic institutions embedded in Confucian values) will open up new frontier in the study of democracy in the modern world.

Even though some of the chapters were written several decades ago, I find their analyses quite timely and highly relevant to understand the contemporary development of East Asia. I think King's selected essays included in this volume stand the test of time.

For example, Hong Kong recently is experiencing a political crisis, as a new generation youngsters protesting against Hong Kong and mainland government and advocating the separation between Hong Kong and mainland China after the Umbrella Revolution. Researchers wonder whether the recent political crisis in Hong Kong is similar to "the elite–mass gap" that King talks about in Chapter 7, and whether the Hong Kong officials would set up a new institution (like the City District Office Scheme) to bridge the gap between the Hong Kong government and the post-nineties young generation. Researchers also wonder whether the present political crisis can be resolved by strengthening the functions of political communication, political socialization, and political integration in Hong Kong society.

Another example: the chapters in this volume also helps us to understand why the Chinese is so good in cultivating *guanxi* in Chinese communities all over the world, and why *guanxi* became so widespread in China after 1978. King's observation that "the widely cursed phenomenon of 'going through the back door' will not go away so easily until market rationality and the rule of law is firmly established in the Chinese economy and society" remains as valid today as the chapter was written in the early 1990s.

In sum, I strongly and enthusiastically recommend this volume to those who are interested in studying Confucianism, modernization, and democracy in mainland China, Hong Kong and Taiwan. I am thankful to Ambrose King to have a chance to read the book manuscript before it appears in print.

Alvin Y. So

Chair Professor, Division of Social Science

The Hong Kong University of Science and Technology

October 2017

1 The Individual and Group in Confucianism: A Relational Perspective

Confucius developed a humanistic ethics in a man-centered world.[1] For a Confucian, the basic concern is the social life here and now. How to establish a secular harmonious world is the basic theoretical and practical question the Confucians have to address. Confucians focus on the organic relationship between the individual and society and consider the two inseparable and interdependent. As we shall see, the problem is that "society" is only vaguely defined, as is the idea of "group" if one is referring to a unit larger than the family.

Ren, "perfect virtue" (James Legge), or "benevolence" (D. C. Lau), is the highest attainment of moral cultivation.[2] In Confucian ethics, *ren* can only be achieved by the efforts of the individual self (*ji*). This means that Confucius regards the individual as an active self which is capable of reaching a state of moral autonomy and achieving sagehood. The cornerstone of Confucian ethics, *shu*, or "reciprocity," in the last analysis can only be accomplished or performed by the individual self.[3] According to Confucius, *shu* means that "what you do not want done to yourself, do not do to others." In fact, *shu*, or the emphatic capacity to take the role of others, is the architectonic concept in Confucian ethics.[4]

In this sense, Confucian ethics is heavily characterized by what may be called "self-centered voluntarism," which we will discuss later. Not surprisingly, Confucianism is distinctly concerned with the concept of self-cultivation.[5] Indeed, the moral autonomy of the self is unequivocally affirmed by Confucians. To be a gentleman (*junzi*), one must be able to assert oneself against all kinds of pressure, from both within and without.

Let us turn our attention to the relationship between the individual and the group. To start with, Confucians never see the individual man as an isolated entity; man is defined as a social being.[6] Indeed, as Hu Shi quite correctly states, "In the Confucians' human-centered philosophy, man cannot exist alone; all actions must be in a form of interaction between man and man."[7] Without doubt, "to be a man among men" is Confucius's fundamental aim. There can be no fulfillment for the individual in isolation from his fellow men. Men would be nothing if it could not be placed in the context of the social world. The fact is that "*ren* can only be cultivated and developed in inter-human relationships, i.e., in a social context."[8] From the Confucian viewpoint, the most fundamental relationships are the *wulun* (five social dyads, or five cardinal relations). These five relationships and their appropriate tenor are *qing* (affection) between parent and child; *yi* (righteousness) between ruler and subject; *bie* (distinction) between husband and wife; *xu* (order) between old and young; and *cheng* (sincerity) between friends.[9] The five cardinal relations have been considered the basic norms of Chinese social order. C. K. Yang writes:

> These five cardinal relations, centering upon kinship
> ties, formed the core of social and moral training for the

individual almost from the beginning of his consciousness of social existence until he became so conditioned to it that his standard of satisfaction and deprivation was based upon it.[10] The five cardinal relations thus comprise the "central value system," to use Bellah's concept, of Confucian society.[11]

Among the five cardinal relations, three belong to the kinship realm. The remaining two, though not family relationships, are conceived of in terms of the family. The relationship between the ruler and the ruled is conceived of in terms of father (*junfu*) and son (*zimin*), and the relationship between friend and friend is stated in terms of elder brother (*wuxiong*) and younger brother (*wudi*). True enough, the true cardinal kinship relations are only the major family relationships, and there are many more. In the *Erya*, the oldest dictionary of the Chinese language, there were more than one hundred specific terms for various family relationships.[12] Many non-family social relationships were patterned after the family system in terms of structure and values. For example, the relationship between teacher and student operated on a simulated father-and-son basis and thus formed a quasi-kinship bond. The Chinese family system as such was thus viewed as "the social system of China."[13] Talcott Parsons has termed China a "familistic" society, one in which the family, and the kinship system deriving from it, has an unusually strategic place in the society as a whole.[14]

In the Confucian family system, the father–son relationship is most important. The principle of *xiao* (filial piety) is at the very center of personal, family, and social existence.[15] While there are other cultural ideals in the Confucian teaching, "filialism was the source of the predominant identity of traditional China, a basic ideal against which any other form of self-image had to be judged."[16] It should be mentioned that in the Confucian value system, each individual role is not placed in an absolute hierarchical context. The five pairs in the five cardinal relations were originally symmetrical (i.e., equal) relationships. But in the influential *Xiaojing*, the *xiao* concept was pushed into the center of the Chinese ethical system. There was no recognition of the independent existence of the individual, the individual was submerged into the familistic ethics.[17] The symmetrical father–son relation thus became asymmetrical in nature.[18] Furthermore, this asymmetrical authority relationship, which became a socially accepted version of the Confucian family ethics, was given institutional support by the Chinese legal system. Throughout the dynasties, as is well documented and argued by Qu Tongzu, Chinese laws underwent a process of "Confucianization" where by the hierarchical harmony of the family was upheld as an unquestionable value.[19] John C. H. Wu writes:

> Traditionally, a Chinese seldom thought of himself as an isolated entity. He was his father's son, his son's father, his elder brother's junior . . . in other words, an integral member of his family. He was a concrete individual person who moved, lived, and had his being in the natural milieu of the family. . . . Each family had a head, to whom his wife, his children, his daughter-in-law, his grandchildren, and the domestics owed unquestioning obedience. I know of no other system of law that is so meticulous in enforcing the duties of filial piety.[20]

To be sure, the individual is not wholly absent in the Chinese family. This is true particularly in comparison with the role of individual in the Japanese family, where the individual was completely submerged by the family as a unit.[21] However, the emphasis on hierarchical harmony in the Chinese family inevitably tends to place structural constraints on the individual. Kenneth Abbott writes: "Individualism exists, but it is interiorized and cannot be socially expressed. . . . Self-cultivation differs from self-actualization in that the first is orderly and the second is spontaneous."[22]

In the family, the individual is hesitant to take a self-assertive stand for fear of being viewed as disruptive of harmony. Richard Wilson argues that the Chinese social system is distinctive in its singular focus on group loyalty and the intensity with which ideals of loyal behavior (such as sacrifice for the collective good) are held.[23] Regarding the status of the individual in the family, C. K. Yang's analysis finds that

> the Western concept of individualism . . . runs directly
> counter to the spirit of the traditional Chinese family and
> is incompatible with the traditional loyalty to it. . . . Self
> cultivation, the basic theme of Confucian ethics traditionally
> inculcated in the child's mind from an early age, did not
> seek a solution to social conflict in defining, limiting, and
> guaranteeing the rights and interests of the individual or in
> the balance of power and interests between individuals. It
> sought the solution from the self-sacrifice of the individual
> for the preservation of the group.[24]

Yang's analysis shows that individual autonomy was indeed emphasized in the Confucian conception of man. But the basic fact is that the individual had to be socially and structurally located in the family, which was the primary social reality for Chinese in traditional times. The family, not the individual, was continually stressed as a hierarchical whole. Liang Shuming's claim that "the greatest shortcoming of Chinese culture is that the individual can never be discovered" is therefore understandable.[25] Zhang Dongsun also views the individual in Chinese culture as a "dependent being."[26]

Indeed, it is no accident that Kang Youwei saw the "abolition" of the traditional family as a condition for proper performance of modern public duties,[27] and that Tan Sitong vehemently attacked the *gangchang* (moral laws) and made an uncompromising call to "burst out the net" of Confucian social bonds.[28] During the May Fourth Movement, a cultural attack was launched on filialism, resulting in a questioning of the Confucian family norms of obedience and authority, at least in the intellectual circles.

Elasticity of the Group

The strong group orientation of the Chinese is treated as an almost unequivocal fact by most, if not all, social scientists, particularly sociologists. The group, so the sociologists of Durkheimian persuasion would argue, has an autonomous life of its own, external to the individual. The Chinese family as the predominant social unit has a structural force which bends the individual to a role of dependency. This sociological fact can hardly be denied. There is a limit, however, to the function of social structure in shaping the individual's behavior. The structural conception of human society, though not wrong, is simply not sufficient. H. Blumer writes from a symbolic interaction viewpoint: "Social organization is a framework inside of which acting units develop their actions. Structural features, such as 'culture,' 'social system,' 'social stratification,' or 'social roles,' set conditions for their action but do not determine their action."[29]

A structural analysis of Chinese behavior (especially Chinese family behavior) will tend to produce an over-Confucianized view of Chinese society. By "over-Confucianized" we mean that the individual's action is consciously or unconsciously interpreted as the result of a complete internalization of Confucian norms and values. The fundamental weakness of the structural conception of Chinese society lies in its failure to recognize that the individuals who comprise the society have selves, which are particularly stressed, as shown above, in Confucian ethics.

The Confucian concept of *zhengming* (rectification of names), which means the correspondence of names and reality, aims at achieving social harmony through a well-defined role system. In the Confucian's ritualistic social relations, each person is assigned a proper place. A considerable amount of conduct can thus be explained by roles. But, as Dennis Wrong rightly argues, a human being is never merely a role-player,[30] and Chinese behavior cannot be understood through the sheer analysis of the Confucian values and norms. This is true not only because a complete Confucianization is impossible, but also because there are inconsistent values and norms within the Confucian ethics. Indeed, there are tensions and conflicts between Confucian cultural aspirations and structural norms. The conflict between loyalty and filial piety,[31] the conflict between universalistic virtue (*gong*) and familistic morality,[32] and the very basic tension between *ren* and *li* (propriety)[33] are cases in point. Most conspicuous is the conflict between the value of individual autonomy and the norm of familial obedience. All of these tensions and conflicts occur "when cultural values are internalized by those whose position in the social structure does not give them access to act in accord with the values they have been taught to prize."[34] These are examples of "sociological ambivalence" par excellence, to use Merton and Barber's terminology.[35] The concept of sociological ambivalence makes a significant contribution to the understanding of the dynamics of the structure of social roles.[36] It helps make more intelligible behavior that cannot simply be attributed to fixed Confucian roles and prescriptions. Ralph Turner's conception of role-making is another important corrective to the static and overly deterministic conception of roles.[37] Turner views the role relations as "fully interactive" rather than merely the extension of normative or cultural deterministic theory; actual role transactions are more or less the result of a stable working compromise between ideal prescription and a flexible role-making process—between the structural demands of others and the requirements of one's own purpose and sentiments.[38] In the analysis of Confucian role behavior, Turner's dynamic view of roles is essential, particularly because of the fact that Confucianism attaches a good deal of autonomy to the individual self. The Confucian *ji*, a dynamic entity, is capable of modifying and creating its role relations with others. This recognition of the voluntary nature of the self and the dynamic of role structure is particularly important when we begin to examine the relation between *ji* (self) and *qun* (group).

Confucians classify the human community into three categories: *ji*, the individual; *jia*, the family; and *qun*, the group.[39] For a Confucian, the emphasis is on the family, and for this reason Confucian ethics have developed an elaborate role system on the family level. Relatively speaking, the Confucian conception of *qun* is the least articulate. It should be pointed out that, conceptually, the family is also a group. For the purpose of analytical distinction, "family" might be termed "familial group," while the *qun* is a "non-familial group," or simply "group." Insofar as Confucian theory is concerned, there is no formal treatment of the concept of *qun*. *Qun* remains an elusive and shifting concept. Fei Xiaotong correctly argues that the boundary between *ji* and *qun* is relative and ambiguous; in the Chinese tradition, there is no group boundary as such—the outer limit of the group is the vague concept of *tianxia*.[40] Barbara Ward has also pointed out that one feature of Chinese social structuring is the relative lack of clear boundaries for defining an "in-group."[41] Even the term *jia*, which describes the basic social unit, is conceptually unclear. Sometimes it includes only members of a nuclear family, but it may also include all members of a lineage or a clan. Moreover, the common expression *zijiaren* ("our family people") can refer to any person one wants to include; the concept of *zijiaren* can be contracted or expanded depending upon the circumstances. It can theoretically be extended to an unlimited number of people and thereby becomes what is called *tianxia yijia* ("all the world belongs to one family").[42] The fact that "group" has no definable boundary has, I would argue, significant theoretical implications for the consideration of the issue of holism versus individualism. The very ambiguity or elasticity of the family group would give the individual ample room for maneuver in constructing his network of kinship relations. The boundaries of both the family and other groups are thus very much dependent upon the decision of the *ji* (self).

According to Benjamin Schwartz, there is a set of polarities in the Confucian social ethics. A central one is the polarity of self-cultivation (*xiushen*, or *xiuji*) and the ordering and harmonizing of the world (*zhiguo ping tianxia*).[43] The *Problematik* of Confucianism explored by Schwartz opens up new dimensions of Confucian social thought which await further articulation. It seems to me that Confucian social ethics has failed to provide a "viable linkage" between the individual and *qun,* the non-familistic group. The root of the Confucian *Problematik* lies in the fact that the boundary between the self and the group has not been conceptually articulated.

As has been noted above, Confucians place a high value on the adjusted equilibrium and social harmony. But a closer look makes it clear that the Confucian social order is constructed upon the concept of *lun,* which can be interpreted as a set of rules governing social relations and is primarily concerned with the problem of *bie,* or differentiation among role relations. A noted sociologist sees *lun* as *chaxu,* denoting a differentiated status order. The phrase *bu shi qi lun* means that every role relation is properly in order; more specifically, it means that the role relations are differentiated according to the degree of intimacy attaching to the individual concerned. *Lun* covers a wide range of social relations, in which the *ji,* or self, is at the center.[44] In other words, *renlun* is the sum total of a person's network of role relations, while *wulun* constitutes the basic principle of a person's network of primary role relations. What must be emphasized here is that while Confucian ethics teach how the individual should be related to other particular roles through the proper *lun,* the issue of how the individual should be related to the "group" is not closely examined. In other words, the individual's behavior is supposed to be *lun*-oriented; the *lun*-oriented role relations, however, are seen as personal, concrete, and particularistic in nature. It is here that the nature of the relationship between the individual and the group becomes difficult to characterize simply.

As mentioned earlier, since the boundary of the group very

much depends upon the individual, who is the architect in role-relation construction, all apparently group values and interests also center around the self. Fei Xiaotong calls this *ziwo zhuyi* (roughly translated as "egoism"). In his view, *ziwo zhuyi* was no monopoly of the school of Yang Zhu, who would not give up a hair from his shank even to gain the entire world. Confucianism also subscribed to this concept. However, Fei is fully aware of the difference between the Yang Zhu school and Confucianism; the former, according to him, neglected completely the relativity and elasticity of *ziwo zhuyi*, thus focusing solely on the self, while the latter was fully cognizant of the relativity of the *ziwo zhuyi* and could extend the self to family and country according to the needs of situation.[45] It is no accident that Confucianism, irrespective of its different strains, emphasizes the concept of *ke ji* (overcoming one's self). And *ke ji fu li* (to return to the observance of rites) through overcoming the self is considered to be the way to achieve *ren*.[46] This ethical principle obviously aims at making the individual self-sensitive to its moral relatedness to others. The significant point is that in Confucianism, though the concept of group is recognized, the individual tends only to identify his moral relation with particular individuals of the group, not with the group per se. *Lun* exists only in relation to individuals, not in relation to the group. This singular fact defies the simplistic application of the Western terms "individualism" and "holism" (or "collectivism") to the Chinese phenomenon.

Relational Orientation of the Individual

Among scholars who have interpreted the inner logic of the Chinese social system, Liang Shuming is one of the most perceptive. After painstaking efforts to compare the Chinese social system with others, Liang Shuming came to the conclusion that Chinese society is neither *geren benwei* (individual-based) nor *shehui benwei* (society-based), but *guanxi benwei* (relation-based). In a relation-based social system, the emphasis is placed on the relation between particular individuals: "The focus is not fixed on any particular individual, but on the particular nature of the relations between individuals who interact with each other. The focus is placed upon the relationship."[47] In other words, in the Confucian system, man is socially situated in a relational context—man is a "relational being." Pan Guangdan, a sociologist, has convincingly argued that the Chinese humanistic value system pays enormous attention to the "other man." Confucian thinking, he writes, is deeply concerned with one basic principle, which consists of two primary problems: the kind of differentiation to be made between individuals, and the kind of relations to be established between individuals. He said the totality of these two issues is the principle of *lun*.[48] The essence of *lun* lies in the differentiated relationship between particular individuals. We might thus say that the Chinese individual is a relational being who conceives of the "other man" in concrete and differentiated relational terms. With a relational orientation, the individual is certainly not an isolated entity; he must be a "social" being. However, his "social characteristics" can only be meaningfully expressed through differentiated relational terms. According to Confucians, there are many kinds of relations between individuals: "Some of them are preordained givens, while others are voluntarily constructed, the father–son and brother–brother relations belong to the former type, husband–wife and friend–friend relations belong to the latter type. Every kind of relation is *lun*."[49] Under various kinds of *lun*, each individual has differentiated, particularistic relations with other concrete individuals. Regardless of whether the *lun* is a preordained given or voluntarily constructed, each individual is expected to perform his particular role in the relational context. What should be stressed here is that in the relational context, the individual's relations with others are neither independent nor dependent but *interdependent*. Thus, the individual self is not totally submerged in the relationships. On the contrary, the individual has considerable social and psychological space for action. Indeed, apart from the preordained *lun*, for example, the father–son *lun*, in which individual behavior is more or less prescribed by the fixed status as well as fixed responsibilities, an individual has considerable freedom in deciding whether or not to enter into voluntarily constructed relationships with others at all, and the individual self is also capable of shaping, if not fixing, what kinds of relationships to have with others. In a word, the self is an active entity capable of defining the roles for himself and others and, moreover, of defining the boundaries of groups of which the self is at the center. It is clearly no accident that social phenomena such as *la guanxi* (to establish relationships with others) and *pan jiaoqing* (to relate oneself to others) are so prevalent in Chinese society.[50] These social phenomena attest to the individual's freedom of action in constructing a personal relational network.[51] At this juncture, it must be stressed again that in constructing a personal network, the emphasis is placed on the particular relations between oneself and other *concrete* individuals. The individual interacts with others always on a particularistic relational basis. In this kind of social communication, the Confucian norms of *shu*, or reciprocity, and the so-called *xie zhu zhi dao*, or the "principle of the measuring square" (a more elaborate version of *shu*)[52] have served as a principal ethical guide. The keyword to both *shu* and *ji ju zhi dao* is *tui* (to infer).[53] Indeed, the kernel of Confucian ethics is an ethics of *tui ji ji ren*, which means to infer another's wants and desires from one's own wants and desires. According to the Confucian mode of thinking, one can infer from the self to the family, from the family to the country, and from the country to *tianxia*. However, most of the Confucian values and norms are not universal and comprehensive in nature; even the most all-encompassing virtue, *ren*, can hardly be interpreted as an overall ethical commandment. Fei Xiaotong went so far as to argue that, because of the lack of a well-defined concept of group, Confucianism could not develop a comprehensive, universal system of morality.[54] Fei's argument is probably untenable, but we have to point out that the basic virtues—*xiao*, or filial piety; *ti*, or fraternal subordination of the younger brother; *zhong*, or loyalty; and *xin*, or sincerity—are all moral elements of private personal relationships. Reischauer's observations are pertinent here:

> The Chinese clearly recognized universal principles, but tempered them with strong particularistic considerations. The five basic Chinese relations were all specific ones and not applicable universally. . . . Among the virtues most emphasized were filial piety, loyalty, and love, or human-heartedness, but to the Chinese this love was not applied uniformly to strangers as well as relatives but was carefully graded according to the nature of the specific relationships. There was no thought of loving one's neighbor as oneself.[55]

The Confucian individual knows how he should deal with the other only after he knows what particular relations the other has with him. The uneasiness and discomfort of the Chinese with strangers are widely recognized.[56] This phenomenon can be attributed in part to the fact that "stranger" as a role category is too ambiguous to be located in any *lun* relations of Confucian ethics. It explains why the intermediary is so widely used by Chinese as a cultural mechanism in the social engineering of relation-building. Through the intermediary, the individual is able to associate strangers on relational terms. Indeed, it could be argued that Confucianism does not provide the individual with ethical guidance in dealing with "strangers" with whom one has no particular relations. As a result, the Chinese who appear to conform to the "cult of restraint," to borrow Lifton's concept,[57] might be just as aggressive as any non-Chinese in the world beyond the "concrete" family. Eberhard writes:

> As the Chinese must suppress all aggression within the family, the outer world is the field in which aggression finds its outlet. . . . Only with complete strangers, such as in encounters in a modern big city, or in a foreign country where one is sure that the contact is casual and not lasting, is the individual free and can discharge his aggression directly as the individual in Western society may feel free to do. What counts in such contacts is aggressive intelligence, making the most of every chance as often as one can without risking too much. The biographies of Chinese immigrants, especially Chinese businessmen in other societies testify to this.[58]

Indeed, in the outer world, when the individual faces an amorphous entity called group or society, he finds himself no longer structurally situated in a relation-based social web. In this setting, the Confucian value and norms would seem to him not morally abiding and relevant. The common saying *ren bu wei ji, tian zhu di mie* ("If one does not think of his own interest, neither heaven nor earth will save him"), by no means a socially embarrassing statement, only becomes thinkable and understandable in a relation-free social context. It is a recognizable social phenomenon that the Chinese individual often ceases to be a "social being" in the true Confucian sense in relation to either the stranger or the *qun* (group); that is to say, he often fails to take the stranger or the group as a serious relational object and is thus incapable of relating himself to the stranger or the group in interdependent terms. As a result, the individual might not feel that it is socially restrained or ethically illegitimate to see things from his own moral or strategic perspective. In this sense, Fei Xiaotong's characterization of *ziwo zhuyi*, or "egoism," may be justifiable. And it is no wonder that *ziwo zhuyi* becomes rampant when the individual's life moves further and further away from the family as industrialization and urbanization progress in modern China. Furthermore, the term individualism, not surprisingly, has been unfortunately defined in Chinese society as "individual firstism" or "undisciplined liberalism," meaning "placing personal honors, status and interests above other things."[59] The phenomenon of "individualism" has become so serious in Taiwan, a rapidly modernizing industrial society, that there was in 1981 an intellectual outcry to establish *di liu lun* (the sixth cardinal relation), namely *qunji lun* (the relationship between the individual and the group or the society), in addition to the traditional five cardinal relations.[60] The very idea of seeking to establish a new *lun* for the relationship between the individual and the group or the society testifies again to the fact that, due to the lack of a clearly defined concept of *qun*, the Confucian paradigm has not provided a "viable linkage" between the individual and the group. Thus, neither holism nor individualism could find a central place in the Confucian mode of thinking. However, for good or bad, the Confucian relational perspective did provide the Chinese with a way of creating a longstanding social system in which the individual, who is a relational being endowed with a self-centered autonomy, finds himself placed in a complicated and humanly rich relational web he could hardly afford to escape.

2 Shame as an Incomplete Conception of Chinese Culture: A Study of Face

co-authored with John T. Myers

Introduction

It is accepted as virtually axiomatic by Western and Eastern scholars alike that a key principle governing the conduct of Chinese social life is the concept of "face."[1] So pervasive has the influence of face been judged that a modern Communist Chinese writer, Yao Wenyuan accuses his countrymen of "face-ism."[2] Often allied to the discussion of face in that same scholarly literature is the corollary that its breach occasions personal and, when appropriate, collective reactions of shame (a social reality) rather than guilt (a personal feeling). Social scientists have found the widely assumed invariant relationship between face and shame a handy feature to exercise a penchant for labeling whole cultures in terms of some single characteristic. Thus, one frequently finds Chinese and other oriental cultures labeled as "shame cultures," e.g., the Japanese have been noted as the most outstanding example of this tendency.[3] That specific feature then is judged critical in differentiating oriental cultures from those of the West which are labeled "guilt cultures."[4]

In this chapter, we neither intend to challenge the

important role attributed to face as a key governing principle of Chinese social relations nor to re-analyze *in toto* crucial points of dissimilarity between oriental and Western cultures. Our fundamental aim, however, is to demonstrate that there are significant deficiencies in the widely accepted view that a face-conscious culture, such as the Chinese, automatically implies the dominance of shame as a means of social control. While the face-shame dyad may at first glance seem firmly rooted in the traditional Confucian emphasis on correct social relations, we intend to show that it is in reality an "under-Confucianized" view of Chinese culture. Unlike Eberhard, who endeavours to demonstrate that face-shame is the province of the Confucianized upper stratum and that "guilt" is an important component of the cultural tradition of the lower classes completely independent of face considerations,[5] we will attempt to show that the concept of face itself when operative in specific situations applies at least in theory to all Chinese and is in essence directly related to guilt as well as shame. In the final section of this chapter, we shall consider, albeit briefly, the role of face in contemporary mainland China.

Face

To the foreigner, the Chinese often appear as an exceedingly, if not an excessively, polite people whose social interaction is acutely tuned to the relative statuses and related attributes of the actors. Concern with the minutiae of interpersonal relations and aversion to situations that may produce open conflict are characteristics of Chinese social interaction that may be viewed positively as a sign of an underlying desire for harmony, or negatively as a sign of inscrutability or even deviousness. Invariably, scholars attempting to uncover the logic of Chinese interpersonal relationships have had to grapple with the concept of face and its behavioral implications.

Since the field in which the concept is initially confronted is the social arena, it is understandable that attempts to make sense of it have emphasized those attributes which become visible in such a context. In a basically synthetic definition ably representing accepted wisdom on the topic, the noted sinologist Fairbank avers that face (for the Chinese) has been a social matter by which personal dignity is derived from right conduct and the social approval it has acquired.[6] Loss of face comes from failure to observe the rules of conduct so that others see one at a disadvantage. Personal worth is not considered innate within each human soul, as in the West, but has to be acquired. Face is thus described in terms reminiscent of Durkheim's "social factors," involving not only the choreography of correct social interaction but also bestowing or withholding personal dignity according to its own dictates. If this is indeed the case, then there is no possibility for self-evaluation apart from face itself and the audience that it implies. We hope to show that this contention is of doubtful value.

To date, the most complete and insightful analytic treatment of face has been Hu's seminal study in 1946 in which she closely examines the Chinese terms rendered into English as face. Hu notes that there are two commonly used terms: the first, *mian* (面, often suffixed with *zi*) refers explicitly to possession of prestige deriving from visible "social" success and ostentation; the second, *lian* (臉) refers to the respect of the group for a man with a good "moral" reputation.[7] The attribution differences between the terms are quite significant; a person may possess one or the other, both, or none.

The presence of *mian* does not in itself entail the presence of *lian* or vice versa. *Mian* is predicated on the recognition of a tangible achievement in the sense of high status, political power, high scholarly accomplishment, etc. *Lian,* on the other hand, implies a judgement on the man himself and his sincerity in adhering to the rules of correct conduct. It is obvious, therefore, that one with high *mian* may not, or need not have *lian* and vice versa. The former implies a type of positional success, the latter personal moral character. At this point, it is already evident that Fairbank's definition above refers only to one form of face, namely the *mian* variety.

Although Hu's contention that the dual connotations of the English term "face" are translated into Chinese by two discrete lexemes may be applicable to the Mandarin speaking regions of North and Central China, it is not applicable in the Cantonese and Hokkien speaking regions of South China where the equivalent of *mian* is the only term utilized. One finds in the southern dialects *mian* inserted in situations where the Mandarin speakers would use *lian.*

(1)	要不要臉	*yao bu yao lian*	[Mandarin]
	要唔要面	*yiu mh yiu mihn*	[Cantonese]
(2)	沒有臉見人	*mei you lian jian ren*	[Mandarin]
	冇面見人	*mouh mihn gin yahn*	[Cantonese]
(3)	厚臉皮	*hou lian pi*	[Mandarin]
	厚面皮	*hauh mihn peih*	[Cantonese]
(4)	丟臉	*diu lian*	[Mandarin]
	唔要面	*mh yiu mihn*	[Cantonese]

Agassi and Jarvie, in their contention that *mian* is hardly used in Hong Kong and that *lian* is the only operative term, seem to have basically misstated the issue.[8] In fact, *mian* is used quite extensively to denote situations covered in Mandarin by *lian* as well. Linguists, e.g., Forrest, content that the southern dialects, especially Cantonese, represent a more ancient form of the Chinese language than contemporary Mandarin which is a relative newcomer.[9] It is reasonable to assume that the southern dialects' lack of *lian* indicates that the term is a comparatively more recent lexical development. A current Chinese dictionary lists *lian* as a "popular expression" for *mian*.[10] While the southern dialects, e.g., Cantonese, Hokkien, do not lexically differentiate the dual meaning of face, they nevertheless allow for those differences to be expressed and understood given the specific context of linguistic occurrence. Since the bulk of the field research carried out for this chapter was accomplished in a Cantonese speaking area, i.e., Hong Kong, we shall use only the term *mian* or its compound *mianzi* to refer to face. The two dimensions of *mian* may become clearer if we discuss them with reference to the actual interactive situations in which they occur, especially those involving losing face and gaining face, and the causes and domains of each.

The Social/Positional *Mian*

A key attribute of this form of *mian* is prestige, in itself a neutral term. It is well known that Chinese traditional society was a carefully graded social system with a clear line of demarcation between those who had started to ascend the ladder of success and those with barely a foot on the bottom rung.[11] Prestige was accorded in graded degrees to those situated on various rungs of the ladder. Recognition of this prestige was denoted by the term *mian* or *mianzi*. Thus, such expressions as "to have *mianzi*" and "to have glory on face (*mian*)" indicated that the individual referred to had achieved a position of honor in the society. While *mian* was an either-or quantity in the sense that some possessed it and others lacked it, it was also a scalar quantity for those who did possess it. Those firmly rooted on a higher rung of the ladder would have a greater portion than others on a lower rung. Since prestige and *mian* are difficult to quantify as such, the relative weight was measured in the carefully orchestrated measure of social deference correlated with differentials in social position. Thus, the common expression "I have not enough *mianzi* to accomplish the task" indicates that the speaker is both aware of his own possession of *mian* and also of the relative position that is his.

Mian as a scalar quantity was subject to both decrease and increase. In such a highly structured society, those who have begun the upward ascent were sensitive to the nuance of their relationship to those higher or lower on the social scale. Giving accord to the requirements of face was essential to maintaining one's status and prestige. To lose sight of one's *mian* through inattention to one's relative position in interacting with others was a precarious oversight. If a man of some prestige was requested by his social inferior to mediate for him with government officials or others higher up the social ladder, he would have first assessed his own relative position vis-à-vis the superior and the chances that he may be successful. If he agrees to mediate and is successful, he will have gained face with both parties. If he excuses himself out of recognition that he has "not enough face to do so," he will lose less face with the inferior than if he tried to mediate unsuccessfully. Argument and open contention especially with inferiors is to be avoided. A person who disregards this norm is said "to have no regard for face," either his own or others. Public arguments and disputes are considered the preserve of those who have no *mian* and therefore nothing to lose, and the person with *mian* will avoid situations where such contentions are likely to arise. The major exception to this rule is the older person who has acquired *mian* both in terms of his accomplishment and his seniority. He may state that "I am too old to worry about losing *mian*, and in reality he is given more leeway to disregard the prerequisites of face than the younger person. *Mian* in the social/positional sense, although earned through individual accomplishment, is by no means limited in its extension to the individual achiever. In traditional Chinese society, the family and even the village was a primary focus of identity for its members, the accomplishment of individual members reflected prestige on those wider units as well. This extension of *mian* is attested in such phrases as "try to win face for your father (or ancestors)" and "don't lose face for your village." In the last hundred years as the nation has become the primary source of identity supplanting the family and village, it is not surprising to hear such Chinese leaders as Chiang Kai-shek speak of the nation's loss of face or national shame. In this instance, the loss of face is predicated on the failure of other nations to recognize China's *mian*.

Mian in the social/positional, scalar sense is akin to a credit card in the West. With good *mian* just as with good credit one has extensive purchasing power, although with respect to *mian* the purchases are honor, influence, and deference rather than tangible commodities as such. Both have their limits. Overextension of credit in the West can result in reduction or loss of purchasing power in the same way as overestimation of one's *mian* in China can lead to decrease or total loss of prestige and influence.

Social/positional *mian* acts as a type of externalized sanction with positive and negative dimensions. Internalization of its tenets is not required; what is required is attention to the external details of social life. The details themselves have been spelled out in the Confucian code of correct social behavior which is classified under the rubric of *li* (禮) propriety. The early Confucianists have pushed *li* to such an extreme as to render it a detailed and rigid code concerning clothes, decorum, and numerous trivia of social interaction. Francis Hsu, in commenting on the *mian*-conscious individual, notes that he must be attentive to "the appropriate clothes for the appropriate occasion, the suitable manner for the suitable situation, the commonly recognized deference and subordination between superior and inferior, a mistake in any of these matters could threaten him with a loss of *mian*.[12] Such an attitude almost naturally leads to formalism and ritualism, a consequent referred to by Hu Shi as extrinsic Confucianism.[13] Fei Xiaotong has dubbed *mianzi* "superficial conformity," a *modus vivendi* which almost naturally leads to hypocrisy since external conformity is the only requirement.[14]

Moral *Mian*

The second meaning of *mian* is that of a moral attribute which corresponds to Hu's use of *lian*. Hu defines it as "the respect of the group for a man with a good moral reputation: the man who fulfills obligations regardless of the hardship involved, who under all circumstances shows himself a decent human being. It represents the confidence of society in the integrity of ego's moral character, the loss of which makes it impossible for him to function properly within the community . . . (it) is . . . an internalized sanction."[15]

Mian in the moral sense differs quite markedly from social/

positional *mian* on several important points. Unlike its social counterpart, it is obtainable by anyone in the society, thus it is at least
potentially universalistic in application. It is also not a scalar quantity since it hardly allows for measurable increase or decrease; it is a
fixed quantum, acquired or lost as a unit. Another major difference
is cited by Hu in the contention that moral face does not necessarily require the judgement of others to be lost. "There is no necessity
for ego to confront public opinion: even though there might be only
one person present or none at all, the consciousness of that failure
to live up to the dictates of moral *mian* will be on his mind. This
demonstrates the complete internalization of the social sanction."

This moral sense of *mian* is not a recent addition to Chinese
culture. Dr. Hu Shi argues that the social interpretation of *li*, which
we noted above, was related to social *mian* and has been labeled
by him as extrinsic Confucianism, was only one dimension of the
Confucianism tradition.[16] It should be recognized that the second
or moral dimension of *li* which Hu Shi labels "introspective Confucianism"[17] is equally, if not more, important to all great Confucianists such as Mencius and Xunzi. This dimension is directly
concerned with matters attendant on man's spirit, his virtues,
motives, and the process of self-evaluation. Dr. Schwartz has rightly
observed that the Confucian emphasis on the inner and outer
"realms" alike is an example of one of the major polarities of Confucian thought.[18] In the case of *li* and *mian*, their external or social
aspect refers to the outer realm, and their internal or moral aspect
refers to the inner realms. The implication should not be drawn,
however, that the authors deny the important social contribution
to the inner or moral realm, since the moral norms themselves
are those developed and promulgated by the society; the impor-

tant point of differentiation is that in one realm the norms referred to need not be internalized while in the other internalization is essential.

Two of the most widely read Confucian classics, *The Great Learning* and *The Doctrine of the Mean*, amply testify to the tradition of introspection. In these two classics, *cheng* (誠) or sincerity appeared to be a key concept. It is said, "*cheng* is the way of Heaven, *cheng* is also the way of man"; and "the so-called *cheng* is nothing but to be genuinely honest with oneself." That is to say, one must have sincere motivation. Therefore, "a true gentleman must be sincere with himself when he is alone." In other words, a gentleman doesn't need an audience; he should behave even when by himself. Behaving when alone is meant to integrate the inner and the outer realms. This is indeed the highest ideal one can attain. During the Neo-Confucian period of the Song dynasty and thereafter, the tradition of introspection was expanded and the practice of self-examination, self-discipline, and self-scrutiny advocated.[19] The process of self-examination, of measuring one's moral character, is guided by the norms of behavior internalized in the *liangxin* (良心) which may be variously translated as the conscience or superego. Common expressions indicating the practice of this form of moral self-examination are "conscience does not feel at ease" and its positive counterpart "feeling no guilt when scrutinized by conscience." Moral accomplishment or failure and the accompanying possession or lack of moral *mian* may, though it need not be, known only to the actor himself after the process of self-examination.

Although there are expressions which indicate that lack of moral *mian* is often an observable phenomenon, e.g., "the skin on his face is thin," our main point is that the audience is not a necessary component. It is obvious therefore that Fairbank's statement quoted earlier that "personal dignity is derived from right conduct and the social approval it acquired" is an oversimplification. If social/positional *mian* were the only possible source of personal dignity then it would be correct, but moral *mian* and the tradition of introspective Confucianism indicates that there is another source of such dignity.

Chi—Shame or Guilt?

Having briefly considered face and its various meanings in Chinese culture, we now turn to another concept often identified as the primary means of social control in face-conscious oriental cultures—shame. Ruth Benedict with specific reference to Japan spells out the major defining characteristics of shame and guilt cultures:

> True shame cultures rely on external sanctions for good behavior, not as true guilt do on an internalized commission of sin. Shame is a reaction to other people's criticism. A man is shamed either by being openly ridiculed and rejected or by fantasying to himself that he has been made ridiculous. In either case, it is a potent sanction. But it requires an audience or at least a man's fantasy of an audience. Guilt does not. In a nation whose honor means living up to one's own picture of oneself, a man may suffer from guilt though no man knows of his misdeed and a man is feeling of guilt may actually be relieved by confessing his sin.[20]

Hsu succinctly reiterates the same theme in the statement that,

> the individual in the . . . Western cultures . . . tends to look

> more to internal forces for guidance of his actions, while
> the individual in the . . . Eastern cultures tends to look more
> to external circumstances for guidance. This makes the
> difference between guilt and shame.

The constant note struck in both of the above quotations is that shame cultures emphasize the external, the social judgements of others; and the guilt cultures put more weight on the internal, the personal assessment of one's worth.

Our intent in this section of the chapter is to show that the realities of Chinese cultural behavior are much more complex than its facile classification as a shame culture would lead one to believe. A major factor contributing to the problematics of this type of classification may be isolated in the extreme difficulty one often encounters in finding exact English lexemes into which Chinese expressions can be translated. The Chinese term *chi* (恥), often translated into English as shame, in effect has a possible connotation of guilt. Eberhard warns us,

> We can say . . . the traditional elite of China had an ideology
> in which shame played an important role, but not in the
> conventional sense of amoral shame. On the contrary, shame
> in Confucianism was a moral concept and was internalized,
> together with the precepts of the code of social behavior.
> In essence then, shame and guilt operate in the same way.[21]

The one aspect of Eberhard's statement that we find open to misinterpretation is his implication that shame was the exclusive possession of the traditional elite. The concept of *chi* has long been important in Chinese culture and has ordinarily been expressed as having "a sense of *chi*." The having "a sense of *chi*" is esteemed as a virtue and is included as one of the traditional eight constant virtues along with love, righteousness, propriety, wisdom, sincerity, and modesty. Mencius, in a statement indicating that this virtue was viewed as potentially universal in extension and not the exclusive possession of a social elite, insists that "a man without a sense of *chi* . . . is not a man." That same philosopher in the tradition of introspective Confucianism saw it as the fountainhead of "unlimited self-cultivation" and "self-perfection." The influential classical works, *The Great Learning* and *The Doctrine of the Mean*, testify to the importance of "a sense of *chi*."

Because it is a virtue, the "sense of *chi*" is inherently a moral concept; it emphasizes one's awareness of moral norms which should govern conduct and the consequences of failure to act in accordance with them. Although in popular usage it may be appealed to as an admonition for observance of the prerequisite of social/positional face, a more precise usage limits it to the domain of moral face. Social/positional face, since it is basically amoral, is in no need of moral awareness to guarantee its prerequisites. A "sense of *chi*" may not be present in the man with high social/positional face any more than moral *mian* itself. Moral *mian*, however, implies the presence of a "sense of *chi*," in the same way that virtue implies an avoidance of vice. The two concepts differ only in their relative emphasis; moral *mian* emphasizes the positive dimension of correct moral conduct, and a "sense of *chi*" emphasizes one's awareness of the consequences of failure to live up to the norms.

A "sense of *chi*" is likewise a product of the tradition of introspective Confucianism. The man with a "sense of *chi*" need not have an audience to follow its dictates. It is this aspect that no doubt caused Eberhard to insist that shame in Chinese culture is not a categorical classification but one with an admixture of guilt, for as the psychologist Erikson defines it, guilt is a "sense of badness to be had all by oneself when nobody watches or when everything is quiet."[22] The concept and possibility of guilt was not peripheral in China; it was constantly nurtured, fostered, and exhorted in the tradition of introspective Confucianism. In this sense, then, those who seek to paint a picture of China as an almost exclusively shame-conscious culture are guilty of presenting an "under-Confucianized" picture of Chinese culture.

Face-Shame in Contemporary Mainland China

Our treatment of face-shame has to this point more direct relevance for China prior to 1949, contemporary Taiwan, and Hong Kong. What is its position in the new society of mainland China? We shall offer some preliminary thoughts on the topic recognizing that little actual research explicitly into it has been accomplished.

Since 1949, the government of mainland China has carried out systematic attacks on selected traditional features of Chinese culture, especially Confucianism which is regarded as the archaic cultural prerogative of the gentry class. The attacks, however, have not been totally unique to the current government; they actually began in the late Qing dynasty and gained momentum in the May Fourth Movement of the early Republic. The latter movement has often been called the "New Culture Movement" emphasizing its attempt to re-evaluate all traditional ideas.

There are two aspects of the more recent situation which are indeed relatively unique. The first is that it is sponsored and administered by the whole political apparatus of the government and is under the direct control of the ruling party. Secondly, the scope of the attack is so broad that it filters into all segments of society, especially the peasants and the workers. The intensity of the attack on traditional practices has recently been heightened in the Chinese Great Proletarian Cultural Revolution and the "Criticize Confucius and Lin Biao Campaigns."

The basic intention has been to rebuild Chinese culture and society along lines idealized in the concept of the "New Socialist Man." This "New Socialist Man" is one who works for the masses rather than for personal or family honor; a pertinent characteristic of the "New Ideal Man" is that he has no room for face in his makeup. A. S. Chen in commenting on contemporary Chinese literature notes: "The portrait of the new citizen naturally leaves no room for saving face. The question of face . . . is completely absent. . . ."[23]

It is no accident that one fails to encounter positive treatises on face in the normative literature; Mao Zedong in 1947 explicitly stated that he was opposed to "a concern with each other's human feelings and face." Lu Xun, a Chinese writer, seems to think that the Chinese people's traditional concern with face was carried to excess largely through the influence of the hypocritical upper classes. Yao Wenyuan, a powerful instigator of the Great Proletarian Cultural Revolution, advocates the destruction of face-consciousness which to him represents the moral system of the landlords, capitalists, and their lackies.[24] The new moral ideals should be that of the working class exemplified in the concept of "sincerity."

Lifton suggests that whereas traditional Chinese culture emphasizes moderation, balance, and harmony, i.e., a "cult of restraint," the contemporary culture stresses spontaneity, conflict, and aggression, a "cult of enthusiasm."[25] He further points out that the primary technique utilized to promote the new ethos is thought reform, a technique which strives at eliciting feelings of guilt rather than shame. The intent is to promote guilt as a primary means of socialization eradicating previous reliance on the face-shame complex.

What aspect of face is actually being attacked? Obviously central focus has been on social/positional face, the scalar quantity, itself a prerogative of success in the traditional society. The moral dimension of face, although undifferentiated in the polemics of restructuring Chinese society, persists and in fact appears to form the bases for techniques utilized in the restructuring process. The moral dimension is not the unique prerogative of any one culture whether oriental or Western, it corresponds to a fundamental human response to problematic aspects of the life situation. During the Great Proletarian Cultural Revolution, the Red Guards institutionalized the use of "public shame" as a weapon for political socialization and struggle. Solomon reports that the public shaming of a social offender is still much in use among the Chinese today.[26] In this process, the question of loss of face as a scalar quantity is not explicitly at issue since in the new society no man is, in theory, to have weightier prestige than another; what is in fact crucial is that the individual be made aware of his failure to meet the moral standards of the society. Whether confessions of guilt that are forthcoming actually meet the requirements spilled out by Erikson is itself a problem since one can easily feign such an attitude to satisfy the requirements of the public forum: successful or not, however, the intent is to produce individuals who are constantly willing to subject their activities to the scrutiny of self-evaluation.

What we may indeed be witnessing in mainland China is the demise of the use of the term *mian* precisely because of its popular over-identification with social/positional prestige, but even though moral *mian* disappears as a term, the reality to which it has traditionally referred remains as viable as ever. The specific normative content of moral *mian* may change, but the practice of self-examination and group evaluation on moral grounds continue as a viable component of the new socialist society. Indeed, it is this strain of the Confucian tradition, introspective Confucianism, that is fostered and preserved in a society which continues to attack the tradition which gave birth to it.

Conclusion

Our intention in this chapter has been the modest one of demonstrating that the concepts of face (*mian*) and shame (*chi*) have often been interpreted too rigidly by students of Chinese culture. The tendency has been to speak of Chinese culture one-dimensionally as a face-conscious one in purely the social sense and a shame-conscious one on the behavioral level. Our contention has been that such categorical statements reify and conceptually freeze concepts which in Chinese are extremely fluid with a wider domain of application than their English counterparts.

As De Vos has convincingly argued in the case of Japan,[27] so we have tried to demonstrate that a single dichotomy between the Chinese face-shame complex and the Western sin-guilt one fails to do justice to the complexities of the Chinese understanding of the key terms utilized in posing such a dichotomy. *Mian* and *chi* are not merely external sanctions lacking potentiality of internalization;

the long tradition of intrinsic Confucianism testifies not only to the possibility of their being internalized as individual moral guidelines, but insists that internalization is a moral necessity. We have not implied that face-shame in a purely social sense was unimportant in traditional Chinese society, but we claim that in itself it was incomplete; yet, it has been this partial component of the traditional complex that has been emphasized by those who have branded China as a "shame" culture. It reflects in essence an "under-Confucianized view of Chinese culture."

3 The Confucian Paradigm of Man: A Sociological View

co-authored with Michael H. Bond

Introduction

While we fully appreciate that Chinese culture is a far from homogeneous system,[1] it seems to us that Confucian values have nevertheless played a predominant role in molding Chinese character and behavior. Therefore, it is legitimate to anatomize the structural pattern of Chinese attitudes and behavior by analyzing the Confucian paradigm of man, although this method is neither exclusive nor exhaustive.

Admittedly, Confucianism, which is enormously rich and complex, defies any simple characterization, and there are different articulations of Confucian theory of society and the individual. Most of the literature, sociological or not, depicts Confucianism as a social theory and a social force that tends to mold the Chinese into group-oriented or, more specifically, family-oriented and socially dependent beings.[2] Unquestionably, this view has a good deal of sociological truth and has been more or less home out to date by empirical studies.[3]

Nevertheless, the typical presentation grasps only a part of the total complexity. In this chapter, we attempt to show that the Confucian paradigm of man has the theoretical thrust as well as a built-in structural imperative to develop a person into a relation-oriented individual who is not only socially responsive and dependent but also capable of asserting a self-directed role in constructing a social world. This feature of Confucianism has been relatively neglected in theoretical analyses and unexplored in empirical research.

The Confucian Conception of Humanity

The fundamental fact of Confucianism is that it is primarily a secular social theory, the foremost purpose of which is to achieve a harmonious society. Indeed, harmony is the most treasured social value.[4] But how is a harmonious society possible? To this question, Confucians invariably answer that if every individual were to act towards others in a proper way, then an orderly world would be achieved. The proper way is prescribed by the dictates *li* (propriety), a set of rules for action.[5] In sociological terms, Confucianism perceives the ideal society as a massive and complicated role system. The conception of role system is in fact embedded in the doctrine of *zhengming* (rectification of names).[6]

"Let the ruler be a ruler, the father a father, the son a son," and so forth.[7] The guidelines for instantiating these various roles are defined by *li*, which can be conceptualized as the grammar of relationships.

In a thought-provoking article, Francis Hsu argues that personality is a Western concept rooted in individualism, and he proposes that the central ingredient in the human made of existence is man's relationship with his fellow men.[8] Accordingly, Hsu proposes the *ren* (human-heartness) approach of Confucianism in contrast to the Western approach, which focuses on anomic individuals and their intrapsychic dynamics. Indeed, it seems to us that the Confucian conception of man cannot be neatly characterized by Western concepts of individualism or holism and should be considered in its own terms.[9]

In Confucian social theory, the individual is never conceived of as an isolated, separate entity; man is, by Confucian definition, a social, or interactive, being.[10] Using the words of Hu Shi, the late contemporary Chinese philosopher, "In the Confucian human-centered philosophy, man cannot exist alone; all actions must be in a form of interaction between man and man."[11] Not unlike Emile Durkheim, Confucians (at least, Confucians of Xunzi's persuasion) see society as a humanizing agent: to them, being human is conditional on a man's being obedient to social norms in daily interactions.[12] It is no accident that the Chinese character *ren* means two men. As Lin Yusheng put the matter, "*Ren* can only be cultivated and developed in inter-human relationships in a social context."[13]

Indeed, Confucius, the founder of Confucian School, is concerned with the nature of humanity rather than the polar concepts "individual" and "society."[14] Liang Shuming presents a perceptive thesis that the traditional Chinese society is neither individual-based nor society-based, but relation-based.[15] Liang writes that in a relation-based social system, "the emphasis is placed on the relation between particular individuals."[16] The focus is not fixed on any particular individual but on the particular nature of the relation between individuals who interact with each other.[17] Put differently, in the Confucian paradigm of man, man is socially situated, defined, and shaped in a relational context. In brief, man is a relational being.[18] A relational being is sensitive to his relations with others, above, below, or on equal footing with him. He sees himself situated symbolically in the web of a relational network through which he defines himself.

It must also be acknowledged, however, as de Bary correctly notes, that "the relations alone . . . do not define a man totally. His interior self exists at the center of this web and there enjoys its own freedom."[19] Confucians recognize and attach great importance to the *ji* (self). While stressing, on the one hand, the importance of relations between and among individuals, Confucians emphasize, on the other, that the individual is not simply a being shaped and determined by his role-relational structure. Ultimately, the individual is more than a role-player mechanically performing the role-related behavior prescribed by the social structure. To use median terminology, the individual consists of a self (*ji* in Confucian terms) that is an active and reflexive entity. Confucians assign the individual self the capacity to do right or wrong, and, ultimately, the individual alone is responsible for what he is. This voluntaristic view of the individual is crystallized in the unique Confucian concept of *xiuji* (self-cultivation). Self-cultivation is a process that involves a subtle interplay between role and identity. And in the process, the ideal of sincerity is essential. The attainment of sincerity is the way of men. *The Doctrine of the Mean* says, "He who attains to sincerity is he who chooses what is good and firmly holds it fast."[20] For Confucians, sincerity is indispensable to the achievement of true self. In the eyes of Confucius, nothing is more unbearable than a *xiangyuan* who was condemned as "the thief of virtue" simply for his lack of moral autonomy and courage in being unable to hold a consistent stand towards right and wrong.[21]

The Confucian paradigm of man, in short, is sociological but not sociologistic. It basically sees man as a relational being, who achieves his humanism through interaction with other particular individuals. His self-image and character are shaped by his role in this relational structure. But the individual is not merely a player of roles prescribed by *li*; he has an active self that is capable of shaping the role-relationship he enters. To this often neglected aspect of Confucianism, we return in the final section of this chapter.

Family Structure and the Individual

The preceding analysis shows that in the Confucian paradigm the individual is conceptualized as a relational being. According to Confucians, certain relationships are of paramount importance. They are the so-called Five Cardinal Relations (*wulun*), namely, those between sovereign and subject, father and son, elder and younger brother, husband and wife, and friend and friend. Of these five basic dyads, three belong to the family and the other two are based upon the family model.[22] In Confucian social theory, the family occupies a central position; it is not only the primary social group but it is the prototype of all social organizations.[23] In the words of Feng Youlan, "The family system was the social system of China."[24] In earth-bound China, family was the primary reality of the Chinese people. Apart from the kinship system, there was rarely a secondary organization or association outside the family to serve the individual's social needs.[25] Indeed, there was no major aspect of traditional social life that was not touched by the ties and influence of the family. It is then entirely understandable why the Five Relations were predominantly familistic in conceptualization and role relationships were couched in kinship terms.

It should be emphasized that in the original Confucian paradigm of the Five Relations, role relationships were symmetrical and interdependent. Each party in the relation was expected to perform his role according to the norms prescribed by *li*. In these role dualities, each actor was required to honor his role requirement. Otherwise, his counterpart was not obliged to honor his responsibility. This implicit contract lay at the heart of the doctrine of Rectification of Names.[26]

After the East Han dynasty, however, the concept of *san'gang* (three bends) gradually emerged as the dominant ideology for the political system as well as the family. According to *san'gang*, the ruler and father were given absolute authority over the subject and the son, respectively. Additionally, the father's position was buttressed by the Confucian virtue of *xiao* (filial piety). It is convincingly argued by Hu Shi that this principle of filial piety was only later elaborated in the hands of Confucius's disciples, especially Zengzi. What *ren* was to Confucius is what *xiao* was to Zengzi and later Confucians. Confucius certainly did not fail to recognize that the father–son relation was one of the basic human relations. Yet, it was the later Confucians who attached singular importance to the father–son relationship. They came to conceive of filial piety as the foundation of *ren*, elevating *xiao* as a preeminent virtue.[27] According to Hu Shi, Confucius's social philosophy of *ren* was transformed into a social philosophy of *xiao*, and *xiao* became the most powerful social dictate.[28] Indeed, filial piety had become so powerful and pervasive that Feng Youlan called it "the ideological basis of traditional [Chinese] society."[29]

It was only logical that the father–son relationship became what students of Chinese society called the model structural unit.[30]

Lifton is certainly right in saying, "Whatever its strains filialism was the source of the predominant identity of traditional China, a basic ideal against which any other form of self-image had to be judged."[31]

Nevertheless, it should be remembered that status and authority in the Chinese family was not solely based upon filial piety; it was also based upon age and the principle of kinship proximity. The veneration of age can be seen as a value concomitant to filialism. According to Confucian teaching, family members should be arranged into proper hierarchic order by their age, with age referring both to generational and chronological age. These two factors formed the foundation for the hierarchy of status and authority in the family. Outside the family, the principle of kinship proximity operated, requiring that children be trained to distinguish the degree of *jin* (closeness) and *shu* (distance) in their contacts with his kinsmen in order to show the proper amount of deference and obedience. As C. K. Yang writes: "The interlocking operation of these three factors, generation, age, and proximity of kinship resulted in a system of status and authority that assigned to every person in the kinship group a fixed position identified by a complex nomenclature system."[32] Thus, we can see that under the sway of Chinese familism, each individual was locked into an elaborate role structure. Throughout his life, the individual constantly struggled with problems concerning his relations with others in this complex kinship circle.

At this juncture, it should be pointed out that the general value of *he* (harmony) was emphatically stressed at the family level.[33] That the family thrives and prospers where there is harmony is a deep-seated tenet of conventional Chinese wisdom. Indeed, family harmony itself became a goal. Given and primacy of family models throughout society, harmony became the touchstone for all interpersonal behavior, and the way to achieve this harmony was through the practicing of *li*.

To speak of *li* is to speak of conformism, that is, conforming with the rules. These rules structure family relations into hierarchical dualities: son–father, younger brother–older brother, wife–husband, nephew–uncle, and so forth. Children are taught respect for this ordering throughout the socialization process but particularly after about age five.[34] Interpersonal communication is nonreciprocal in the sense that children are disciplined not to take initiative in respect to adults and they are not supposed to talk back to parents or other elders. This pattern of passivity is expressed in the Chinese phrase for obedience, *tinghua* (listen to talk).[35] In child-rearing practices, a fundamental concern is to inhibit open emotional expression of hostility or aggression towards authority or even peers.[36] There is in fact no prescribed and sanctioned way for the expression of such feeling and behaviors.[37] This lack is certainly consistent with the logic of filial piety. Restraint (*zhi*) is a highly desirable trait in Chinese culture. Controlling emotions is a condition necessary for proper behavior; it is believed that if a man is under the undue influence of passion, he will be incorrect in his conduct and incapable of objective assessment.[38]

Lifton labels the Chinese cultural pattern—moderation, balance, and harmony—a cult of restraint.[39] Self-expression or the strivings for autonomous behavior on the part of the children are discouraged or suppressed as nothing more than selfishness.[40] This is certainly fundamental to the concept of *keji* (conquering or overcoming one's individuality).[41]

At this point, it should be mentioned that the social forces pressing for hierarchical order are not without their counterpoint. Confucian teaching does recognize the legitimacy of non-conformism. As Rubin rightly points out, the ideal Confucian is one who aims at harmony, not uniformity; and in the *Analects*, "the message concerning obedience is balanced by one concerning disobedience."[42] This potential for disobedience functioned socially to help individuals mobilize resources for overpowering tyrannical leaders who had exceeded the bounds of legitimacy. In fact, the right of rebellion against tyrannical leaders was fully endorsed in Confucian social-political thought.[43] Therefore, Confucianism can hardly be accused of being an intellectual system lacking concepts of individualism.[44]

The self-oriented precepts became especially vital for the individual when he was caught in a dilemma resulting from divided loyalties. Traditional Confucian scholar-bureaucrats were often under cross pressures coming from the family group, for which the ethical principles were particularistic, and from bureaucratic organizations, for which the ethical principles were universalistic. There was no easy solution for the individual scholar-bureaucrat in passively conforming to ready social guidance; the resolution of such conflicting demands required active struggle and individual choice.[45] We believe that the extensive explorations into Chinese conformity have failed to tap the potential for disobedience in the Chinese by constructing demonstrations, where no serious moral choices were involved. Hopefully, this incomplete picture of the Chinese as dependent and conforming will be fleshed out by studies more sensitive to the full range of the Confucian influence.

One further word about Chinese conformity is that it is often nothing more than surface conformity, that is, compliance without internalization.[46] Chinese persons are not subject to the same pressures for consistency between inner beliefs and outer behavior as are Westerners.[47] One generally responds to the dictates of the situation rather than to the dictates of one's self.[48] Such behavior is not construed as hypocritical or insincere as it would be by Westerners; rather, it is a culturally sanctioned mechanism enabling the individual to maintain a harmonious relationship with the external world. In a way, formalistic conformity has a ceremonial function in maintaining social harmony.[49]

This observation is not to deny that Chinese have a sense of self with associated attitudes, beliefs, and opinions. We have not yet, however, begun to investigate when these internal characteristics come to be relevant in guiding behavior. Until we do so, comparisons of conformity in Chinese and Westerners will be incomplete.

The Problematic of the Confucian Paradigm

One of the enduring observations of Western analysts is that Chinese people have a strong sense of belonging to a group. Wilson writes, "What differentiates the Chinese is the singular focus of Chinese group loyalties and the intensity with which ideals of loyal behavior (such as sacrifice for the collective good) are held."[50] Compared with the individualistic culture of the West, this can hardly be debated.[51] However, in comparison with the Japanese, the Chinese seem to us less group centered. Nakane perceptively points out:

In the Japanese system all members of the household are in

one group under the head, with no specific rights according to the status of individuals within the family. The Japanese family system differs from that of the Chinese system, where family ethics are always based on relationships between particular individuals such as father and son, brothers and sisters, parents and child, husband and wife, while in Japan they are always based on the collective group, i.e., members of a household, not on the relationship between individuals.[52]

Perhaps, the source of the difference between Chinese and Japanese culture is the consideration given within Confucianism to the individual.

The Confucian version of individualism has, however, a relational emphasis. As Bodde summarizes it, "Confucian 'individualism' means the fullest development by the individual of his creative potentialities—not, however, merely for the sake of self-expression but because he can thus best fulfill that particular role which is his within his social nexus."[53] This particular role is often uncongenial to the development of individual autonomy and initiative. The family produces structural effects that tend not only to make child develop a dependency social orientation towards authority but also to make the members develop a group orientation towards the family. In traditional China, it was the family, not the individual, that was the important unit in social transactions.[54] Whenever there was conflict between individual members and the family, "it sought the solution from the self-sacrifice of the individual for the preservation of the group."[55] Family socialization practices were marked by a particular stress on the cultivation of collective consciousness and responsibilities of the members. This same strategy is being used in contemporary China to sharpen the individual's sense of responsibility towards that larger group of the commune, district, and the country.[56]

The much-discussed concept of face is a case in point.[57] Face concerns are certainly no monopoly of Chinese people.[58] Part of what differentiates the Chinese concept of face from that of the Westerner, however, lies in the fact that face is more a concern to the family than to the individual. Face-losing or face-gaining concerns not only the person directly involved but also the family.[59] Such sayings as, "The children's misbehavior is the fault of the father," or, "The ugly things [of the family] should not go out of the family gate," underscore the sense of joint responsibility and shared fate involved in family membership. One's face is a collective property. For this reason, children must be taught that, "A man needs face like a tree needs bark." Believing this, children are likely to be cautious and avoid any rash behavior that may adversely reflect both on them and on their family.

We have briefly outlined the hierarchical and collective pressure inherent in Confucian social philosophy. The family, as the primary social reality for Chinese, was chiefly responsible for socializing its members to function within these restraints to achieve harmony. Often this harmony was purchased at the price of individual interests, despite the considerable emphasis given by Confucian teachings to the need for individual development and cultivation.

It is understandable, then, why scholars advocate the discovery of the individual as the main theme of Confucius,[60] yet hold the view that the individual can never be discovered in Confucian culture.[61] Indeed, this is the problematic of the Confucian paradigm.[62] We venture to argue that the Confucian paradigm for man is not totally compatible with Confucian familistic structure and concerns. And it is here the so-called three contradictions of the Confucian tradition argued by Solomon become crystallized.[63] These contradictions and their practical resolution have never received adequate attention from scholars. We hope that this chapter helps stimulate that interest.

The Self and Relation-Construction

In the preceding analysis, we argue that the Chinese individual was locked into a hierarchical and cohesive family structure. There is no denying that family harmony was supported by asymmetrical norms of *xiao* (obedience): we should not, however, overlook the fact that family harmony was also maintained by care and intimacy among the family members. Warmth and mutual love are outstanding characteristics of the Chinese. Consistent with this caring is the probability that the Chinese family has greater tolerance than most for deviant behavior.[64] So, family life was not an oppressive burden by any means for its individual members.

However, the structural restraints of the Chinese family have produced a tendency to subordinate the individual to the wishes of superiors as well as to those of the group (family), and it is no accident that the self's emancipation was widely believed to be possible only through normative and structural changes in the family system.[65] With the increasing influence of Western individualistic values since the early twentieth century and the inexorably evolving forces resulting from industrialization and urbanization, the Chinese family system has slowly, but definitely, been eroded.[66]

Moreover, it is not only that the internal family structure has been weakened, the individual's life space has been extended more and more from this primary group into secondary groups. As a result, the Chinese individual is no longer tightly locked in a family structure but finds himself in quite a new social situation where the individual is given a much broader scope for self-expression. To put it differently, the individual is now relatively freer from the restraints of familism, thus shifting the Confucian agendas to a new and different structural base. And it is here that we turn our attention.

To be sure, social relations were never confined exclusively to the sphere of the family in traditional China.[67] Of the Five Cardinal Relations, the Confucian paradigm explicitly recognizes relations among friends. The Chinese proverb, "Relying on parents at home, and on friends outside of home," testifies clearly to the recognition of the need for transcending the family boundary in coping with life situations. Of course, friendship is a universally recognized human phenomenon. What is probably a distinctive characteristic of Chinese friendship is that its nature is always couched in kinship terms. That is, relations among friends are constructed along the pattern of elder brothers and younger brothers: Friends treat each other as brothers. So, three friends became the three blood-brothers immortalized in *The Romance of the Three Kingdoms*. Expressions such as, "Friends are as close as brothers," and, "Within the four seas, all men are brothers," emphasize this familistic conception of friendship. So, the less well articulated form of relationship is modelled along the lines of a more familiar *lun*, that of elder brother and younger brother.

Nowhere does Confucius discuss relations among strangers. Not surprisingly, Chinese people are uneasy in such social transactions. Abbott writes, "Heavy reliance on the family and primary group seems to make functioning in outside groups in Chinese society an uncomfortable process even for people with healthy ego-structure and who enjoy associating with others."[68] In the case of the Chinese, the individual's discomfort with strangers lies partly in the fact that he is unable to relate to strangers through any *lun* prescribed by Confucian ethics. Because Confucian ethics are particularistic, but not universalistic, in nature,[69] the stranger as a role category is too ambiguous to be placed in any role structure. This is one reason why Chinese have used the intermediary widely as a cultural mechanism in social relation-construction. Solomon, who is aware of this phenomenon, writes, "Given the importance which Chinese attach to status deference in social contact, in instances of dealings with unknown individuals they tend to seek out a mutually known third party who understands the 'face' expectations of all involved to mediate the relationship."[70] We might also add that the third party acts as a bridge to integrate one's relationship to the other indirectly into some prescribed *lun*.

Given the hierarchical nature of the established *lun*, the individual would be relatively uneasy relating with a friend or peers of equal or near-equal social status.[71] In this respect, Fairbank observes: "An equal relationship has little precedent in Chinese experience. Their relation (to politics) began with the observation that the order of nature is not egalitarian but hierarchic."[72] This aspect of Chinese relation-construction has important implications for interactions between Chinese and persons from more egalitarian cultures. Mutual accommodation is probably required. The strategy of adopting a Western given name in dealing with Westerns is one such adaptation and is in part a device for managing this unusual relationship between equals.

Another important feature of relationship building is that once outside the rigid role requirements of the immediate family structure, the individual self has considerable freedom in constructing the relational network. What cannot be overemphasized is that the boundary of the Chinese relation network is highly elastic in the sense that it can be expanded or contracted according to the decisions of the self.[73] It is significant to note that even the Chinese basic and primary social group, *jia* (family), is in fact an elastic entity. It can mean only the members of a nuclear family, or it may also mean all members of a lineage or a clan. This ambiguity or elasticity of the family gives the individual ample room for maneuver in kin-relation network construction. What constitutes the boundary of family is very much dependent upon the purposes of the ego. Chinese kinship relations, C. K. Yang writes, "take on the form of a series of concentric circles with Ego as the Center."[74] At the center of the elastic relation network, as Fei rightly argues, there is always the self.[75]

The self-centered voluntarism of the Chinese, which is underdeveloped in the family system, manifests itself in various ways when the individual is free from the bonds of the family. Eberhard is not incorrect, though exaggerating somewhat, when he says,

> As the Chinese must suppress all aggression within the family, the outer world is the field in which it must find its outlets. . . . Only with complete strangers, such as encounters in a modern big city, or in a foreign country where one is sure that the contact is casual and not lasting, is the individual free and can discharge his aggression directly as the individual in Western society may feel free to do. What counts in such contacts is aggressive intelligence, making the most of

every chance as often as one can without risking too much. The biographies of Chinese immigrants, especially Chinese businessmen in other societies, testify to this.[76]

It is a widely recognized social phenomenon that Chinese individuals unabashedly show a kind of egocentric behavior outside the family, particularly in a non-kin social context.[77] Instead of Western individualism, one finds what is called individual firstism, meaning "placing personal honors, status and interest above other things."[78] We are here indeed suggesting that when the Chinese individual is not structurally situated in a relation-based social web, Confucian values and norms cease to be morally relevant. The popular saying, "If one does not think of his own interests, neither Heaven nor Earth will save him," can hardly be slighted as of no social consequence. Indeed, this egoistic aspect in the development of the Chinese individual, though utterly non-Confucian, is rooted in the very body of the Confucian social theory, which gives a central place to the individual self.[79] Ironically, this type of Chinese characteristic, though often seen as pathological, seems to be socially acceptable in competitive societies.

What interests us here, however, is the relation-construction project, which seems to be of vital importance for the individual engaged in social engineering in a modern world. As mentioned above, the Chinese individual has a strong relationship orientation, which conceives the other person in concrete, differentiated terms. According to the Confucian paradigm, every individual is related with others in the context of *lun*; some *luns*, such as the father–son relation, are preordained givens, while others, such as the friend–friend relation, are voluntarily undertaken. In the former type, the individual has little or no option; he is expected to perform his prescribed roles in these structured relations. However, in the latter type, the individual is very much on his own; he is the initiator of social communication; his is the architect in relation-construction.

It is in this vortex of voluntary network building that the Chinese have demonstrated impressive and sophisticated skills. As one Western anthropologist notes, "Chinese culture has developed inter-personal relationships to the level of an exquisite and superb art."[80] In Western societies, one noted Chinese sociologist writes, "People struggle for rights, while in China, people are concerned with relation construction, affectionate ties."[81] This Chinese concern makes very good sense, of course. In a society where civil law was relatively undeveloped[82] and bureaucratic corruption was rampant,[83] a reliable friendship network was of considerable advantage in protecting one's personal and family interests.

It is therefore no surprise that in effecting a social transaction, personal relational networks, which are based upon particularistic ties, have taken precedence over universalistic legalistic relationships.[84] It is surprising perhaps, this cultural phenomenon has not only survived in socialist China but has become increasingly rampant. "Walking through the back door" and other practices are almost the norm rather than the exception in mainland China.[85] The phenomenon is so widespread that a new term, *guanxi xue* (relationology), has been coined for it.[86] However, it should be noted that this phenomenon is no monopoly of the mainland Chinese; it is a phenomenon of all Chinese communities. In the achievement-oriented and highly competitive, capitalist society of Hong Kong, this relation-oriented behavioral pattern continues to be a viable cultural phenomenon co-existing with the universalistic, rational pattern of behavior. It is important to bear in mind that traditional familism has been eroded in Hong Kong due primarily to vast institutional processes of industrialization and urbanization. The ascriptive aspect of Chinese familism is fading.[87] A new kind of familism in which utilitarian considerations are the hallmark of relation-construction has emerged in Hong Kong.[88] Due to war and geographical mobility, traditional kinship ties have ceased to have an impact on individual family members. This structural loosening allows for greater flexibility to kinsmen's selectivity in their relation-construction.[89] In Hong Kong, the Chinese individual has not infrequently constructed relation networks through the mobilization of kinship ties, ethnicity ties, friendship ties, and work ties.

So, regardless of the political setting, the Chinese cultural dynamic continues to operate. This kind of highly personal relation construction constitutes an important cultural strategy for securing social resources towards self-advancement. To be sure, it is not merely a rational, calculative process; such "engineering" is conditioned by Confucian norms of *bao* or reciprocity.[90] What we argue is that the Chinese individual living under Confucian guidelines is entirely capable of asserting a self-directed role in constructing vast relational networks outside his family. The individualism forming a part of Confucian social philosophy can be realized in this important social arena. Undoubtedly, there are many other such arenas. We hope that this chapter with its relative emphasis on Chinese individualism may stimulate others to examine these other social avenues for self-expression among the Chinese. Previous analyses of Chinese culture have been guilty, we believe, of focusing exclusively on the dependent aspects of Chinese behavior. Such unbalanced presentations are not in keeping with the Chinese imperative of "keeping to the middle way."

4 *Guanxi* and Network Building: A Sociological Interpretation

No one who has had firsthand experience with Chinese society could fail to note that Chinese people are extremely sensitive to *mianzi* (face) and *renqing* (human obligation) in their interpersonal relationships.[1] Likewise, no one who has lived in mainland China, Taiwan, Hong Kong or any other overseas Chinese society could be totally unaware of a social phenomenon called *guanxi* (personal relationship). It is no exaggeration to say that *guanxi, renqing* and *mianzi* are key sociocultural concepts to the understanding of Chinese social structure. Indeed, these sociocultural concepts are part of the essential "stock knowledge," to use Alfred Schutz's terminology, of Chinese adults in their management of everyday life.[2] It is perhaps surprising that, despite the tremendous modernization of social and economic life taking place in mainland China, Taiwan, and Hong Kong in the past decades, these sociocultural concepts still play significant roles in shaping and influencing the social behavior of the Chinese. It is striking to note that although the Chinese Communists in mainland China have repeatedly launched vigorous campaigns—including the Great Proletariat Cultural Revolution—to attempt to uproot "feudal" elements of the Chinese culture, these concepts, *guanxi* in particular, remain strong; they even threaten the formal and official ideological system of Marxism-Leninism. Liu Binyan, a former senior reporter of the *People's Daily*, writes:

> In Bing county, you simply cannot clearly figure out the *guanxi* [personal relations] among people. It seems that in everyone's body there is a particular switch. If you touch a person, it will unexpectedly affect a large number of persons. . . . There are complicated and overlapping relations between and among people, weaving a thick and tight social web. Whatever "-isms" or principles, whatever policies or program guidances, as soon as they touch this social web, they lose their function immediately, just like being suddenly electrocuted.[3]

Fox Butterfield, a former foreign correspondent for *The New York Times*, has the following observations:

> I began to appreciate how differently Chinese order their mental universe than do Westerners. We tend to see people as individuals; we make some distinctions, of course, between those we know and those we don't. But basically we have one code of manners for all. . . . Chinese, on the other hand, instinctively divide people into those with whom they already have a fixed relationship, a connection, what the Chinese call *guanxi*, and those they don't. These connections operate like a series of invisible threads, tying Chinese to each other with far greater tensile strength than mere friendship in the West would do. *Guanxi* have created a social magnetic field in which all Chinese move, keenly aware of those people with

whom they have connections and those they don't.
They explain why the Communist leadership, which
was so grateful to Richard Nixon for helping make the
breakthrough in Sino-American relations, could never
understand Watergate and why Peking even sent a special
plane to bring Nixon back to China for a visit after his
disgrace. In a broader sense, *guanxi* also help explain how
a nation of one billion people coheres.[4]

The ever-present social phenomenon of *guanxi* is not confined to
mainland China. Various field workers convincingly testify to the
prevalence of *guanxi* in other Chinese societies.[5]

I attempt here to give a sociological interpretation of *guanxi*
and network building, first, to see how *guanxi* is conceived in Confucian social theory; second, to analyze the ingredients of *guanxi*
construction and the social skills needed in the establishment and
maintenance of personal networks; third, to analyze the function
of *renqing* in network building; and fourth, to describe strategies
of *guanxi* avoidance and *guanxi* disengagement, which are built-in
cultural mechanisms to ensure universalistic rationality for the management of economic and bureaucratic life.

Guanxi in Confucian Social Theory

Confucian social theory is concerned with the question of how to
establish a harmonious secular order in the man-centered world.
According to Confucianist philosophy, the individual is never an
isolated, separate entity; man is defined as a social or interactive
being.[6] It is no accident that the Chinese character *ren* (benevolence) means two men. Indeed, there is no concept of man as sep-

arate from men. Hu Shi states: "In the Confucian human-centered philosophy man cannot exist alone; all action must be in a form of interaction between man and man."[7] *Ren*, the highest attainment of moral cultivation, would be nothing if it were not placed in the context of the social relationships among men. Tu Wei-ming writes that "the original Confucian intention . . . is the moralization of the person in human relationships."[8] Francis Hsu notes:

> The Chinese conception of man (also shared by the Japanese but pronounced *jin* as opposed to the Chinese term *ren*) is based on the individual's transactions with his fellow human beings. When the Chinese say of so and so, *"ta bu shi ren"* (he is not *ren*), they do not mean that this person is not a human animal. Instead, they mean that his behavior in relation to other human beings is not acceptable. . . .

> But the concept of *ren* puts the emphasis on interpersonal transactions. It does not consider the individual psyche's deep cores of complexes and anxieties. Instead it sees the nature of the individual's external behavior in terms of how it fits or fails to fit the interpersonal standards of society and culture.[9]

What constitutes proper human relationships is the central problem in the Confucian project. Liang Shuming, comparing the Chinese social system with Western ones, asserts that Chinese society is neither *geren benwei* (individual-based) nor *shehui benwei* (society-based), but *guanxi benwei* (relation-based). In a relation-based social system, Liang writes:

> The focus is not fixed on any particular individual, but on the particular nature of the relations between individuals

who interact with each other. The focus is placed upon the relationship.[10]

In a nutshell, man is a relational being in the Confucian system.[11] True, the word *guanxi*, which is a relatively modern expression, is not found in the Confucian classics; instead, the word *lun* is used. *Lun* means order[12] or, more specifically, "differentiated order" among individuals. Pan Guangdan points out that the Confucian concept of *lun* is basically concerned with two problems: the kind of differentiation to be made between individuals, and the kind of relations to be established between individuals.[13] Confucian social order is constructed upon the concept of *lun*, which is primarily concerned with the problem of *bie*, or differentiation among role relations.

The phrase *bu shi qi lun* means that every role relation is properly in order. To be more specific, it means that role relations are properly differentiated according to the nature of relations between particular individuals. Social order and stability rest on differentiation rather than homogeneity.[14] Furthermore, Fei Xiaotong sees *lun* as *cuxu*, which refers to differentiated and graded relations according to the degree of intimacy attaching to the individual concerned.[15] The closer the other is to the individual, the more intimate their relations will be. It is true also in the reverse situation. Here, it should be mentioned, according to Confucians, there are many kinds of relations between individuals of which the well-known five cardinal relations are the most fundamental. These five relationships and their appropriate tenor are *qing* (affection) between parent and child; *yi* (righteousness) between ruler and subject; *bie* (distinction) between husband and wife; *xu* (order) between older brothers and younger brothers; and *xin* (sincerity) between friends. Among the relations, "some of them are preordained givens, while others are voluntarily constructed; the father–son and brother–brother relations belong to the former type, husband–wife and friend–friend relations belong to the latter type."[16]

It is here that we touch on the very nature of the individual in the Confucian social theory. The question is: What is the role of the individual in the process of relation construction? In particular, what is the role that the individual plays in those relations which are voluntarily constructed? Apart from the preordained relation, for example, the father–son *lun*, in which individual behavior is more or less prescribed by fixed status as well as fixed responsibilities, an individual has considerable freedom in deciding whether to enter into voluntarily constructed relationships with others. Most of the literature, sociological or not, depicts Confucianism as a social theory that tends to mold the Chinese into group-oriented or, more specifically, family-oriented and socially dependent beings.[17] Without question, this view has a good deal of sociological truth. Nevertheless, this typical presentation grasps only a part of the total complexity.[18]

Confucianism attaches a good deal of autonomy to the individual. The expression *wei ren you ji* testifies that achieving the highest virtue (*ren*) is, in the final analysis, in the hands of *ji* (self). Admittedly, in the Confucian relation-based social system, the focus is not fixed on any particular individual but on the particular nature of the relation between individuals. However, as de Bary correctly notes, "the relations alone . . . do not define a man totally. His interior self exists at the center of this web and there enjoys its own freedom."[19] It is important to bear in mind that the Confucian individual is more than a role-player mechanically performing the role-related behavior prescribed by the social structure. To use Meadian terminology, the Confucian individual consists of a self (zi) that is both an active and a reflexive entity. In relation construction, it is the individual who is capable of defining roles for himself and others, and is always at the center.[20] Precisely because of the voluntaristic nature of the self, the Confucian individual is the initiator of social communication in the non-preordained, *lun* relation with others outside the family structure. Indeed, he is the architect in relation construction.

It is necessary to examine the relation between *ji* (self) and *qun* (group) if the dynamic relation construction of Chinese behavior is to be more fully appreciated. In Confucianism, as was mentioned, the voluntaristic nature of the self is fully recognized, while the conception of group is the least articulated. Fei Xiaotong convincingly argues that the boundary between self (ji) and group (qun) is relative and elastic.[21] In the Confucian mind, there is no group boundary as such.[22] The term *jia* (family), which is the basic social unit, is an elastic entity; it sometimes includes only members of a nuclear family, but it may also include all members of a lineage or a clan. The common expression *zijiaren* (our family people) can refer to any person one wants to include; it is entirely up to the individual to contract or expand the boundary of the concept of *jia*. It can theoretically be extended to an unlimited number of people and thereby becomes what is called *tianxia yijia* (all the world belongs to one family). The elasticity of the boundary of the group (the family or other collectives) gives the individual enough social and psychological space to construct his *guanxi* with an unlimited number of other individuals on kinship or fictive kinship bases.

At this juncture, the definition or an English translation of *guanxi* is in order. *Guanxi*, which J. Bruce Jacobs defines as "particularistic tie," is basically a kind of personal connection. In recent years, a new interdisciplinary field of personal relationships has emerged.[23] J. Clyde Mitchell, in one of the pioneer works on the social network, writes:

> The point of anchorage of a network is usually taken to be some specified individual whose behavior the observer wishes to interpret. Which individual is taken will turn on the particular problem that the observer is interested in. . . . This has led to the specification of this type of network as ego-centered though the term "personal network" may be more acceptable.[24]

It seems to me that either "particularistic tie" or "personal network" does carry the meaning of *guanxi*, but neither fully grasps the complicated and rich meaning of the word. A Chinese anthropologist argues well that the concept of *guanxi* should be kept and incorporated into modern social science literature.[25] Indeed, if a new science of relationships is going to be developed, *guanxi* is a concept that can hardly be excluded.

The Individual, Attribute, and Network Building

I hope I have made it clear that Confucian social theory has the theoretical thrust of developing a person into a *guanxi*-oriented individual. The Chinese preoccupation with *guanxi* (relationship) building has indeed a built-in cultural imperative behind it. It is not surprising, therefore, that the Chinese in their everyday life have demonstrated impressive and sophisticated skills in network building. La Barre, an anthropologist, notes: "Chinese culture has developed interpersonal relationships to the level of an exquisite and superb art."[26]

Let us take the way in which the Chinese construct their personal networks a step further. Chie Nakane, a Japanese anthropologist, has provided us with some very useful analytical tools. She uses two terms, *attribute* and *frame*, as contrasting criteria of group formation. According to Nakane, "Groups may be identified by applying the two criteria: one is based on the individual's common attribute, the other on situational position in a given frame. . . . Frame may be a locality, an institution . . . [it] indicates a criterion which sets a boundary and gives a common basis to a set of individuals who are located or involved in it." On the other hand, "attribute may mean, for instance, being a member of a definite descent group or caste." And "attribute may be acquired not only by birth but by achievement."[27] In making her point, Nakane illustrates the contrasting principles of family formation in Japan and China:

> The Japanese family system differs from that of the Chinese, where family ethics are always based on relationships between particular individuals such as father and son, brothers and sisters, parent and child, husband and wife, while in Japan they are always based on the collective group, i.e., members of a household, not on the relationship between individuals.[28]

Nakane asserts that the formation of social groups on the basis of fixed frames is characteristic of Japanese social structure. As for the Chinese system, the principle of attribute is indeed much more applicable; in fact, a few Chinese anthropologists have found that the concept of *fen lei* (similar to the concept of attribute) is the constitutive rule of Chinese social structure.[29] That is to say, Chinese group consciousness is formed on a set of criteria—such as kinship, native place, dialect, religious belief—as a base for group identification. Wang Songxing argues that, unlike the Japanese, the Chinese have "pluralistic" identifications with other individuals or social groups according to the "attributes" the individual has in common with other particular individuals or social groups. The more attributes the individual has, the more *guanxi* he is able to establish. The more *guanxi* he has, the more advantageous his position in mobilizing resources in order to achieve his goals in a competitive world.[30] *Guanxi* is established through social interaction between two or more individuals. *Guanxi* building is a work of social engineering through which the individual establishes his personal network. The existence of *guanxi* depends on the existence of the attributes shared by the individuals concerned. The shared attributes are what Jacobs calls "a base of *guanxi*." He writes, "In Chinese culture (and perhaps cross-culturally), a base for a *guanxi* depends upon two or more persons having a commonality of shared identification."[31] In Chinese societies, the most common shared attributes for building networks are locality (native place), kinship, co-worker, classmate, sworn brotherhood, surname, and teacher–student.[32] It should be remembered that as the base of group identification, the shared attributes are not constant or unchanging; people can form a group on the shared attribute of kinship at one time and on the shared attribute of dialect at another time. Moreover, the nature of shared attributes is quite elastic in the sense that they can be contracted and expanded; for example, locality can refer to a natural village, a county, a city, or a province. It can even be stretched to mean a regional grouping of provinces (such as *Hebei Shandong tong xiang hui*).

In network building, *la* (pulling) *guanxi* is the social phenomenon Chinese are most familiar with. "Pulling *guanxi*" means to establish or strengthen relations with others when no pre-established relation exists between them, or where a pre-established relation is remote. Ways of pulling *guanxi* are varied and have developed in mainland China into such a subtle and complicated "science" of the management of human relations as to be called *guanxi xue* ("relationology").[33] "Walking through the back door" (*zou hou men*) is widely known to be the most effective and necessary way to get things done through personal networks (*guanxi*) in today's Communist China. Butterfield observed the following:

> Ling's tickets to these films were classic back-door deals. As Chinese friends described the workings of the back door, these exchanges usually do not involve money. That would be considered bribery and therefore illegal. Instead they are based on the traditional use of *guanxi*, the cultivation of contacts and connections among friends, relatives, and colleagues. The longer I stayed in Peking, the more I sensed that almost anything that got done went through the back door.[34]

Chu and Ju's important and comprehensive survey, which was carried out in Shanghai and Qingpu (a rural county outside Shanghai) in 1988,[35] clearly shows that people perceive *guanxi* to be essential to social-economic life. When asked to rate the importance of network connections in Chinese society, an overwhelming majority of the respondents said that network connections are: very important (42.7 percent); important (26.9 percent); or somewhat important (22.8 percent). Only a few (4.9 percent) said that they are not very important, and still fewer (2.6 percent) said that they are not important at all. Furthermore, when asked to respond to the following: "Suppose you have a problem. If you follow the normal channels, it will take a long time, and the result may not be satisfactory. Do you think you should try to go through some connection?," over two-thirds of the respondents (71.7 percent) said they "should first try some connections." Only one in five (19.6 percent) would rather follow normal channels, saying they "should not try connections"; the remaining 8.8 percent were not sure.[36] The findings confirm the prevalence of the practice of *guanxi* in mainland Chinese society today. The same survey also shows an interesting phenomenon: younger people seemed to attach greater importance to *guanxi* than older people. Almost half of the young people (46.0 percent) said it was very important, as compared to 35.1 percent of the older people.[37] Only 5.0 percent of the young people said it was either not very important or not important at all, as compared to 13.6 percent of the older people. Indeed, as Chu and Ju pointed out, the practice of using *guanxi* to get something done in a hurry has always existed in Chinese society, but it has now reached almost epidemic proportions.[38]

At this point, it might be appropriate to discuss, in brief, how the practice of *guanxi* has evolved in Communist China over the last four decades. The Chinese Communist Party, as soon as it gained control over the mainland in 1949, launched a series of campaigns and movements with the purpose of transforming the traditional norms of personal relations in China from what Vogel calls "friendship" to "comradeship."[39] Friendship in Vogel's ideal construction is a particularistic or private morality, while comradeship is a universalistic ethic. Comradeship was taken to mean the embodiment of a citizen's public spirit in the socialist state. In a sense, comradeship is an ideal based on universalistic socialist values, which were supposed to transcend those particularisms based on kinship, locality, and so on. In short, the Chinese Communists intended to create the new Socialist man for the new Socialist society. Among the many Confucian-feudal elements they were determined to eradicate, *guanxi* was on the priority list. According to Vogel, the Communists' gigantic project of value transformation was achieved largely through fear. It is worth mentioning that the Chinese Communist Party had struggled to effect a revolutionary change in the 1950s and 1960s by using "organization" to destroy and replace the institutional structure of the Chinese traditional social system. By the end of the 1960s, Communist China had become, to use Franz Schurmann's perceptive (though somewhat exaggerated) expression, "a China of organization."[40]

The party-state structured the society into an all-inclusive, functional collectivity called *danwei*. In mainland China, almost every working adult belongs to a *danwei*, which provides its members with extensive goods and services.[41] The relation between the individual and *danwei* is near total and the high degree of individual dependency on the *danwei* has created a "culture of organized dependency," as Walder demonstrated.[42] During the Cultural Revolution of 1966–1976, the Party's domination over society reached its highest point. It attempted to bring all aspects of social life under its control through the concept of the "all-round dictatorship over the bourgeoisie." The Party not only tried to monopolize activities in the public sphere, it even tried to eliminate the private sector. The Cultural Revolution marked the culmination of the totalitarian tendency at the brink of "revolutionary feudal totalitarianism."[43] During this period, despite the unabashed ideological rhetoric on public or proletarian morality, the social order and public civility were seriously eroded. Distrust existed in all relationships, and a pervasive amorality and cynicism prevailed. An extreme form of instrumentalism colored norms of behavior in personal relations.

In the aftermath of the Cultural Revolution, under the new slogan of the Four Modernizations (particularly with the advent of economic reform advocated by Deng Xiaoping), a drastic change in social-political life took place, accompanied by a retreat of political power from its increasingly deeper penetration into civil society and the economy. The operation of the market was accepted as a supplement to a planned economy. Tang Tsou writes, "In short, civil society is being revived and the relationship between political power and society has changed."[44] With the resurgence of market and civil society and the low institutionalization of law and administrative regulation, people who are freed from omnipresent fear for the first time in their lives are eschewing socialist values and ideals and are returning to traditional behavioral patterns now officially sanctioned in the privatized social-economic spheres. Thomas Gold argued in 1985 that at both the micro and the macro levels, "instrumentalism and commoditization had supplanted both friendship and comradeship as primary characteristics of personal relations. It located the causes of this situation in certain aspects of the Cultural Revolution and current development-oriented reforms."[45] In present-day China, both traditional and socialist moral values are cast in doubt, practical utilitarian concerns have gained an upper hand.

Starting in 1977, the socialist modernists in China were anxious to re-establish universal standards and universalistic ethics, and they did make some progress. For example, examinations were instituted as the basic criterion for admission to universities and schools. The appointment of friends and relatives was widely attacked in the media and some officials became more cautious about this practice. However, "It was not uncommon, for example, for official A to appoint a relative of official B and for official B in return to arrange an appointment for a relative or friend of official A. Or official C, believing their connection would be useful, sometimes hired a relative of high official D without any intervention by official D."[46] Vogel, in writing about Guangdong in 1989, observed that "the cultivation of personal connections, long a prominent feature of Chinese society, was moderated beginning in the late 1970s by the new concern for universal standards, but at the same time *guanxi* blossomed to play a new instrumental role for entrepreneurs taking advantage of market opportunities."[47] However, "in Guangdong in this early but dynamic stage of commodity society, when markets were not yet fully opened, the new desire to make things happen led many entrepreneurs to use *guanxi* to achieve what was otherwise impossible."[48]

Renqing and Network Building

As discussed above, in the Confucian social theory the individual self, as a dynamic and reflexive entity, is at the center of relation construction. Apart from natural relations (that is, father–son, brother–brother relations), non-natural relations are voluntarily constructed with the individual self as the initiator. Indeed, Chinese *guanxi* building can be characterized as an ego-centered social engineering of relation building. We have shown that one's *guanxi* or personal network is based on the attributes shared by people. However, if there is no interaction between individual A and individual B, and if A wants to establish *guanxi* with B, whether or not B has common attributes with A, B is a "stranger" to A. Under such circumstances, an intermediary (*zhongjianren*) is often used as a cultural mechanism in *guanxi* building. Through the intermediary, the individual is able to associate with the "stranger" on relational terms. In the Chinese art of relation management, that is, the establishment and maintenance of *guanxi*, *renqing* plays an important role.[49] It should be pointed out that *renqing* is different from *ganqing* which is merely sentiment, or an affective component of all human relations. *Ganqing* is personal, while *renqing* is social. Yang Liansheng renders *renqing* as "human feelings," which, he writes, "covers not only sentiment but also its social expressions such as the offering of congratulations or condolences or the making of gifts on appropriate occasions."[50] Robert Silin's translation "human obligations" is probably closer to the meaning of the word *renqing*.[51] *Renqing* can be interpreted as the norms of *Chinese* interpersonal relationships. The Confucian norms of interpersonal relationships are fundamentally based upon the concept of *shu*, or reciprocity, which Max Weber takes as the foundation of Confucian social ethics.[52] J. H. Weakland writes:

> The system of reciprocal aid in Chinese life—except within the circle of the family and very close friends where mutual help is at least assumed to occur with no question of exchange at all—is centered around the concept of *renqing*.[53]

True, "in part *renqing* can be equated with the content of the Confucian *li* (propriety). The emphasis in the concept of *li* is on the individual's responsibility to know and act on certain prescribed rules of behavior."[54] If a Chinese is accused of "knowing no *renqing*," it means that he is lacking *li* and is incapable of managing interpersonal relationships. The Shanghai and Qingpu survey shows that *renqing* is still playing an important role in Communist China. When people were asked: "Suppose a relative wants your help to ask someone to do something. You are able to do it, but it will give you some inconvenience. What will you do?," over two-thirds of the sample (70.9 percent) would offer to help; very few (8.0 percent) would decline. Some others (5.1 percent) said they would help if the request was for a good cause. When a similar question regarding *renqing* for friends was asked, 64.3 percent of the sample would offer to help. Quite a few (14.3 percent) said it would depend, and 11.4 percent said no.[55] It is not surprising that kinship is a more weighty factor than friendship in people's interpersonal relationships.

It is worth mentioning that there are two basic types of interpersonal relationships or *guanxi*. One is economic exchange (economic *guanxi*), the other is social exchange (social *guanxi*). In a strict sense, *renqing* hardly enters into economic *guanxi* since economic exchange is dictated by impersonal market rationality. On the other hand, in social *guanxi*—which is diffuse, unspecific, and is ruled by the principle of reciprocity—*renqing* plays a central role. In social exchanges among Chinese, *renqing* serves as a medium. The common expressions "to give you a *renqing*" (*song ge renqing*), "to give me a *renqing*" (*ta gei wo yi ge renqing*), "he owes me a *renqing*" (*ta qian wo yi ge renqing*), or "I owe him a *renqing*" (*wo qian ta yi ge renqing*) show clearly that *renqing* is a kind of resource or social capital in interpersonal transactions. Because of the intricate relation between *renqing* and *guanxi*, the two some-times become interchangeable; for example, the saying "there is no *renqing* between us" is equivalent to saying "there is no *guanxi* between us." Cultivating *renqing* is a prerequisite to establishing or sustaining *guanxi*. The degree of *renqing* between two persons is usually a good indication of the "closeness" or "distance" of *guanxi* between them. A Chinese typically feels that he is locked into *renqing wang* (web of human obligations) or *guanxi wang* (web of personal networks).

Guanxi Avoidance and Universalistic Rationality

We have discussed at length the social phenomena of *renqing* and *guanxi*. Indeed, they are important tissues in the Chinese social structure. There is a general impression, correct or not, as observed by Liu Binyan, Butterfield, and others, that the Chinese are hope-lessly interlocked in *renqing wang* or *guanxi wang*. True enough, Chinese individuals have commonly utilized this kind of highly per-sonal relation construction as a cultural strategy for securing social resources toward goal attainment. However, we must be reminded that this is only a partial picture of the Chinese cultural dynamic of network building. In the Chinese cultural system, there are also cul-tural mechanisms to neutralize or to freeze the practice of *renqing* or *guanxi* in order to carve out room for instrumental rationality, which is necessary to maintain economic and bureaucratic (in the Weberian sense) life. To engage in *renqing* or to establish *guanxi* with others usually means a heavy social investment. Once one is inside the *renqing wang* or *guanxi wang*, he is locked into an intri-cate relationship of interdependence with others. He is, in this case, socially obliged to respond to any request for help from others. As such, the individual will lose autonomy and freedom. Therefore, it is not surprising that some Chinese have consciously tried to avoid relating themselves too intimately with others in order to avoid this dependence."[56] A student of Chinese society, describing the quality of interpersonal relationships in a town called Lukang in Taiwan, points out the importance of social distance:

> The aim seems to be a lot of amiable, matey, but not intimate ties with as many people as possible. People give the impression of being hesitant about getting too close, too deeply involved with or committed to anyone else. Amiable relationships may break down if too much is expected of them.[57]

The Chinese folk wisdom that one should not allow oneself to be a debtor in *renqing* transactions is meant to enable one to preserve some space for autonomy of action. In other words, it will enable individuals to have enough freedom in deciding whether to establish personal networks with others. *Guanxi* is a form of interpersonal relationship which is predominantly based on particularistic criteria. Talcott Parsons, writing on the nature of Confucian ethics, writes:

> Its ethical sanction was given to an individual's personal relations to particular persons—and with any strong emphasis only to these. The whole Chinese social structure accepted and sanctioned by the Confucian ethic was a predominately "particularistic" structure of relationships.[58]

It became necessary to freeze or to neutralize, if not to eliminate, "particularistic" elements in interpersonal transactions when universalistic rationality was needed, e.g., in the domains of economic and bureaucratic life. In traditional China, there was no shortage of cultural mechanisms for preventing the practices of *guanxi* or *renqing*. In imperial times, there was a system according to which employment of an official in his native place was prohibited and likewise the employment of relatives in the same bailiwick.[59] Max Weber described it as an ingenious "patrimonialist means" of imperial control.[60] We could well argue that the latent, if not explicit, function of this system was to prevent the official from being overly pressured by the particularistic demands of his relatives or friends, thus maintaining bureaucratic rationality. Using similar cultural logic, businessmen in olden times were inclined to leave their hometowns to do business far away. This again was to ensure that business could be conducted according to market principles, freeing the parties from interference by the particularistic pressures of *guanxi*.[61]

Fei Xiaotong's study of market town behavior is most illuminating. In his study of rural China, he observed that within the same village, neighbors usually walked miles to the market town to carry out their transactions there instead of at their front doors. As a result, the particularistic role relations between neighbors became impersonal and they could then do business with each other as "strangers." Setting accounts straight is a kind of exchange considered legitimate between strangers without regard to other elements of social relations.[62] De Glopper's findings in contemporary Taiwan are also worth noting:

> In ideal terms, people in Lukang describe the sum of their social relations with a set of discrete categories. There are business relations; there are kinship relations; there are

neighborly relations; and there are what are usually called "social" relations. Each of these has its own principle and purposes, its own satisfactions and problems.

He continues:

The small businessmen in Lukang desire to maximize their autonomy and freedom of choice, and prefer limited, functionally specific relations to diffuse ties, fused with personal relations.[63]

As a matter of fact, within Chinese society the folk culture, if not the great Confucian tradition, has long developed what may be called a "compartmentalization" strategy to separate the functionally specific economic exchanges from the functionally diffused social exchanges.[64] This compartmentalization strategy is applicable even to the relationships among the most intimate kinsmen (brothers). The folk saying goes, "Among good brothers, neat accounts are a must" (*hao xiongdi ming suanzhang*). According to this folk logic, the functionally specific economic rationality takes precedence over the functionally diffuse particularistic norm in the brother–brother relation, a *lun* in the five cardinal relations. The rationale underlying this logic is, of course, not to damage the cardinal relations; on the contrary, it is intended to protect the cardinal relations from being damaged by the potential conflicts arising from possible muddy economic transactions. In the course of my field study of small factories in Hong Kong, I heard time and again the saying *shu huan shu, lu huan lu* (money is money, *guanxi* is *guanxi*) meaning people are adopting a "business is business" strategy in their economic exchanges.

In this connection, it is interesting to note that people in

Communist China today, though fully aware of the importance of *guanxi*, tend to condemn those who use it deviously to serve either personal or organizational (*danwei*) purposes. When asked to identify what constitutes leadership qualification for their *danwei*, over half the respondents (59.1 percent) in the Shanghai and Qingpu survey considered having "good outside connections" to be the least important. Why is it that leaders who have good connections (*guanxi*) are rated so negatively? Chu and Ju give the explanation:

> We think that the highly negative rating of this qualification was not so much a reflection on the leaders themselves, but rather a condemnation of the widespread current practice. While everybody was playing the game, many deplored it.[65]

At normative levels, people seemed to hold a view that devious use of *guanxi* is morally wrong. They are not condemning *guanxi* or *renqing* as such; they are condemning it when the practice of it is in conflict with more universalistic ethical concerns. While honoring *renqing* in their interpersonal relationships, as mentioned above, people seemed to think that it should be used conditionally. Chu and Ju's study shows that a large majority of respondents (82.2 percent) would refuse to vote for somebody they knew nothing about even if a good friend asked them to do so. Moreover, it is argued that, "despite the widespread use of network connections in society, there is a near universal wish among the Chinese people that the country be ruled by law because they believe that law brings justice to society."[66] I am inclined to think that Chinese in Communist China, like their compatriots in Taiwan and Hong Kong, have felt a need for universalistic rationality in the emerging market and civil society.

Conclusion

In the preceding pages, I have intended to demonstrate that *guanxi* is part of the "store of knowledge" of Chinese adults in their management of everyday life. To know and to practice *guanxi* is part of learned behavior—of being Chinese. As a sociocultural concept *guanxi* is deeply embedded in Confucian social theory and has its own logic that may be said to form and constitute the social structure of Chinese society. Though Confucian social theory has a tendency to mold the Chinese into group-oriented and socially dependent beings, it must be emphatically argued that Confucianism does attach a good deal of autonomy to the individual. The Confucian individual is the initiator of social communication outside the family structure; he is the architect in *guanxi* building. *Guanxi* building is the Chinese version of network building, which is a phenomenon found in all cultures. Chinese *guanxi* building can be characterized as an ego-centered social engineering of relation building. We have shown that *guanxi* building is based on shared "attributes" such as kinship, locality, surname, and so on, which are the building blocks the individual employs to establish "pluralistic" identifications with multiple individuals and groups. Indeed, network building is used (consciously or unconsciously) by Chinese adults as a cultural strategy in mobilizing social resources for goal attainment in various spheres of social life. To a significant degree, the cultural dynamic of *guanxi* building is a source of vitality in Chinese society.

For a long time, the social phenomenon of *guanxi*—like that of *mianzi* (face) and *renqing*—has been perceived as undesirable or dysfunctional for China's modernization and development. *Guanxi* is deplored by Chinese modernists, Communist or not, who believe that *guanxi* is a private and particularistic morality, and that what China needs is a universalistic ethic. However, we have pointed out that, within the Chinese cultural system, there are mechanisms to neutralize or to freeze the practice of *renqing* or *guanxi* in order to carve out room for the universalistic rationality that is necessary for the management of economic and (in a Weberian sense) bureaucratic conduct. There is no sign that *guanxi* building as an institutionalized mode of behavior is disappearing in modernizing Chinese societies, like Taiwan or Hong Kong. In the modernizing Chinese societies where market rationality and law are becoming the predominant value, the scope of *guanxi* practices has been narrowed and circumscribed and its strategy subtly transformed. The practice of *guanxi* per se is not necessarily incompatible with modernization. What is interesting to note is that the devious practice of *guanxi* for personal or organizational purposes in Communist China today has reached an unprecedented level. The widespread phenomenon of "going through the back door" (to get things done through *guanxi*) has indeed become a social epidemic. It is clear that the gigantic value transformation effort undertaken by the Chinese Communist Party—in order to create a new socialist man for the new socialist society—has ended in failure. The Party's efforts—primarily through the use of fear—to eradicate "Confucian-feudal" elements, including the practice of *guanxi*, have not succeeded. During the so-called Second Long March of the Four Modernizations, which began in 1978, a drastic change has occurred in social-economic life. The market is being partially reinstituted and civil society is being revived. The often criticized traditional behavioral norms are now officially sanctioned in privatized, interpersonal relations. During this rapid transition stage, when the socialist universalistic values are cast into doubt and the market is not yet fully operational, *guanxi* blossoms to play a new instrument which enables people to achieve what has usually denied them through normal channels. There are, however, clear signs that people in mainland China are condemning the devious use of *guanxi* for personal or organizational gains. Nevertheless, the widely cursed phenomenon of "going through the back door" will not go away easily, not until the day when market rationality is fully operational, and law becomes the rule of everyday political life.

5 The Role of Intellectuals in Chinese State Socialism

Intellectuals and the Communist Revolution

Since the late Qing dynasty, after China was repeatedly assaulted by Western imperial powers, Chinese intellectuals have engaged in the search of national power and wealth.[1] The 1911 revolution established the first Republic in Asia, but it failed in creating a modern Chinese state.[2] The May Fourth Cultural Movement, a Chinese version of "Enlightenment," was aimed at the emancipation of individuals from the sociocultural domination of Confucianism and feudalism. The slogans of "Democracy" and "Science" of Western liberalism were embraced with enthusiasm by a sizable number of intellectuals and university students. However, China, as a connective, was faced with what was called "total crisis."[3] Western liberalism with validity based on individualistic reason was considered by radical intellectuals not as powerful a candidate for a total change as Marxism which couched its validity in collectivist reason. Marxism was perceived by intellectuals, like Li Dazhao, to have provided a "fundamental solution" for the Chinese problem. In a world context, socialism was then ascending as an intellectual wave for the

future and in the context of China in the 1920s, Marxism, as a special brand of socialism, was indeed the ideology that could satisfy
most the psychological need of the Chinese intellectuals. Most Chinese intellectuals of the early twentieth century could not be anti-tra-
ditionalistic as well as nationalistic at the same time. Therefore, a
"Marxist turn" of Chinese intellectuals was unsurprising. As Meisner points out: "To become a Marxist is one way for a Chinese intellectual to reject both the tradition of the Chinese past and Western
dominations of the Chinese present."[4] The 1917 Bolshevik revolution, as a historic testimony to the theoretical relevance of Marxism-Leninism to the non-Western world, brought to radical Chinese
intellectuals a revolutionary message of hope for national salvation.[5] During the 1920s, Chinese intellectuals, radical or liberal,
were more concerned with national salvation than with individual
emancipation embodied in the Enlightenment promise.[6] It was no
accident that Marxism eventually became the "opiate" of the intellectuals in China as it was in many other non-Western countries.

The Chinese Communist Party (CCP), which started its revolution in the name of the proletariat, was hardly a party of the proletariat. In fact, the CCP was rather a mass party of intellectuals.
The party leaders, especially the high-level cadres, were intellectuals
par excellence.[7] It is worth mentioning that, as pointed out by Tu
Wei-ming, for Chinese intellectuals, "the sense of urgency and the
psychology of uncertainty, intertwined with an acute awareness that
one's own fate is inextricably tied to the destiny of the nation have
caused political questions to predominate over all other interests in
the perpetual Chinese intellectual search for self-definition."[8] The
intellectual's involvement and participation in the Chinese communist revolution were, in a Marxist sense, engaged not only in

interpreting the history, but also changing it. The contributions of intellectuals to the ultimate victory of communism in 1949 are not the concern of this chapter. What I try to do here is to provide an analysis of the role of intellectuals under state socialism after 1949, with an emphasis on the intellectuals I role as carrier and innovator of culture in two periods of critical change in Chinese Communist history.

Intellectuals under State Hegemony

In Communist China after 1949, Marxism-Leninism was "an ideology in power," to borrow Bertrand Wolfe's expression.[9] Under Marxism-Leninism, Communist Chinese aspired to build a total state.[10] In a total state, the state is identical with society and co-existent with it. Mao's signification of Marxism, like Lenin's "de-Westernization" of Marxism, was a victory of oriental despotic propensities over occidental democratic tendencies. After 1949, Mao successfully established a party-state hegemony to a degree unimagined by dynastic empires. The party-state, not unlike the imperial universal kingship, enjoyed, to use Schwartz's words, "an encompassing jurisdictional claim"[11] over every sphere of sociocultural life, thus creating, especially during the period of the Cultural Revolution, a state-dependent society. In the realm of culture, totalism, not pluralism, was the hallmark of China under Mao's rule.[12] The Chinese intellectuals throughout Chinese history had held what could be called a statist belief that the state should have a moral duty or moral mission "to cultivate the people" (*jiaohua*). Marie-Claire Bergere argued in her book, *The Golden Age of the Chinese Bourgeoisie, 1911–1927*, that China's bourgeoisie had a perception "that the state is indispensable to the constitution of a society and that liberalism itself must be a product of the state."[13] The statist belief was even more pronounced among the cadre-intellectuals of Communist China. Indeed, this belief became their "habits of the heart." Timothy Cheek perceptively pointed out that intellectuals in China shared a mental "frame." This "frame" or set of fundamental assumptions presupposes "the primacy of culture, the importance of educating with proper culture what was viewed by Chinese leaders as a largely passive general public, and the role of the educated elite as the transmitters, the propagandists of a single orthodox culture for the masses."[14]

Under party-state hegemony, intellectuals were all incorporated into the party-state bureaucracy. Indeed, all Chinese intellectuals, be they writers, scientists, professors, journalists, or other forms of mental-workers, were state employees, one way or another. It is not incorrect to say that "In contemporary China, if you are not some kind of establishment intellectual, you are not a legitimate intellectual at all.[15] While being establishment intellectuals, they were invariably attached to a *danwei* (work unit) which provided or decided their income, research funds, promotions, and even their personal or family's living, medical care, etc. Leaving the *danwei* not only their status would be lost, but their very physical existence would come into question. As a result, intellectuals developed a "personal dependence" on the establishment.[16] In a strict sense, in Chinese state socialism, there was no possibility of having what Robert Merton calls "unattached intellectuals."[17] Mao Zedong metaphorically described the awkward situation of intellectuals in the "new China" by saying: "with the skin gone, to what can the hair attach itself?" According to Mao, in the past the intellectuals depended on five skins for a living, namely, imperialist ownership, feudal ownership, bureaucratic-capitalist ownership, national capitalist ownership and small producer ownership, but these five skins which had been the targets of democratic revolution and socialist revolution have been removed. Mao said in 1948: "All these five skins are now things of the past. . . . What skin is there now? The skin of socialist public ownership."[18] Mao said again in 1957 in the same vein:

> The intellectuals must transform themselves into proletarian
> intellectuals. There is no other way out for them. "With the
> skin gone, to what can the hair attached itself?" In the past
> the "hair," meaning the intellectuals attached itself to five
> "skins," that is, depended on them for a living. . . . At present
> what kind of skin do intellectuals attach themselves to?
> To the skin of public ownership, to the proletariat. Who
> provides them with a living? The workers and peasants. . . .
> the intellectuals from the old society are now without a base,
> they have lost their former social and economic base, that
> is, the five skins, and they have no alternative but to attach
> themselves to a new one.[19]

Mao was not wrong—intellectuals in China's state socialism had to be attached to the party-state for a living. All the famous intellectuals, including those erstwhile independent May Fourth intellectuals, such as Wu Han and Dang Tao, were establishment intellectuals. The expression in the *Books of Odes* that "Of all the subjects of the earth, there are none who are not the servants of the King," was applicable with greater force to the fate of intellectuals under Chinese state socialism.

Given structural conditions as this, it is not fruitful to take a dichotomous conception of the interests between the party-state and the intellectuals. Intellectuals were not outside of the state; they were inside the state. When they became cadres, their status was not unlike the scholar-officials of the imperial age. Furthermore, in traditional times, it was still possible to be an intellectual without being incorporated into the imperial bureaucracy.[20] But, in state socialist China, it was almost inconceivable to be an intellectual without being attached to a *danwei*.

A further point has to be made if we want to know the different roles intellectuals played in Imperial China and in state socialism. In the imperial time, great Confucian literati more often than not upheld *daotong* (or Confucian Way) as a principle against *zhengtong* (or political system). In China's state socialism, *daotong* and *zhengtong* are tightly merged into one. Party-state is the embodiment of Communism (Marxism-Leninism). In the system of state socialism, Marxism has become what Kolekowski calls "Institutional Marxism," meaning "(Marxism) a doctrine defined purely formally, its content being in every case supplied by the decrees of the Infallible Institution."[21] In other words, Marxism or truth is what the office and officer says. It is only natural that struggling for power has become in China inseparable from what is called "struggling for lines." Whoever has the power decides what Marxism is or what Marxism is not. Almost invariably in every Communist state, but particularly in China, intellectuals become the "instrument" in the power struggle of political leaders. As such, intellectuals' relationship with the party-state is complicated and intriguing. True enough, at one level, we could speak of the party-state in conflict with intellectuals. Nevertheless, at another deeper level, we find that intellectuals were and are often intricately allied with political factions and power-holders in a fashion of vertical patron–clientele relationship. When there was a conflict between political leaders, if not resolved privately, the conflict broke out into the open and manifested itself in subtle or not-so-subtle debate conducted in the open behind a veil of symbols, nuances and metaphors. The debaters were intellectuals who acted as surrogates for leaders who did not want to confront each other directly.

Building a New Socialist Culture

From the day the People's Republic of China was established in 1949, Mao Zedong had almost his way in ruling the China mainland until his death in 1976. In summarizing Mao's life, Stuart Schram has stated that Mao's effort, culminating in the Great Proletarian Cultural Revolution, was "to change the face of China both by shaping the country's society and economy so as to turn it into a powerful modern nation, and by transforming the pattern of thought and behavior of the Chinese People.[22] For Mao, China's road to national development was the road of socialism.[23] Mao's lifelong project was, thus, in short, to build a socialist China. Admittedly, Mao's approach to "building socialism" placed great importance on the reconstruction of the social and economic structure. He nevertheless always viewed the transformation of Chinese culture as indispensable, if not a prerequisite, for the task. Indeed, to him, the task of "building socialism" would not be possible without having a total transformation of Chinese culture. Mao declared in 1940:

> We communists of China have for years been struggling not only for the political and economic revolutions, but also for

the cultural revolution. . . . The aim of all our efforts is the building of a new society and a new nation of the Chinese people. In such a new society and new nation, there will be not only a new political organization and a new economy, but a new culture as well.[24]

It is no surprise that the question of ideology figures so prominently in Mao's writings. Mao was a kind of Marxist who attached tremendous importance to the conscious factor in the human affairs. For him, as Schwartz stated, "the survival of socialism (and attainment of communism) was not assured by the socialization of property. Only the internationalism of a socialist (and communist) ethos could assure ultimate victory."[25] The subjects of ideological remolding or thought reform were all sectors of people. However, the intellectuals were its main target. According to Mao, intellectuals, including writers, artists, scientists, technicians, professors and teachers "are all educating students, educating the people." "Being educators and teachers, they have the duty to be educated first."[26] The necessity of remolding for intellectuals was, to quote Mao again: "Because we want the bourgeois intellectuals to acquire the proletarian world outlook and transform themselves into proletarian intellectuals."[27]

Mao Zedong who, before his ascendance to the leadership role in Zun Yi Meeting had been despised and criticized by "big intellectuals" in the party,[28] had a deep-rooted distrust in and contempt for intellectuals. Mao wrote in 1957, "All wisdom comes from the masses. I have always said that it is intellectuals who are the most ignorant."[29] Worse than this, Mao never really thought intellectuals could be trusted. He described them as "a tuft of grass at the top of the wall swings right and left in the wind."[30] He said that Chinese intellectuals' acceptance of socialism was due to the fact that "they have no alternative; they cannot but accept it. But in their mind they are not convinced."[31] Throughout Mao's era, campaign after campaign was launched aiming at the ideological remolding of intellectuals. They were, namely, Zheng Feng campaign, anti-rightist campaign, socialist education campaign, etc. These campaigns, though different in emphasis and intensity, were a variegated form of thought reform against intellectuals. Robert Lifton suggested that the fundamental aspect of thought reform was the replacement of filial piety which constituted the central moral value of traditional China by a new form of filial piety directed towards the regime. In short, thought reform was a psychological process of identity-destruction and identity-reconstruction. It was designed to transform Chinese people from a "filial son" to a "filial communist," that is, the "new socialist man."[32]

Mao's assumptions about the extreme malleability of the human character and his totalist vision of change or what J. L. Talmon called "the sustained and violent effort to make all things new" could hardly have found support from psychiatric experience.[33] To what extent the thought reform succeeded in transforming Chinese intellectuals into "filial communists" is a moot question though many an intellectual, like Feng Youlan, was made to believe that he was willing to accept Marxism as the guiding ideology to his work.[34] What can be said is that thought reform had a near-complete success in silencing the intellectuals. The most famous, but by no means a typical case was Fei Xiaotong, the internationally known Chinese sociologist/archaeologist. After his essay on "The Early Spring of the Intellectuals" was attacked and labeled as "reactionary bourgeois academic authority" in the Anti-Rightist Campaign, he stopped writing anything scholarly in the fields of sociology and anthropology for eighteen years.[35] Under Mao's China, Marxism was upheld as the paradigm. Intellectuals in arts, humanities and social sciences had to present their ideas and debate issues within a Marxist paradigm. Other ideas and ideologies had to be evaluated according to Marxist criteria.[36] Not long after the People's Republic was inaugurated, Hu Shi and Liang Shuming who were seen respectively as representatives of Western liberalism and Chinese Confucian tradition came under fire. Western liberalism and Confucian tradition were attacked as two main reactionary thoughts.[37] Confucianism, which was the main target of the May Fourth Intellectuals, never had a chance of recovering its status as a living ideology in Mao's China. In the early communist period, there was no shortage of scholars studying Confucianism, but for them, Confucianism was merely an academic interest and invariably, the works on Confucianism were cast in a Marxist straitjacket. True, during the Hundred Flowers period in the 1950s, quite a number of books and articles were published, and some interesting ideas, like "abstract inheritance" of Feng Youlan, were developed and debated;[38] but throughout Mao's era, especially during the Cultural Revolution, Confucianism was condemned as a feudal ideology. It can be argued that Confucianism as a social ethic still had a real living meaning to contemporary Chinese people. The "museum" image of Confucianism by the late Joseph Levenson[39] is, to say the least, problematic. However, Mao's vision of new socialist culture, which is probably not more than what is called "Sinification of Marxism," accorded not too much room for Confucianism as his once comrade, Liu Shaoqi, would have.[40]

For Mao, "Sinification of Marxism," which was a slogan Mao put forward in 1938, meant "Concrete Marxism" that has to take on a "national form." He said, "the Sinification of Marxism—that is to say, making certain that in all of its manifestations, it is imbued with Chinese peculiarities."[41] The thought of Mao Zedong, as an amalgam of Marxism with a Chinese element,[42] was enshrined as early as 1945 in the party constitution's preamble as a "guidance" of the party, and in the Culture Revolution, it was transformed from an ideology into, using Schram's words, "a kind of Marxist Koran endowed with magical virtues."[43] The cult of Mao and his thought was such that no intellectual was able to advance anything theoretically significant and creative, contributing to the development of socialism or Chinese socialist culture. In the "One Voice Hall" (Yi Yan Tang) of Chinese state socialism, Mao Zedong was indeed the only theorist, while hundreds and thousands of intellectuals and new "proletarian intellectuals" were, sadly or not, doing no more than writing "footnotes" for works of the "Greatest Theoretician," a title with which Liu Shaoqi once willingly honored Mao Zedong.[44]

Mao's approach to building a new socialist nation was to engage China in both social and cultural revolution.[45] Apart from rapidly carrying out the transformation of ownership of the means of production through a series of policies of collectivization, culminating in the establishment of commune system, Mao unceasingly worked towards the transformation of cultural values of the Chinese people through mechanisms such as mass campaigns, mass movements, "thought reform," "study groups,"[46] etc. Needless to say, this was a very complicated and gigantic task of ideological engineering. It was not simply a task to uproot the feudal (i.e., Confucian) or the bourgeois values; it was, more importantly, to institutionalize a new secular socialist value system. Harmony was believed to be one of the core values of Chinese culture.[47] Mao had, according to Richard Solomon, "seen conflict as the basic process of social change, and hostility as the motivating force by which politically passive peasants will struggle to build themselves a new world."[48]

Under the Maoist state socialism, the traditional concept of ideological tolerance, *yitu tonggui* (divergent roads to a common end) was regarded as a camouflage for reaction.[49] Ideas and ideologies other than socialism in the first thirty years of communist rule were not tolerated, as C. K. Yang, a prominent Chinese sociologist, writes on the Communists: "No sociopolitical movements based on other forms of idealism in modern China demanded the same complete break with the past as the price of admittance to its rank."[50] Therefore, not only the competing secular ideologies, namely Confucianism and Western liberalism, were vehemently attacked, Chinese theistic religions, Buddhism and Daoism, were also suppressed. Indeed, Communist ideology was made to serve as a "monotheistic faith"[51] for the Chinese people. And all existing cultural values, rites and rituals were supposed to be transformed and replaced. James L. Waston advanced an argument that the deciding character of "Chineseness" was based on particular standardized rituals rather than on proper ideas or, to use his terminology, on "orthopraxy" rather than orthodoxy.[52] He writes:

> Besides attacking the foundation of traditional mortuary
> rites, Communist authorities attempted to introduce a new set
> of socialist rituals, based roughly on Soviet models. . . . The
> results of the Maoist preoccupation with orthodoxy are by

now universally recognized: disruption, disintegration, and anomie on a massive scale. It would appear that the construction of a new cultural identity through the imposition of a centrally-controlled ideology was an unmitigated disaster for China.[53]

Sixteen years have passed since Mao's death, yet it is still not possible to have a consensus among students of China on what extent Mao succeeded in developing a new socialist culture. But there are indisputable signs indicating that it is a far cry to say that Chinese intellectuals have acquired new values or behaviors. The publications of the Hundred Flowers period clearly demonstrated that intellectuals, once given the "freedom" to speak out, did not lose time to criticize the regime. Though the content of the criticisms never really went as far as to question, challenge, let alone or reject the system, they, like earlier idealistic Confucian scholar-officials, did forcefully articulate the gap between the system's ideal and the political-administrative reality.[54] What they advocated was to rectify the wrongdoings of party leaders and to put an end to the devious tendencies of the system. Moreover, in the mid-1960s, intellectuals even showed moral courage in criticizing the "Great Helmsman" and his radical rural policies. Wu Han, then Vice-Mayor of Beijing, showed just this kind of courage by writing "Hai Rui Dismissed from Office." In fact, the debate between Wu Han as well as the like-minded intellectuals and Maoist intellectuals marked the beginning of the political struggles of the Cultural Revolution. In this sense, the debate between opposing camps of intellectuals involved so-called "struggle between two lines." "Struggle between two lines" could be a life-and-death ideological conflict among intellectuals. In a nutshell, it was an ideological debate on who was the legitimate heir for true Marxism-Leninism. The self-legitimization of Communist China, like that in other socialist countries ruled by a communist party, was based on Marxism-Leninism. Marxism-Leninism was, to use a traditional Chinese expression, *daotong* of the Communist party-state. Intellectuals engaged in the conflict sometimes genuinely believed in their own interpretation of Marxism-Leninism as the true version, while their ideological opponents were the revisionists of some sorts of *daotong*. To the intellectuals who were involved in "struggle of two lines," what they argued was not whether they should be loyal to the "system" or *daotong*. What was at issue was the true system, or true *daotong*. Critical intellectuals' critiques until the downfall of Gang of Four were not aiming at rejecting the "system," but at making the system true to its *daotong*.[55] This was the case during the Cultural Revolution of 1966–1976 and also at the time of Mao's death in 1976. A divided leadership often split the intellectuals and pushed them into opposing ideological camps. When their political patron triumphed, they entered into the center of power. This happened to radical intellectuals when Mao became the sole leader during the Cultural Revolution, and they were pushed to the periphery of power and met their downfall after Mao's death.

What is worth mentioning is that the process of ideological debate, with its great waste of intellectual resources, sometimes makes possible the emergence of more than one vision of reality, heightening the fundamental issues, i.e., Red versus expert, facing a modernizing country like China.[56] There is no doubting Mao's unceasing cultural change efforts brought considerable impact on the pattern of thought and behavior of the Chinese people. Godwin

Chu and Ju Yanan, in their countrywide survey study on mainland China in the 1980s, *The Great Wall in Ruins*, suggested that the traditional cultural system, metaphorically identified as the Great Wall, has been deeply eroded, and a new pattern of thought and behavior has taken root.[57] However, one could argue, what the centrally controlled Maoist non-theistic ideology had created is a "flat cultureless culture," as Myron L. Cohen writes:

> Hegemony in modern China receives no commonly accepted legitimization through culture, rather it represents the culture of the barracks, a culture of compliance, of slogan, posters, and mobilizations conveying messages and commands rather than meaning. This form of flat cultureless culture was most emphasized during the various movements or campaigns (*yundong*) which were especially characteristics of the first three decades of the Communist era.[58]

Three years after Mao's death, the New Realism Literature of 1979–1981, which flourished during a brief thaw, was most revealing in terms of the candid and critical attitudes of the authors toward the Communist system. Representative authors, like Bei Dao, Gu Cheng, Wang Xizhe, to name a few, were members of the first generation of Chinese to grow up under socialism. They were reared on Maoist ideology, and were not antagonistic to socialist ideals. However, "their works now suggest a deep sense of disillusionment—a loss of absolute faith in the Political Ideals taught to them in their youth. They not only condemned particular events or individuals in the People's Republic's history, but also questioned the ideological foundation upon which the socialist regime has relied.[59] Mao's ideology was quickly losing its magical appeal among intellectuals.

Intellectual and Post-Mao Modernization

The collapse of the so-called "Gang of Four," immediately following the death of Mao in 1976, marked a turning point in the history
of China's state socialism. In 1978, Deng Xiaoping, who has been
down three times, managed a dramatic comeback, and launched
the Four Modernizations program or what he often calls the "second revolution" which placed utmost importance on productivity.[60]
Deng is a thoroughgoing pragmatist and instrumentalist. His most
celebrated saying is a homely metaphor to the effect that it does not
matter whether a cat is black or white so long as it catches mice.
He, opposing to Mao, is anything but an ideologue. Deng ignores
or defies many of the precepts most cherished by traditional Marx-
ists; he is unrepentant in combing communism and capitalism.[61]
Deng set about to replace Maoism with his uninspiring formulation of "socialism with Chinese characteristics." Deng's concept of
"socialism with Chinese characteristics" has no theoretical core,
yet it embraces both the values of socialism and nationalism, thus
enabling it to have an appeal to the Chinese intellectuals of different ideological persuasions. However, Mao Zedong Thought, the
state ideology for the past three decades, did not fade away along
with the collapse of the "Gang of Four." The task facing Deng and
his supporters was to demystify and demythologize Mao. Without
a process of de-radicalizing Maoism, Deng's "second revolution"
would find legitimation difficult. The Chinese intellectuals who
had long been disenchanted with Mao Zedong Thought embraced
Deng's reform and modernization program with varying degrees
of enthusiasm. Indeed, they are too willing to be involved in the
process of de-Maoification. It should be pointed out that the fate

of intellectuals has experienced a drastic change since 1978 under Dengist leadership. Half a million intellectuals, who had been pilloried as rightists in 1957, were re-evaluated. Ideologically, intellectuals as mental workers were reclassified as an integral part of working class. In the last Mao decades, they were condemned as the "stinking number nine" (*chou laojiu*), the dregs of society. As the Dengist leadership appreciated the value of expertise for China's modernization, intellectuals became for a time the "sweet number nine."[62] In fact, the role of intellectuals in the post-Mao period was essential in the process of de-Maoification through their ingenuous reinterpretations of Mao Zedong Thought, giving primacy to his theory of knowledge. This rationale basically implies a shift from the emphasis on the substantive conclusions of Mao Zedong Thought to a stress on its use as a method of analysis.[63] The epistemological postulate that "practice is the criterion for testing truth" was elevated to the most fundamental postulate of Marxism, thus making Mao Zedong Thought not a criterion, but as an object itself to be tested and assessed.

This postulate of the methodological master-principle was developed and written by Sun Changjiang, a ghost-writer for Hu Yaobang.[64] It should be said that in the post-Mao era, intellectuals indeed made important contributions to the development of the so-called "cultural heat." What is more, a considerable number of intellectuals were actively engaged in developing new ideological formulations for the advancement of "Enlightened Marxism" and "Socialism with Chinese characteristics." The latter type of intellectuals, though seldom becoming star intellectuals or cultural heroes, have helped the Dengist leadership in changing the face of China's economy and culture. They are not ideological "technicians," like intellectuals in Mao's era, merely writing "footnotes" for Mao's works. It was through the reinterpretation and reformulation of Marxism-Leninism and their "surgical operation," to use Schram's expression,[65] of Mao Zedong Thought by these intellectuals (more precisely, Marxist intellectuals) we saw in 1980 marking a new turn in Chinese state socialism. Tang Tsou has the view that under Deng's reform, there was a genuine retreat of politics from the control of society.[66] He wrote:

> The practical and operational consequences of the current ideological discourse are to allow economic forces and other social groups a degree of autonomy in order to ameliorate many of these adverse effects of politics. Politics is still given a primary role to play in economic development, but the market and other social forces will also be allowed to play their own roles in the economy and society.[67]

Indeed, the Dengist leadership has consciously moved away from the concept of the total state. Intellectuals were beginning to question the wisdom of the statist belief which not only has been accepted as part of the Marxist project ever since Kantsky, but has also been the shared political orientation of Confucian intellectuals. Vivienne Shue writes:

> The new party state center did not, could not, and plainly did not wish to, control everything . . . that in the contemporary Chinese state–society relationship, the state is at long last breaking down.[68]

The economic reforms have reduced the state's persuasive influence. Robert F. Ash in his analysis of the state's role in agriculture argues that "since 1978 the state's economic involvement in the agricultural sector has declined markedly,"[69] and by the time of the Thirteenth National Party Congress (October 1987), "the notion of assigning some policy independence to 'society' was finding limited recognition at the theoretical level."[70]

In the 1980s, intellectuals began to search for independence and authority outside of the party-state. The first salon to claim public existence as a political entity was the *minzhu shalong* (Democracy Salon) established in Peking University on May 4, 1988 by Fang Lizhi and others. After 1983–1984, a number of *minjian* magazines and research institutes came into existence with the backing of private or semi-private sources. To name a few, the *Jingjixue Zhoubao*, an economic weekly, was a truly *minjian* periodical; the famous *Beijing Shehui Jingji Kexue Yangjiusuo* (Beijing Research Institute for Sociology and Economics), established by Chen Ziming, was supported by an array of smaller *gongsi* (companies). As pointed out above, intellectuals' autonomy and independence was made almost impossible because of the fact that they were state employees, or to use Mao's expression, they have to attach to the only "skin," that of private ownership. However, with the existence of private enterprises becoming legitimate under new policies, the intellectuals discovered the potential for having new "skins" to attach to. Admittedly, the cellular organization of the *danwei* that kept the individual in communal bondage was not deeply altered by the reform. Intellectuals were not fully ready to break the so-called *tiefanwan* (iron rice bowl). Michel Bonnin and Yves Chevria point out:

> They (intellectuals) maximized the advantages of *tiefanwan*
> by not breaking with their *danwei*, while counting at the same

time on the new opportunities in the public sphere, much as the writers had done by getting state wages plus royalties on their sales, but on a greater scale.[71]

Nevertheless, there were intellectuals, though not a large in number, breaking *tiefanwan* by seeking full-time jobs in the non-state sector. A case in point was Zhou Duo who left his job in the Sociology Department of Peking University to join the research center created by the Stone Company.

Prior to and during the Democracy Movement in 1989, the appearance of autonomous organizations was an important testimony to the emergence of civil society, though embryonic in nature. Among these groups, the Beijing Association of Intellectuals established by Yan Jiaqi, Bao Zunxin and other intellectuals and the Beijing's Workers Autonomous Federation were the most prominent. Deng's reforms, though limited in scope and one-sided in nature,[72] unquestionably gave more weight to the long-ignored "society" vis-à-vis the state. Although only to a small extent, there appeared a process of "de-establishing" the status of intellectuals in terms of decreasing the degree of personal dependency on the party-state.

It is questionable whether any non-party or non-state agents could offer an alternative to the existing hierarchies of party-state power. But the significance cannot be unnoticed that intellectuals like Jin Guantao, Yan Jiaqi and Fang Lizhi established what was in China a "civil discourse." Never since 1949 have intellectuals been allowed much "public sphere"; and in their "civil discourse," the critique was no longer confined to the shortcomings or wrongdoings of the bureaucracy or officials. Intellectuals began to question, criticize and challenge the "system," the *daotong*, i.e.,

Marxism–Leninism–Mao Zedong Thought. After having experienced the "holocaust" of the Cultural Revolution, Chinese intellectuals reached a high level of self-reflexibility, developing what Tu Wei-ming calls "communal critical self-consciousness." A process of secularization rapidly developed among intellectuals with regards to Communist ideology in general and Mao's Thought in particular. Maoism as a "non-theistic faith," though not totally losing its mystic power among the populace, seldom found audience among intellectuals. There were a few exceptions like "leftist" party ideologues, Hu Qiaomu and Deng Liquan. The Chinese intellectuals who had been marginalized in the Maoist era found themselves back in the mainstream of society.[73] Outside of the state, they managed to find ways to articulate ideas and ideals far from the Marxist or Maoist paradigms. They no longer were concerned whether what they said was in conformity with party lines or not. The Communist Party proved unable to assert the cultural hegemony it enjoyed prior to 1978.[74] As a matter of fact, during Deng's period, there were no clear party lines to speak for as "the Chinese communist party lost its unified voice and monopoly on truth,"[75] resulting in ideological dislocation.

In the cultural marketplace of the reform period, as Peter Woody, Jr. argues, political thought was given to "fade."[76] Of intellectual fads, humanism (Western type), democratic liberalism, scientific rationalism and non-authoritarianism[77] captivated most main-line intellectual sentiments. Cultural pluralism, rather than cultural totalism, was the hallmark of the intellectual landscape during the so-called "cultural heat" of 1983 through 1989. It was said that "the problems with intellectuals nowadays is not that they have no ideas, but that they have no common ideas."[78] If there was a focus of concern among intellectuals of different intellectual persuasions, it was their obsession with the future of China.

Intellectuals, like the writer Wang Ruowang and the journalist Liu Binyan, unambiguously attributed the problem plaguing China to Confucian feudalism and Marxist-Leninist totalitarianism. This diagnosis of China's current sickness was powerfully presented in a six-part television series titled *He Shang* (The River Elegy) in 1987, as a response to the dismissal of the party's Secretary-General, Hu Yaobang, seen by many as the most liberal and reform-minded of party leaders. *He Shang* was produced by a talented team of critical young intellectuals; its message was cruelly clear. The Yellow River Culture is dead and the only hope for China's revitalization is to embrace the culture of the Blue Ocean which means modern Western civilization. The tone of *He Shang*'s attack on Chinese tradition was strikingly similar to the "Down Confucius Shop" of the May Fourth Movement and its unconditional embrace of Western values was only a dramatic version of Westernization, of the intellectuals in the twentieth century. Intellectuals were inclined to believe that the root of China's problem was in the realm of culture. What China needs is a cultural project of "New Enlightenment." Indeed, for most critical intellectuals, what contemporary China should have is a "New May Fourth."

Not unlike May Fourth intellectuals, most contemporary intellectuals are iconoclastic and anti-traditional. Their critique is encompassing and sometimes totalistic. The difference between the New May Fourth intellectuals and their predecessors in May Fourth is that while the latter rejected Confucianism, the former reject both Confucianism and Marxism-Leninism-Maoism. True enough, intellectuals of China today are still not free from the tension between *Qimeng* (Enlightenment) and *Jiuguo* (National Salvation), but they are not prepared to sacrifice the former for the latter as most of their predecessors did in the early twentieth century. The moral courage of intellectuals under Deng's era is hardly in doubt, but their level of intellectual sophistication regarding issues such as democracy and science is hardly higher than that of their May Fourth predecessors. In a dispassionate analysis of the writings of intellectuals participating in the Democracy Movement, Andrew Nathan points out that the concepts of democracy and science they articulated were one-sided or blatantly naïve. He writes about Fang Lizhi, a renowned astrophysicist and democracy fighter, as follows:

> For Fang, science is able to make the same kinds of all-embracing claims to certainty as the dialectical materialism that it displaces. Even the old idea of cosmic harmony reappears when Fang argues that the beauty of a certain mathematical concept is evidence for the inevitability of democracy, on the grounds that both the formula and democracy demonstrate the principle of harmony that is the essential nature of the universe.[79]

As was mentioned, intellectuals under Deng's era played a considerable role in effecting a "cultural heat." The "cultural heat" of the 1980s, revived the cultural discourse of the May Fourth Movement. The significance of "cultural heat" has been subject to various interpretations.[80] In the words of Richard Kraus:

> The most obvious cultural achievement of the reform decade was enormously increased diversity in arts products, especially for urban Chinese. Not only were new works offered, but formerly banned art was revived, and a new

wave of foreign culture was introduced to Chinese audiences, who tried to cram a whole century of "bourgeois" Western art into a single decade, with US television series abstract expressionism, and psycho-analysis tumbling into each other in a sometimes confusing, but tremendously energetic way.[81]

The "cultural heat" was seen as the second current of intellectual emancipation since the May Fourth Movement.[82] Its content defies any generalization. Nevertheless, the underlying theme was clearly the century-old intellectual preoccupation: "Whither Chinese culture?"

At this juncture, let me say that the narrative of the intellectual as cultural carriers or innovators of the reform period cannot be complete without mentioning the role intellectuals played in transforming Chinese state socialism from within. The role of intellectuals who remained in the party-state was just as significant as those who came out of the party-state in the great transformation that has unfolded since 1978. Above, I have discussed how the intellectuals helped Deng Xiaoping's ideological engineering to discredit the radical utopianism of Mao through the "truth criterion controversy." To be sure, the "surgical operation" of Mao Zedong's Thought would not be possible without the efforts of the Marxist intellectuals. As a matter of fact, if not because of the cooperation of the Marxist intellectuals working under the reformist leaders, like Hu Yaobang and Zhao Ziyang, Deng's "second revolution" could not have gone this far, or, perhaps, even happened at all. The reformist leaders were the pivot around which intellectuals made their contributions in effecting a series of change in the economy and polity. The remarkable group of Marxist intellectuals, including Su Shaozhi, Wang Ruoshui, Li Hanglin, Yu Guangyuan, to name a few, spared no time in articulating their own interpretation of Marxist ideology. On the occasion of the centennial of Karl Marx's death (March 14, 1983), the highly respected establishment intellectual, Zhou Yang, openly advocated Marxist humanism and raised the issue of alienation in socialist society. On December 7, 1984, the editorial of the *People's Daily* proclaimed that "we cannot ask writings of Marx and Lenin to solve all our current problems." Su Shaozhi, the former Director of the Marxist and Leninist Institute of the Chinese Academy of Social Sciences and Wang Ruoshui were among the first Marxist intellectuals who put forward a series of theoretical propositions reformulating Marxism-Leninism with the purpose of providing a theoretical base for a positive ideology for China's reform and modernization. Ideas coming from Su and Wang included: Socialism must be humanistic; Marxism must be committed to greater openness and compatibility with other strains of thought; the economic reforms cannot succeed without a corresponding political reform; social science must be independent; freedom of inquiry must be legally guaranteed; etc. Above all, Su Shaozhi advanced a point that the process of building socialism in China has to be reconsidered.[83]

During the 1987 Thirteenth Congress of the Communist Party, seen as the watershed of Deng's reform, the "theory" of the "primary state of socialism" figured prominently in the political report of Zhao Ziyang, then Party Secretary General. The theory of the "primary stage of socialism" argues that building socialism involves different stages. What China can have in the present period is the "primary stage" which would require at least one hundred years. The central task for this primary stage is modernization and to develop productivity is the master-principle of all efforts.

It can be well argued that the theory of the "primary state of socialism" is the singular breakthrough in ideological engineering of the Chinese Marxist intellectuals. This theory found renewed confirmation and amplification in the so-called theory of "socialist market economic system" adopted by the Fourteenth Congress of the Communist Party in October 1992, three years after the tragic Tiananmen repression. At the Fourteenth Congress, Deng Xiaoping's reform ideology was upgraded and upheld as "Deng Xiaoping Theory," enjoying as much, if not more, status than Mao Zedong Thought. It is no exaggeration that Deng's Theory has provided a tremendous impetus for China's economic development. My rather lengthy treatment of the Theory of the "primary stage of socialism" here is not only for its intrinsic importance, but also to reiterate a point that China's restructuring of its economy and culture could come only from the transformation of the party-state itself. The "re-functionalization of ideology," to use Peter Ludz's phrase, was made viable mainly through the works of the Chinese Marxist intellectuals who worked within the party-state apparatus. It should be pointed out that the theory of the "primary stage of socialism" originated from no other than Su Shaozhi, an establishment intellectual par excellence.[84] Up to the eve of the bloodshed of Tiananmen in June 1989, Chinese intellectuals in the years of the General Secretaryship of Hu Yaobang and the Premiership of Zhao Ziyang had "love affairs" with power-holders of the party-state bureaucracy, resembling the relationship between intellectuals and the bureaucracy in some countries of Eastern Europe in the 1960s.[85] Although intellectuals and bureaucrats in China never formed one new, unified dominant class, there was a kind of detente between them. Chinese intellectuals, unlike intelligentsia in the Soviet Union, never had a political culture of the refusenik, and were much more inclined to join the party-state to change it from within. They tended to collaborate with inner-party reformist "to liberalize society prior to any maturity of civil society."[86] Chen Yizi, once the confident of Zhao Ziyaug and now in exile in the US, and many like-minded intellectuals, willingly participated in the political process within the establishment and made substantial contributions to Deng's reform. Bonnin and Chervier write:

> They thought that their being within, as carriers of new ideas and symbols of new social powers, was a sign of change in the state as significant as the reforms engineered by the state and the possibility given to various social groups to operate in a new public sphere without the official structure.[87]

As known to everyone, the reform work of the Chinese intellectuals, within or without the party-state apparatus, came to a halt following the tragic crushing of the Democracy Movement. However, with Deng Xiaoping's "socialist modernization with Chinese characteristics" regaining its ideological supremacy in the recent Fourteenth Congress of Communist Party, there is every sign that China will accelerate its effort to travel a road to modernization further and further away from Marxism-Leninism-Maoism. With renewed, active participation of the Chinese intellectuals in the second wave of Deng Xiaoping's reform, there is a real possibility that China will be the first socialist country to make, willy-nilly, its "exit" from communism.

6 "Modernization" and "Modernity": The Construction of a Modern Chinese Civilizational Order

Any consideration of China's cultural modernity must begin with a rethinking of traditional Chinese civilization in its orientation and the problems that it has to face in the modern age. As many scholars have pointed out, Chinese civilization developed relatively independently in its ancient stage. The German philosopher Karl Jaspers sees China as one of the few high civilizations among India, Greece, and the Near East that formed the "axial age" before the Christian epoch.[1] Each of these civilizations had its unique development and cultural orientations, and exerted tremendous influences on the subsequent ages. From the pre-Qin times to the late Qing dynasty, China remained a long and continuous civilization dominated by Confucian values, despite the assimilation of foreign cultures and the adoption of foreign elements into the culture of the "Middle Kingdom." Ancient China, of course, was a nation, but in a sense very different from the modern "nation state." It was a political-cultural entity developed independently, based more on cultural than ethnic distinctions. In other words, ancient China was a "civilizational state," with a peculiar cultural order, and made up a world of its own. In the past three thousand years, there were certainly contacts between the Chinese world and its outside, but the current concept of "world system" did not exist in traditional China. In traditional China, the civilizational order was particularly manifested in terms of *huangquan*, or the Chinese idea of "universal kingship," which emphasized its "universal jurisdictional claims over the land under the heaven," and Chinese values were wittingly or unwittingly adopted as the measure of the degree of civilization. In the course of time, there had been changes in the realms of politics, economics and culture, but the basic character of Chinese civilization, especially with respect to social structure, ways of life and deep meaning structure, remained intact till the late Qing. "Pre-modern" China was truly a unique form of civilization. Having impacts on Japan and Korea, it may be regarded as the very form of East Asian civilization as a whole.

Modern Challenges from the West

In the mid-nineteenth century, the Chinese civilizational order was faced with an unprecedented challenge. Essentially, this challenge did not just come from the West; for more precisely, it came from "modern" Western civilization, that is, the Western civilization that have gone through modernization. Modern Western civilization first made its presence in China and East Asia in the forms of imperialism and colonialism. At that time, Chinese intellectuals like Li Hongzhang and Yan Fu felt that it was the greatest turn in three thousand years of Chinese history or an unprecedented epochal change ever since the Qin and Han times. Trying to understand this "greatest turn" or "epochal change" was a rather slow process. In the past hundred years or so, the Chinese understanding of the essence of the Western "challenge" grew only gradually. In fact, the Chinese response to the challenge from modern Western civilization means, to use the most encompassing term, China's modernization, or the renewal and further development of traditional Chinese civilization.

The first wave of China's modernization was the "*Yangwu Yundong*" (Westernization Movement) led by officials like Zeng Guofan, Li Hongzhang, and Zhang Zhidong in the second half of the nineteenth century. These early reformers merely saw the material and technological sides of modern Western civilization, putting their efforts on mining and building ships and guns. Kang Youwei and Liang Qichao, leaders of the Reform of 1898, went further and saw the urgency of "studying Western principles," thus touching on the "institutional" aspect of modern Western civilization. The "*Sturm und Drang*" movement in the course of China's modernization is the Revolution of 1911 led by Dr. Sun Yat-sen, which toppled the monarchy and established the Republic. This must be counted as an epoch-making event, because it transformed China, for the first time, from a "civilizational state" into a "nation-state." The centrality of Chinese civilizational order was the political system, which was already undermined during the late Qing.[2] When the civil service examination system was abolished in 1905, a pillar of the edifice was dismantled. And the whole political order was completely destroyed by the Revolution of 1911. The significance of the Revolution, as a scholar has pointed out, "lay in its negative achievement—the extinction of the monarchy which was not just a national kingship of the European type but the universal kingship of the Son of Heaven."[3] No doubt, the Revolution of 1911 was a sign of China's turn toward the "modern," and more importantly, it indicated the decomposition of the political order of the age-old Chinese civilization. After the Revolution, China was no longer the same China. The Revolution was a modern type of political revolution, for it broke through the previous state of dynastic changes, which lasted two thousand years. It did not turn China into a successful republic, not to say a real democratic state. Yet it is politically significant because the idea of "kingship" was replaced by the law of "people's rights," and the theory of "Heavenly Mandate" by the discourse of people's rights as the legitimate and proper basis of the political order. After the collapse of the Manchurian monarchy, China began a journey on a long and winding road in search of a modern form of nation, or a political order for modern Chinese civilization, which is inseparable from China's response to the West.

In Search of a New Order in Globalization

In respect of China's modernization, the May Fourth New Culture Movement is as important as the Revolution of 1911. Championing "Science" and "Democracy," the New Culture Movement had a strong flavor of the European Enlightenment. It was, as John Dewey puts it, a "revolution in thoughts."[4] Its main spirit was to "re-evaluate" the value system of traditional Chinese civilization. All the slogans, such as "down with Confucianism," "to hell with rites," "do away with filial piety," "cannibal rites" and "anti-feudalism," aimed at attacking the Confucian moral-political order which provided the foundation of traditional Chinese civilization. The chief aim of this movement was the liberation of the individual, freeing the individual from the bondage of traditional society and freeing the individual mind from the Confucian ethical system. As a result, revolutionary changes took place in the Chinese family and in Chinese values. True enough, the new thoughts promoted by the May Fourth Movement were not entirely new for they might be found in earlier reformers, such as Liang Qichao, Tan Sitong and Sun Yat-sen. By the time of the May Fourth Movement, however, they had already become common convictions of many a new intellectual. Science and democracy, the twin goal-value of the May Fourth Movement, one must point out, were borrowed from the West. Hu Shi's view of "complete cosmopolitanization" (*chongfen shijiehua*) clearly demonstrates that the civilizational order of traditional China must turn from a "Chinese" one to that of the "world."[5] But one must also note that the "cosmopolitan" cultural order in Hu Shi's mind is defined as well as dominated by the Western model. The fact is modernization only took place once and in Western Europe, and up till now the modernization process originated from Western Europe remains the only and dominant model modernity for the whole world.

Globalization as Modernization

From the late Qing dynasty to the present, China's effort in modernization has traversed the entire course of the twentieth century. In twentieth-century China, there were too many events that hindered or twisted the course of modernization. Prominent examples include warlord period, the Japanese invasion, the Chinese Civil War, and the Cultural Revolution. Today, Chinese societies, including mainland China, Taiwan, Hong Kong and Macau, are all consciously modernizing themselves. Whether the road of socialism, as taken by mainland China, or the road of capitalism, as taken by Taiwan, Hong Kong and Macau, are essentially self-conscious routes of modernization; China's modernization is part of the "globalization" of modernization. Modernization, as mentioned above, originated from Western Europe. The globalization of modernization can be seen as a process whereby the modern form of civilization of the West diffuses all over the world. Globalized "standards of civilization," in effect, are the "universalization" of the Western particularism[6] as exemplified by the institutionalization of World Time and the Gregorian calendar. In a "late stage" of modernization today, the phenomenon of globalization of modernization is no longer limited to the economic realm, or what Wallerstein calls the "capitalist world economy" as a result of capitalist expansion.[7] In respect of politics, the form of "nation-state" in Western Europe has become a basic structure in the world political system today.[8] More significantly, with respect to cultural values, ideas which first emerged in the West, like democracy, human rights, rights of homosexuality and sexual liberation also increasingly become globally accepted. There was never, and will never be a "monadic modern civilization." Yet one cannot but be struck by the fact that the particular form of Western civilization, especially the particular form of American civilization, has exerted greater and greater global influence since the 1950s.

Modernization in the Global Scale

In regard to China's modernization, Taiwan and Hong Kong won the reputation of "little dragons" in the late twentieth century due to economic success, while the economic development in mainland China after the Cultural Revolution also made enormous progress under "Open-door Policy." Back in the nineteenth century, the founders of sociology, Marx, Durkheim, and Weber, were all concerned with a single explanation for the origin of the "modern" as manifested in technological and bureaucratic organizations, which in Marx is "capitalism," in Durkheim "industrialism," and in Weber "rationalization." Modernization, of course, is a multidimensional process of social transformation, but the transformation in the realm of economy (from agriculture to industry) did play a central role in the transformation of society as a whole. Economic transformation, whether in terms of the mechanism of capitalism or of industrialism, depend on what Weber called "rationalization," especially in the form of "instrumental" or "means/ends" rationality (*Zweckrationalität*) that he observed shrewdly. In the dynamics of the market under capitalism, "instrumental rationality" is particularly intensely manifested, and can be empirically verified with reference to the modernization of Taiwan and Hong Kong.[9]

In the 1990s, vigorous processes of modernization, especially in the realm of economy, have already been found in Chinese societies. Japan, another nation in East Asia, is indeed fully modernized. The American sociologist Peter Berger claims that East Asia has made a "second case" of "capitalist modernity" after the model of Western Europe.[10] He says that "modernity" in East Asia is different from that of the West in its nature and particular manner of manifestation. Undoubtedly, the modernization of East Asia is already a success and a fact, which calls for a rethinking of the problem of modernization, and of modernity among scholars in particular.

Contestation with Modernization

Although modernization has become a global phenomenon, there have been various kinds of "counter-modernization" and "de-modernization" movement all over the world since the 1960s, in developed as well as developing countries. These movements represent, fundamentally, discontent with "modernity," which, as manifested today, is dominated by instrumental rationality. The world of modernity, to use Weber's words, is the result of "disenchantment of the world." Modernity does have a liberating function. Increasing autonomy of the self as an individual is the main concern of modernity and "alienation," "meaninglessness" and "homelessness" are prices we have to pay.[11] More significantly, while modernization originated from rationalization, the inflation of "instrumental rationality" is in fact a reaction against reason.[12] The German sociologist Jürgen Habermas points out that there is "colonization of life world" in modernity today.[13] Such discontents with modernity have led to the de-modernizing impulse, which in particular, strongly expressed in environmentalism and movements involving mystic religions. Today, while modernization is vigorously set in motion in all countries, the "de-modernizing impulse" is also in full swing in its effects. One must point out, however, that the "de-modernizing impulse" suffers from intrinsic and extrinsic limitations, and it is impossible to stop or reverse the processes of modernization.[14] Modernization does generate "pathologies," yet one must not forget the opportunities and "benefits" it has brought to the human kind.[15] Even more importantly, in regard to social development, one simply cannot find any viable alternatives to modernization. The voice of Octavo Paz, Mexican poet and the 1991 Nobel

Laureate for Literature, is perhaps representative of this view:

> While modernization is the only rational and in fact
> inevitable path for Mexico, it will fundamentally change
> and displace the moralism that Mexicans have lived with for
> centuries. And not all of these changes of family values, life
> goals and societal norms are positive.[16]

On the one hand, Paz feels that Mexico is "condemned to modernization," and on the other, he asserts that Mexico is "condemned to modernize." For him, Mexico has no future unless it modernizes, but modernization is indeed no gospel. In the case of China, can we deny that it, too, is "condemned to modernization" and "condemned to modernize"? In order to set foot in the modern world, can ancient civilizations like China and Mexico not self-consciously take a modern turn?

The "modern turn," in fact, has been China's choice in the past hundred years or so. But we must ask: did the modernization of China follow exactly the same route as that of the West? Is the modernity pursued by or appeared in China a replica of the West? More importantly, can China develop a form of modernity different from that of the West? This, of course, concerns the problem of universality of Western modernity.

In certain respects, China's modernization is an intentional imitation of the West. As one can clearly see in the discussion above, Chinese intelligentsia and political elites in the late nineteenth and early twentieth centuries took the model of Western modernization as a model and paradigm. In the late Qing dynasty, there were views that advocated the preservation of traditional Chinese values. The idea of localism embedded in the saying, "Chinese studies as the fundamental structure, Western learning for practical use" (*zhongxue wei ti, xixue wei yong*) put forth by Zhang Zhidong and others, had been temporarily adopted as a measure that calls for a balanced and structured way to handle the complex relations between "the local / the Chinese" and "the global / the Western." But since the New Culture Movement of 1919, many have accepted, consciously or unconsciously, Hu Shi's belief in "complete cosmopolitanization." In the past hundred years, Chinese intellectuals started off with the preservation of the *ti* (essence or fundamental structure) of "Chineseness" (*zhongguo zhi wei zhongguo*) in respect of spiritual values and permitted only "practical application" (*yong*) of West knowledge. *Ti* means a cultural tradition, or the kernel of traditional Chinese civilization. However, in pursuit of a powerful and prosperous nation, changes occurred with respect to "practical application," and eventually even the Chinese "essence" was abandoned. New "applications" and new "essences" were sought in a modern Chinese civilization.[17] Intentionally China did imitate Western modernization, but empirically China's modernization did not and could not simply follow the Western route. As a latecomer, China's experience of modernization was radically different from that of the West with regard to the foundation on which the process began, the agents in the process, the strategies of development, different intensities of the pressure of time in the course of development, and the cultural conditions. Even within different Chinese societies, namely Taiwan, Hong Kong and mainland China, the experiences of modernization were very different. Strictly speaking, China's modernization cannot and in fact did not follow the Western path. One can say that, only in terms of "visions" of modernization, China has long been using the Western model as the standard for a new civilization. Of course, one must note that the visions of a modern culture, or more precisely, of a culture "surpassing the modern," as depicted by the Communists in this century is distinct from the capitalist model of modern civilization. Still, Communism, in the last analysis, came also from Enlightenment in the West. Marx's cultural hero, after all, is Prometheus, and what Communists cherish most is the "ideal of development."[18]

Globalization as an Inevitable Result of Modernization

In the literature on modernization, the dominant theoretical view is that, despite different points of departure, all modernized societies will become similar or even the same with respect to the ultimate form of "modernity." "Theories of modernization" prevalent in the 1950s, 1960s and even 1970s have a strong propensity toward this conception of linear evolution. "Theories of modernization" is deeply influenced by the American sociologist Talcott Parsons, whose theory of social change is fundamentally an evolutionary view. Parsons believes that all modern societies have only one origin, that the "rationalization" processes which account for modernization of Western Europe have "universal" implications, and that these modernization processes are necessarily "directional" rather than arbitrary. He thinks that this course of development will become the main trend in the next century and perhaps even further in future, resulting in the establishment of societies of what he calls the "modern type."[19] In sociology, the clearest example of seeing modernization as a global phenomenon of linear evolution is the "theory of convergence" proposed by Clark Kerr (1964) and his

colleagues. Kerr's view is that all societies on the road of industrialization, due to the very logic of industrialization, will eventually
converge with respect to the industrial system and related social and
cultural forms. "Theories of modernization," especially "theory of
convergence," see the Western European experience of modernization not only as the "first case," but also as the universal "paradigm"
of modernity.[20]

Nowadays, "theories of modernization" and "theory of convergence" have already received severe criticism. Tested against
the phenomenon of development in East Asia's modernization,
however, one cannot say that such theories are devoid of empirical
support.[21] In fact, all modernized societies in terms of institutional
structures, be they industrial, occupational, educational or urban,
do show the phenomenon of "convergence." Besides, pathologies
of modernization, one kind or another, also cropped up. According to The Economist, in the course of East Asia's (especially Taiwan's and Hong Kong's) modernization, there have been increases
in crime rate (especially juvenile delinquency) and in the rate of
divorce, while family values are undermined by the market system
and there are other signs of social decadence. All these phenomena differ from those in Western modernization only in degree and
not in kind. What afflicted and keeps on afflicting modern Western
societies can hardly be avoided in the course of modernization in
Asian societies. In view of developmental trends, mainland China
and India are expected to repeat some predictable patterns as experienced in England during the eighteenth and nineteenth centuries.[22]
True enough, the characteristics of modernity found in East Asia
now to a certain extent, share much commonality with those of the
modern West. Commonality, nevertheless, does not entail homo-

geneity. More and more Asian scholars now believe that Asian democracy is different from Western democracy in the way Asian management is different from Western management. Asian democracy and Asian management, like Asian arts, Asian architecture and Asian food, are "specific categories" distinct from those of the West.[23] In short, Asia can and should have her own modernity distinct from that of Western Europe. The significance of this argument is not limited to academic discourse, for it marks the confident self-reflection of Asians in quest of a modern civilizational order. Asians in the late twentieth century are no longer willing to accept or believe in Western modernity as a universal paradigm of modernization. Since the late nineteenth century, Asians (including Chinese) have been "condemned to modernization" and "condemned to modernize," wittingly and unwittingly modelling on the West. It is interesting to note that in the processes of the globalization of modernization, Asians nowadays begin to question the universality of Western modernity as a model. Based on their unique experience and in their new vision, many affirm that Asia can and should have its distinct form of modernity.

Localized Modernity in Asia?

Can China or East Asia truly develop a model of modern civilization distinct from the Western model of modernization? This is an assumption as much as a theoretical question. The American sociologist Peter Berger's answer is obviously affirmative. Berger's view is based on the consideration of culture. He believes that Confucian ethics is a cultural resource for the construction of East Asian modernity. Today, many scholars are directly or indirectly exploring the possibility and necessity of a particular form of East Asian modernity, highlighting especially Confucian ideas as a useful resource.

Modernity is an extremely complex sociocultural system, and its genesis and development cannot rely on any single factor, be it economic interest, ideology, geographic environment, or the particular character of an individual leader. Although Parsons believes in the universality of Western modernity, he sees culture as the highest cybernetic level accounting for social change. He even calls himself a "cultural determinist."[24] In an essay on modernity, Charles Taylor (1992) points out that the "a-cultural theory of modernity" had dominated the discourse of modernity in the past two centuries. That is to sap the cultural factor that has been neglected in the discussion of modernization and modernity. Max Weber may be considered a founder of this kind of discourse, for his theory of rationalization is a prime example of the a-cultural theory of modernity. Followers of this theory, Taylor says, believe that traditional Western societies went through a "transformation" into the modern form, and this transformation is a culture-neutral mechanism. They see modernity as the growth of reason, like the growth of scientific consciousness, secularization and the development of instrumental rationality, and they define modernity in terms of changes in social processes, such as social movements and industrialization. In the "a-cultural theory of modernity," all cultures must inevitably go through this social transformation, and any culture, including the Chinese of course, will experience some definite forms of change along the way like the secularization of religions and the challenge and erosion of the ultimate values by instrumental reasons. In brief, modernity is believed to be culture-neutral. Taylor strongly argues against such a view and he asserts that the understanding of Western modernity based on the assumption put forth by the "a-cultural theory of modernity" is one-sided and distorted. Its limitation lies in the attempt to see everything modern as derived from the "Enlightenment package," and it may thus be called the "Enlightenment package error." Taylor, of course, does not suggest that the "cultural theory of modernity" can explain all aspects of modernity. Rather, he thinks that a theory of modernity which is devoid of a cultural consideration can hardly fully deal with the most urgent task of social sciences today, that is, to see the full gamut of "alternative modernities" that are in the making in different parts of the world.

Taylor's criticism of the "a-cultural theory of modernity" serves in effect as a reminder to all theorists that the form Western modernity takes is not necessarily universal in its application. On the other hand, one must also not try to define the "transformation" from the tradition to modernity solely in terms of cultural change, or else one will oversimplify the issue and miss the point of seeing the complexity of the transformation. For example, one must reckon with the fact that efficacy offered by modern science and technology is one thing any society will understand and try to obtain. Any society, which does not recognize the importance of science and technology, will lose its place in the global battle of competition for survival. There is "universality" in modernity, but it does not follow that all forms of the modern cultural order are "homogenous." One important component of Western "modernity," Berger points out, is individualism. In the Western experience, capitalism and individualism are inseparable. However, what one finds in East Asia is a "non-individualistic version of capitalist modernity." Berger's study provides an important clue for the exploration of "modernity" in East Asia and China.[25] In his analysis of Japan's modernization, Tanase Takao of Kyoto University puts forth a thought-provoking view: Japan's case is "modernization without being modern." His main argument is that although Japan has successfully completed her "modernization" in three important domains, namely, industrialization, democratization and individualism, one must also note that the market mechanism in Japan is still under strict government control. Despite the institutionalization of democracy, Japanese politics is infiltrated by authoritarianism, and that the new values the Japanese discover in the self is "my-home-ism," without any traits of Western individualism at its core.[26] Tanase Takao's observation demonstrates that Japan's modernization is modernization without being modern. On the other hand, one may as well contend that the Japanese form of modernity is distinct from its Western counterpart. That is to say, the Japanese form of modernity, while sharing some of the "universal elements" of global modernity (industrialization, democratization and individualism), also bears characteristics peculiar to Japan. Today, East Asia, including the few Chinese societies (such as Taiwan and Hong Kong), is undergoing modernization and in the process exhibiting some features of modernity different from those of the West. How to understand and analyze these "alternative modernities" must be a very meaningful and challenging task for social scientists.

Chinese Modernization in the Midst of Globalization

Chinese modernization cannot be seen simply as the quest for power and prosperity. More fundamentally, it is a historical process whereby China searches for a new civilizational order. Though China is "condemned to modernize," her "modern turn" is as much "destined" as is a matter of choice. The form of modern civilization as a result of modernization is a particular type of new civilization, which is essentially different from pre-modern civilizations.[27] This new civilization has its origin in the "globalization" of the West, and that is why the Western form of modernity holds such a dominant position in global modernization. Now in different parts of the world, different cultures are experiencing the impact of this "transformation," in which the "universal elements" of modernity may appear and be redefined. The modern character of this new civilization, nonetheless, is increasingly facing criticism and resistance, and it has even triggered off a global "nostalgia" for older civilizations.[28] The central issue today is not only the reflection upon modernity but the need for exploring pluralistic forms of modernity. What has made the Western form of modernity the dominant form is the culture and advancement of science that Western Enlightenment has brought forth. But despite the universal appeal of such Enlightenment values of freedom, equality, democracy, and fraternity, the "Enlightenment mentality" has been severely criticized. To completely oppose spirit of Enlightenment is not what we should do, but to claim that everything modern belongs to and necessarily comes from Enlightenment is a cognitive error. The objective of China's modernization is to construct a new civilizational order and it is not possible that the spirit of Enlightenment has played no role there. And yet Chinese modernization does not need to subscribe to the whole "Enlightenment package." In this respect, part of the resources for the construction of Chinese modernity should and must come from the cultural tradition of China as a high civilization of the "axial age." China surely needs a modernized new civilization, but what form of such a civilization will take remains a question.

There is not much freedom of choice regarding China's "modern turn," but it does not entail that there is absolutely no room for creativity. The Chinese and East Asians (and including all non-Westerners) should, in the course of modernization in economics, politics and culture, self-consciously adjust and broaden their vision of modernity. While imitating or borrowing from the modern Western model, they should not blindly accept it as the standard for all new civilizations. In the process of constructing a new modern Chinese civilizational order, we must not simply accept all values put forth by Enlightenment but re-evaluate them critically. All in all, building a new modern Chinese civilizational order involves not only a process of deconstructing the cultural tradition but also a process of reconstructing it. For the new Chinese civilization, after all, needs to be both "modern" and "Chinese."

7 Administrative Absorption of Politics in Hong Kong: Emphasis on the Grassroots Level

Hong Kong is one of the few Asian cities which have become rapidly urbanized and industrialized in recent decades. In the last twenty years, Hong Kong has been transformed from a British colonial entrepôt to a city of world significance with a population of four million.

There is a growing literature arguing that Asian urbanization has distinct characteristics and thus differs from Western urbanization. This difference is often believed to have resulted from the differing growth patterns of their seminal cities. Most students of the city use technology as the strategic variable to delineate types of cities. Indeed, the Western city differs in large measure from the Asian city in that the former resulted from technological industrial expansion while the latter did not. However, cities in both the West and the Orient have been multifunctional, and there are very few contemporary cities so heavily committed to industrial activities that a great majority of the labor force is engaged in it. Therefore, apart from technology, other variables such as value and power, especially power, should be taken into account. More often than not, the contemporary Asian cities are created and shaped primarily by power variables. As a matter of fact, Hong Kong, along with many other major Asian cities, has been the result of foreign domination or enterprise. They were created and shaped by the colonial powers for political and economic reasons; they did not grow out of an indigenous urban process. In this sense, Hong Kong is, using Redfield and Singer's concept, a heterogenetic city, and it fits well into McGee's description of the so-called "colonial city."[1]

Hong Kong's urban characteristics cannot easily be described by the rural-urban continuum theory concepts which grow out of the grand tradition of dichotomous social change. The grand dichotomous conception of social change, despite its usefulness as a heuristic model, is primarily a useful typology, rather than a theory of social change. Moreover, it is probably time-bound and culture-bound. The concept of Asian urbanization, however, it seems to us, can hardly be applied to Hong Kong. In this chapter, we are primarily concerned with the political implications of urbanization. In the West, urbanization has often been linked to democracy by political theorists. Max Weber, one of the pioneering students of the sociology of the city, held that the city, as a political community, is a peculiarly Western phenomenon and the source of the modern conception of "citizenship," which itself is the source of democracy.[2] Later, Harold Laski's view that "organized democracy is the product of urban life" was further elaborated by S. M. Lipset.[3]

But it would be a gross mistake to assume that what holds true of the historical relationship between urbanization and democracy is necessarily true in the cities of the Third World. The cities of the Third World are in a situation "that is congenial not to democracy but rather to political demagoguery, or to radical movement, and to the eruption of mob violence."[4] There are many things that make the city political life of the West different from that of Third World societies. But, the basic fact is that the rapid increase of population living in urban settlements in the Third World makes the city a field where the major sociopolitical transformation process takes place in a rather short period of time. Karl Deutsch has termed the process "social mobilization" which is "the process in which major clusters of old social, economic and psychological commitments are eroded and broken and people become available for new patterns of socialization and behavior."[5] It is our belief that the social mobilization process is certainly not confined to the Third World city, but it is by definition more dramatically manifested in cities where people have sudden high exposure to aspects of modern life through demonstration of machinery, buildings, mass media, etc. The increased numbers of mobilized population tend to increase their demands for participation in the political system, leading to a phenomenon called "participation explosion." More often than not, social mobilization and participation explosion lead to political instability in the Third World resulting primarily from, using Huntington's concept, the political gap between the rapid social and economic changes and the slow development of political institutions which have dominated the scene throughout Asia, Africa, and Latin America. The political gap is wider in the city than in the countryside precisely because rapid social mobilization takes place in the city and yet non-governmental institutions are weak or undeveloped. As a consequence, "the instability of the city—the instability of coups, riots, and demonstrations—is, in some measure, an inescapable characteristic of modernization."[6]

What has been said above is indeed a rather gloomy view of the political aspect of urbanization in the Third World. However, we are not ready to accept the view that the pattern of political development in Asian cities and other cities in the developing countries is a "deviant" pattern of the Western model. In our view, the reason why Asian political urbanization does not fit the Western model can be explained in two equally valid ways: either it is the particularistic nature of the Asian political urbanization, or it is simply the parochial nature of the Western model itself. The positive political role of cities in Asia can be better understood by viewing the city as a center of change that has contributed to nation-building because urbanization serves to undermine primordial sentiments, loyalties, and identifications with sub-national entities and thus helps to make the development of new and larger political communities possible. Indeed, Asian cities' political function must be understood in terms of the relation between the part (city) and the whole (national societies). This, however, cannot apply to the Hong Kong case. Hong Kong is a city-state: it is a total entity itself. And this makes Hong Kong a special variant of the Asian city, or the colonial city. What concerns us in this chapter is the way Hong Kong's political system has coped with the problem of stability and, especially, the way it has been coping with the "crisis" of political integration resulting from rapid urbanization in recent decades.

Participation, Synarchy, and Elite Integration

In large measure, Hong Kong is an urban polity relatively free from riots and political cleavages. It has achieved a kind of equilibrium in a very intricate political situation. It certainly has not experienced violence on the same scale as many cities in the Third World. It is the argument of this chapter that the kind of equilibrium this colonial city has thus far achieved is largely due to a process which might be called the "administrative absorption of politics." By this we mean a process by which the government co-opts the political forces, often represented by elite groups, into an administrative decision-making body, thus achieving some level of elite integration; as a consequence, the governing authority is made legitimate, a loosely integrated political community is established.

Hong Kong is not a democracy. The British colonial government has never attempted to follow Western democratic models. It has from the very beginning tried to adopt a unique brand of politics of its own. To characterize politics in Hong Kong is far from an easy job. The most widely quoted concept of "government by discussion" is given by Endacott:

> An examination of the working of the Hong Kong constitution shows interested opinion is consulted continuously prior to any important government decision, . . . and that on occasion . . . the general public at large is invited to express its views." Indeed, consultation as practiced by the Government is so extensive that the term "government by discussion" aptly describes one of its leading characteristics.[7]

Endacott's arguments certainly have some insight and validity. However, it is our view that conceptually and empirically the concept of "synarchy" is the key to understanding the art of government and politics in Hong Kong. "Synarchy," to borrow the concept of J. K. Fairbank,[8] implies a joint administration shared by both the British rulers and non-British, predominantly Chinese, leaders. The kernel of synarchy is a form of elite consensual government; it is a grass-tops approach to the problem of political integration. The

British have consciously or unconsciously governed the colony on the synarchical principle by allowing, though limiting, non-British participation in the ruling group.

Synarchical rule has both formal and informal faces. Before proceeding to discuss the formal face of synarchy, it should be noted that the constitutional structure of Hong Kong's political system is in the typical colonial pattern. The British Crown is represented by a Governor who is "the single and supreme authority responsible to and representative of the Queen." The office of the Governor is the central feature of the Government of Hong Kong. The Governor is in a real sense the head of the Government. Strictly speaking, the Governor can govern the colony, if he wishes, with his own will without regard to what the people in the colony think. But the Government does not seem to have an unlimited image of authority; it has tried to gain legitimacy for its authority not from the Crown but from the consent of the ruled by claiming to conform to democratic values, if not to a democratic form of government. It is under this normative "democratic" or consensual framework that the system of synarchy is practiced.

The formal face of synarchical rule can be analyzed through discussing the operation of the three Councils and the civil service system. On April 5, 1843, Hong Kong was granted a Royal Charter which declared Hong Kong a separate Colony. Among other things, the Charter established a Legislative Council and an Executive Council. The Governor is advised by the Executive Council and is bound to legislate through the Legislative Council. These two Councils are not elected bodies; they are composed of both "official members" and "unofficial members." As of now, the total membership of the Executive Council is fourteen; six are "official members," of whom five are ex-officio members, eight are "unofficial members." The Legislative Council has twenty-nine members in total, with fourteen "official members," of whom four are ex-officio members, and fifteen "unofficial members." And fifteen out of the total twenty-three unofficial members are Chinese. All members, with the exception of ex-officio members, are appointed by the Queen or by the Governor on the instructions of the Secretary of State. These two Councils are the top governmental organs through which the people from the community participate in the policymaking and management of public affairs in the Colony. The precise degree of the "unofficial members" influence in the Councils is difficult to assess, but in large measure "on important issues, their opinion has obvious weight and their opposition is avoided," and "in deference to local Chinese opinion, Chinese custom is safeguarded and legislation concerning it is unlikely to be proposed except on the initiative of the Chinese unofficial members."[9] What concerns us is not only the question of whether the unofficial members have influence in the policymaking process, but also the question of who the unofficial members are and whom they represent. It is true to say that the great majority of the appointed unofficial members are men of caliber and that they are sensitive to "the needs of the community as a whole." But the undeniable fact is that the appointed unofficial members were and still are established or emerging socioeconomic elites who are order-prosperity minded and come from a very narrow sector of the population.

With a few exceptions, the Unofficial Members are men of wealth. Among the Chinese Unofficial Members, prior to 1964, over 90 percent are from "established rich" families and are among the small circle of elite in the Chinese community. After the mid-

1960s, another category of persons has been rising—the "new rich," representing the ever-increasing industrial forces. And among the non-Chinese Unofficial Members, about 75 percent are chief executives or managing directors of commanding economic institutions.[10] It is worth noting that in the very beginning of the Colony's history, the British ruling group seemed not too much concerned about the problem of Chinese participation. Although the two Councils were assembled as early as 1844, the first Chinese, Ng Choy (or Dr. Wu Ting-fang) was appointed to the Legislative Council only in February 1880, due to the belief of the Governor Sir John Pope Hennessy that since the Chinese outnumbered the foreigners in Hong Kong, they should be allowed a share in the management of public affairs. And it took another forty-six years to appoint Sir Shouson Chow as the first Chinese member of the Executive Council in 1926. It seems that the concept or practice of administrative absorption of politics is not out of grand design by any person, but rather it grows out of a need to cope with the problem of legitimacy. In the words of an informed Chinese on Hong Kong politics, the appointment of Sir Shouson Chow was not made wholly on personal grounds, "it was evident that political considerations also came in, viz., to pacify anti-British sentiment in China and further encourage the loyalty of local Chinese towards Hong Kong."[11] Chinese participation in the two Councils has steadily increased since the Second World War. This is clearly shown in the Legislative Council: the Chinese Unofficial Members were less than 50 percent between 1945–1950, 62.5 percent from 1960–1963, 70 percent from 1964–1967, 77 percent from 1968–1969, and 84 percent from 1970. The steady increase of Chinese participation in the Councils is a reflection of the growing strength and vitality of the Chinese community on the one hand,

and the sensitive responsive capability of the government to absorb the socioeconomic leaders on the other. The British are not attempting to create a mass-consensual community; they are, however, attempting to create an elite-consensual polity. The normal pattern in elite-consensus building is to co-opt the men with a power base into the polity.

Below the Legislative and Executive Councils, there is the Urban Council, which is the only government organ with a partially elected membership. Prior to April 1, 1973, there were 26 members in the Council—six were ex-officio members and twenty were unofficial members, ten of whom were appointed and ten elected. Despite the fact that the Urban Council's elections are the only occasions for the general public to participate in the formal political process, they have never interested the average person. The striking thing is that ever since the Urban Council elections were reinstituted in 1952, the rate of registration for election has never exceeded 1 percent of the total population and, although up to 30–40 percent of those who register eventually turn up at the polls, only 0.5 percent or less of the total population turn out to vote.[12] The poor turnout in voting is often deplored as a lack of civic spirit and as an exhibition of political apathy. One reason for political apathy, it seems, must be the traditional Chinese Confucian political culture which is more parochial-subject than participant in nature; the ordinary people lack an active self-orientation towards politics in Hong Kong.[13] A more basic reason for the low participation, however, could be found in the political system of Hong Kong itself; that is, the Urban Council is an organ without teeth. It is perceived as involved in a "politics without power," "completely divorced from the dynamism of Hong Kong's economy."[14] It would appear that the Hong Kong Government does not hold that modern democratic politics has to be politics of mass participation. The foremost goal of the Government is to achieve a maximum level of political stability in order to foster economic growth. And the key to that goal is the administration of politics; it is the antithesis to politicization.

Bearing in mind the notion of the administration of politics, we will be in a better position to understand the role of the government bureaucracy in Hong Kong. Insofar as Hong Kong's real and day-to-day governing power is concerned, it lies in the hands of the civil service, headed by the colonial Secretary who, under the direction of the Governor, carries on the general administration. At present, there are 40 government departments. The growth of the bureaucracy is phenomenal: there were just over 17,500 officers in 1949; this increased to 45,000 in 1959; and now its present strength is over 84,500. The bureaucratic expansion is, in short, primarily due to the pressures of urbanization.[15] It is no exaggeration to say that Hong Kong, despite its claim to a laissez faire philosophy, is, in fact, an "administered city" governed by "departmentocracy."

Strictly speaking, there are no politicians in Hong Kong. Gabriel Almond has, expressing a functional view, distinguished four input functions of any political system: political socialization and recruitment, interest articulation, interest aggregation, and political communication.[16] Since there are so few political structures outside of government for the performance of these four input functions in Hong Kong, the bureaucracy of necessity plays a "political" role. And, as a matter of fact, the old orthodoxy of the politics–administration dichotomy is purposefully broken down in Hong Kong; the administrators, especially those at the top level, are encouraged to play the political role. A point should be noted here that the Government is the largest employer in Hong Kong. By January 1972, there were 84,565 officers in total, of which 82,662 were local officers, and 1,903 overseas officers.[17] The data indicate that one in every fifty of the total population was employed within the civil service. Because of this very fact, the bureaucracy has contributed a great deal to the stability of Hong Kong by serving as a mechanism for assimilating the potential "discontented" into the governing machinery. The government bureaucracy has been fairly open to Chinese intellectuals, especially since the 1950s. And, it is mainly in the area of administration that the synarchical rule has been put into practice. From 1952 onward, the local officers who are predominantly Chinese have constituted over 95 percent of the total number of officers. However, the quantitative figures do not give us the whole picture; if we look at the "qualitative" side of the picture, a rather different conclusion will emerge. Although localization of the government bureaucracy has been the publicly stated policy of the Government since 1946, it has proceeded slowly and very unevenly. The pattern of localization is that the lower the categories of officers are, the faster the localization; and the reverse is true. The obvious evidence is that in the Administrative Grade, 64 percent were British, while only 36 percent were local officers in 1970 (although, as compared to 2.3 percent in 1950 and 16.27 percent in 1960, the progress cannot be ignored). On the other hand, in the Executive Grade, 73.4 percent were local officers, while 26.6 percent were British. Insofar as the top rung of the bureaucracy is concerned, the Government is still dominated by British expatriates.[18] In a sense, Hong Kong's administration is a lopsided synarchy, with much Chinese "participation" but little "joint rule." Synarchy has never become fully-fledged.

The discussion of synarchical rule cannot be completed without mentioning the informal side. Synarchical rule does not stop at the direct or formal co-option of political elements into administration; it also reflects indirect or informal co-option.

When the British took over Hong Kong in 1842, Hong Kong was a rural community without a great gentry. However, by the end of the nineteenth century, a viable and rapidly developing community of Chinese had come into being. Because of the ingenuity and great organizational ability of the Chinese merchant class, they were able to build up an autonomous power base outside the polity of the British Government. The wealthy Chinese have demonstrated extreme adaptive capacity in creating high-power associations of various kinds for the purposes of mutual assistance and self-advancement in a rapidly urbanized settlement under alien rule. The Tung Wah Group of Hospitals, the Po Leung Kuk and the Kai-fong are all indigenously developed. The key figures in these Chinese associations are civic-minded men of achievement respected by their community. They have developed an informal system of power and influence parallel to the formal system of the British. The Hong Kong Government has never failed to appreciate the fact that these prominent Chinese could well perform a boundary role between the government and the community, as played by the Chinese gentry in traditional society. The last thing the British want to see is the development of powerful oppositional forces by Chinese or other non-British leaders. In this connection, the British have wisely and successfully absorbed Chinese leaders into the official political circle by either giving them formal membership in the Councils and in the bureaucracy or bestowing on them honors (e.g., Justice of the Peace) and involving them in more than 130 consultative and advisory committees at various Governmental levels. Here again we found that the great majority of unofficial Justices of the Peace among Chinese are successful men in the economic field. The Chinese members of consultative and advisory committees are also by and large successful businessmen. The significant boundary role of the leaders of Chinese associations is well recognized by the Government. It is beyond doubt that the formal and informal administrative absorption of Chinese leaders of important associations is one of the major factors contributing to the stability of the urban community of Hong Kong.

The Integration Crisis and Its Response

What we have said thus far should give us a fairly clear picture of how the continuous stability of Hong Kong is secured through the willingness and ability of the British to change and enlarge the elite circle by co-opting emerging leadership groups. The best example is shown in the Government's readiness to accept the industrial "new rich" into the Legislative Council since the mid-1960s, because from then on the industrial sector has become the backbone of the economy.[19] But it is our contention that elite integration can work relatively well only in a society in which the masses are primarily apolitical, and it probably would not work as well in a society which has undergone the process of social mobilization. This was not fully recognized until two major riots occurred in 1966 and 1967. The 1966 riot, lasting for several days, resulted from a rise in the first-class fare for the ferry between Kowloon and Hong Kong Island. In 1967, a series of uprisings against the colonial Government were triggered, as it is widely perceived, by the Cultural Revolution in mainland China. The riots were controlled and died out rather quickly. What is significant is that these episodes indicate that Hong Kong's equilibrium is rather precarious, and there are underlying factors which are predisposed to react to stimuli for violent and mass behavior. After the 1966 riot, the Government realized that the basic political structure of Hong Kong had been changed with the rising young generation entering into the political strata.[20]

According to the findings of the Government, the cause for the 1966 riot was a "failure of communication" between the Government and people.[21] This finding admits in fact, implicitly or explicitly, that the structure of "government by discussion" which had succeeded in elite-to-elite communication had failed in providing an effective channel for elite-to-mass communication. In a way, Hong Kong's current problem is not so much the gap between the British and the non-British as the gap between the elite and the masses. The riots were symptoms of malintegration between the rulers and the ruled of this rapidly urbanized city.

It seems quite legitimate to view the riots as a kind of communication crisis or, more accurately, integration crisis. The basic reason for the integration crisis can be found in the political structure, which has few political structures performing the basic political functions for the masses in Hong Kong. At present, there are only seven associations which are political in nature. Four of them are registered as political parties: the Democratic Self-Government Party, the Hong Kong Socialist Democratic Party, the Labour Party of Hong Kong and the Liberal Democratic Party, but none of these are of any political significance. Three are registered as "clubs" and "associations": the United Nations Association of Hong Kong, the Reform Club of Hong Kong, and the Hong Kong Civic Association. Of the seven, the Reform Club and the Civic Association, which claim a membership of 30,400 and 10,000 respectively, have dominated the Urban Council elections. But both of these are more concerned with social and economic reforms and are, by nature of their limited resources and organizational ability, hardly effective articulators or aggregators of the interests of the masses. In addition, at the bottom there are seldom any strong grassroots associations which can perform a role of interest articulator for the masses. It is small wonder that, on the whole, ordinary urban dwellers have the tendency to express their sentiments and demands through "anomic" political structures—i.e., riots, demonstrations, strikes, teach-ins, sit-ins, and sleep-ins, etc. Indeed, this becomes increasingly a form of political participation in Hong Kong.

The problematic gap between the elite and the masses is not unique to Hong Kong; it is a very common problem among new nations. Edward Shils is probably the scholar who has given this problem most attention. For Shils, the political integration of the new state depends primarily on the closing of the elite–mass gap, and he suggests that the gap be bridged by the dispersion of initiative. The solution suggested by Shils is, in short, political democracy.[22] In fact, in late 1966, the Working Party on Local Administration appointed by the Governor took a similar view by suggesting the creation of a strong Hong Kong Municipal Council. It in effect proposed apolitical democratic solution. However, the proposal was not implemented at that time; instead, a City District Officer Scheme was instituted in April 1968 as a "stop gap" mechanism in lieu of local government.

Political Absorption at the Grassroots Level: The City District Officer Scheme

After the 1966 and 1967 riots, the government decided that it needed a political machinery to cope with the ever-increasing politicized life of the urban dwellers, especially at the local level. It is here that we see that the City District Officer (CDO) Scheme carries a basically political spirit, for the government's diagnosis of the riots of 1966 and 1967 reflects a belief that the basic problem lies not in the colonial system as such, but in a metropolitan government structure that is too big to manage, too complex and bureaucratized to be intelligible to the ordinary people. Therefore, what the CDO Scheme tries to accomplish is a decentralization and a debureaucratization of the metropolitan Government.

The Ideology Goals and Structure of the CDO Scheme

The CDO Scheme was launched with great fanfare and publicity in mid-1968, immediately after the climax of the 1967 riots. A government-sponsored intensive image-building campaign was successfully carried out to convince the public that the CDO Scheme is something which is genuinely of and for the people. The ideology of the CDO Scheme is a "service ideology": service for the Government; service for the community; and service for the individuals. These are explicitly stated in the Directive to City District Officers.[23]

The explicit goals of the CDO Scheme are many-sided. It is designed to be a political communication agent, a community organizer, a troubleshooter for the people. To put it in more general terms, the CDO Scheme is aiming to counteract the tendency of the metropolitan Government toward centralization and departmentalization. The establishment of the CDO Scheme is to make one person or one office which the residents could recognize as "the government" in their district.

The CDO Scheme was approved by the Hong Kong Government in early 1968. It was decided that ten CDOs would be established in the whole metropolitan area. By the end of the same year, five CDOs were established: Eastern, Western, Wan Chai, Mong Kok, and Yau Ma Tei. The other five, subsequently opened by the end of 1969, were Central, Kwun Tong, Sham Shui Po, Kowloon City, and Wong Tai Sin.

The CDO Scheme is under the general supervision of the Secretariat for Home Affairs. Directly under the Secretary for Home Affairs are two deputies: one is in charge of the traditional duties of the former Secretariat for Chinese Affairs—newspaper registration, trust fund, liquor licensing, tenancy matters, etc.; the other is responsible for the CDO Scheme. Under him are two City District Commissioners, one responsible for the four CDOs on Hong Kong Island, and the other for the six CDOs in Kowloon.

The organization of the ten CDOs are the same. The City District Officer is the head of the office. Under him are two sections: Internal and External, each headed by an Assistant City District Officer. The Internal Section deals mainly with administrative matters, and the External Section with field or "liaison" duties. The number of other staff varies with individual offices. There are usually five to eight Liaison Officers assigned to each office. One is invariably assigned to the Public Enquiry Counter, and a greater part of the rest to the External Section. There are two to four Liaison Assistants in each office to assist the LOs.

The CDO at Work in Kwun Tong Community

How has the CDO Scheme actually performed at the district level?
How has the idea of the CDO Scheme been transformed into
action? We have selected Kwun Tong District for our study. Kwun
Tong District, one of the ten City Districts of metropolitan Hong
Kong, is one of the newest and most rapidly developed urban com-
munities in Hong Kong.

The CDO is not an ordinary functionally specific administrative organization; rather, it is a multifunctional political structure.
What are the functions of the CDO in the Kwun Tong District?
According to our findings, during the three-month period from June
1971 to August 1971, the CDO's activities involve such things as
commenting on the District's development planning; helping to clear
out huts and hawkers; building a playground for children; helping
in relief of typhoon victims; organizing festival celebrations; administering the Fat Choy Special Aid Fund; handling "individual and
family cases"; answering public enquiries; and administering statu-
tory declarations, etc. The CDO's activities are indeed highly func-
tionally-diffuse. They involve just about everything occurring in any
local community, ranging from political to very mundane affairs.

One of the CDO's major functions is to facilitate communication between the governors and the governed, including the input
of intelligence about "public opinion" to the decision-makers in the
government. The CDO is required to produce a report entitled "The
Anatomy" of his District within six months of his appointment. In
the "Anatomy," thorough information about the peculiarities of
the social and economic structure of the district as well as its per-
sonalities is expected to be included. The CDO is often asked by
various Departments to give comments on intended actions, such

as the Development Town Plan of the Public Works Department, and other Government organizations ask it to gather information on social needs for decision-making. For example, the CDO has conducted a "survey" on the needs of the ferry service on behalf of the UMELCO (Unofficial Members of the Executive and Legislative Councils). The methods used to gather intelligence, besides "survey" conducting, are the District Monthly Meeting, the Study Group and "Town Talk."

The CDO holds Monthly Meetings which involve a fairly stable group of local leaders, leaders of Kaifong Associations, Multi-Storey Building Associations (MSB), District Associations, the business and industrial sector, etc.; the representatives of field agencies of Government Departments are also present. It is the primary mechanism of the CDO to collect opinions of local leaders on any issue concerning the Government and the public. From the minutes of the meetings, we find that members present voice their opinions on the procedure of reporting crime to the police, on the improvement of recreational facilities in the district, etc. The CDO is designed to extend the Government's consultation circle at the center to a much wider circle at the peripheral and district level.

The Study Group is rather ad hoc in nature. The people invited to discuss in the Study Group vary from one to another, depending on the topics discussed. The discussants include industrialists, school principals, hawkers, shop owners, taxi-drivers, factory workers, students and others. Sometimes the subjects discussed might include not only matters of a specific nature but also matters of common concern such as traffic problems, corruption, petty crimes, smoke from restaurants, clearance of refuse, Chinese as an official language, etc.

The "Town Talk" mechanism is not officially included in the CDO Scheme, but it is believed to be one of the most important channels for soliciting public opinion by the CDO. It is probably true that the Monthly Meeting or the Study Group are, in practice if not in theory, geared primarily to reach local leaders rather than the ordinary man. The Town Talk is in a sense more oriented toward the "man in the street." The CDO has no specific instructions on whom to consult. As one respondent reported, comments were noted down from casual conversation with whomsoever they happened to talk to, on official or private terms. It emphasizes not the quantitative but the qualitative aspect of the opinions expressed by the people. The keyword is "people"; several officers interviewed repeatedly and separately asserted that the present "trend" was towards contacting the "man-in-the-street."

A second function of the CDO is to articulate the demands made known to them through the Monthly Meeting, the Study Group and Town Talk by people from different walks of life, as well as demands channeled through newspapers and outside "requests." Moreover, interests are articulated by the CDO's self-initiative, based upon its knowledge of the needs and attitudes of the residents of the community. The interests articulated by the CDO are both minor in nature and all-embracing. According to our findings in the period under analysis, the CDO made comments on multi-storey building car parks, cooked food stalls, hawker bazaars, a minibus station, a refuse collection center, and a clinic with regard to the Kowloon Bay Development Plan. The CDO's interest articulation is limited in the sense that it has only recommendation function.

With respect to the redressing of grievances, it has been expressly denied by the Chairman of the Urban Council that the

CDO are ombudsmen.[24] The CDO is certainly not an ombudsman in the original Scandinavian sense which guarantees his independence as an instrumental officer of the legislature. The CDO is not. However, the public image of the CDO as an ombudsman is prevailing, and it is, furthermore, clearly stated in the Report of the CDO Scheme.[25] The CDO's grievance redressing activities can be classified into two major types: redressing of grievances for groups and for individuals. The first type arises out of events affecting a large number of people, such as a clearance operation. This type of grievance redressing is relatively rare; in Kwun Tong District, there were only two instances. One was the Shun Lee Chuen Clearance in which villagers whose huts were due to be demolished demanded compensation from the Government through the CDO; the other was the Typhoon Rose case in which the victims of Sam Ka Chuen demanded a reassessment of the decisions of the Resettlement Department. The individual cases were very large in number in the same period, however, totalling 256. Of these, family disputes accounted for 152, housing 37, and traffic accidents and compensation 24. In all cases, it was the clients who took their complaints to the CDO for assistance.

The CDO referred the two group cases to the responsible departments for reconsideration but they were not favorably reviewed because the departments concerned thought their demands were not in compliance with government policies. In this respect, the CDO could do very little, but it did "explain" the government policies to the two groups in a more personal way. As for the individual cases, 204 out of 256 cases received were recorded to have been settled. In handling individual cases, the CDO acted as middleman between parties in disputes. When individual grievances arose from a Government decision, the CDO could not reverse the original decision, but it had the "power" to bring the case to the responsible departments for a second look, although often all that the CDO could do was "talk things over," and "give advice."

Another function of the CDO is a special set-up called the Public Enquiry Service (PES) Counter, usually manned by an Executive Officer, a clerk, and clerical assistants. The PES set-up is designed to familiarize people with the government bureaucracy. The Hong Kong Metropolitan Government has become more and more technical, complicated, and fragmented; the ordinary people are often bewildered by the intricacy of governmental operations. There exists a kind of "information gap" between the Government and the people. The PES is apparently a useful mechanism to bridge this "information gap," and this is evinced in its enormous use by the people. The number of enquiries received per month by the CDO's PES counter increased from 991 in September 1970 to 5,472 in April 1971. The enquiries cover a wide range of information concerning personal documents, land and housing, employment, taxes, duties and fees, family welfare, education, traffic, medical, and other miscellaneous things.

Another important political function of the CDO may be called political socialization and recruitment. The CDO, in this regard, provides a framework for participation by "responsible" local sectors. Most of the CDO's efforts are geared to structuring the channels of participation for two major categories of people— youth and "local leaders." Different institutional mechanisms have been created to co-opt and socialize them in CDO-sponsored community activities. The Monthly Meeting is the most formal forum. During the three months under study, other mechanisms and activities relating to socialization and recruitment were used. For example, with the help of the Lion's Club and the Army, student volunteers were mobilized to assist in constructing a playground and jetty at Kowloon Bay; they initiated and sponsored, with the support of local prominent people from Kaifongs, schools, and business firms, district-wide sports activities; they worked through voluntary associations in organizing and promoting recreational and festival activities. All these activities were apolitical in terms of their manifest functions; they were primarily recreational in nature. However, these activities were not sheer structuring of leisure time for the local leaders and the youth; they served to channel participation in a "right" way, to develop community-oriented civic consciousness, to transform the young people into "good citizens" and future community leaders, and to create a political culture which is supportive of the political structure of Hong Kong.

An Evaluation of the CDO Scheme

The CDO of Kwun Tong has played a fairly successful boundary role between the Government and the society: as a multifunctional political structure, it has by and large provided institutional channels for political inputs and outputs. The most effective function of the CDO is in political communication, especially the "information output" from the Government to the people. The Public Enquiry Service has undoubtedly performed a vital role in transmitting and spreading knowledge of the aims and purposes of the government to the people, and has helped to make the government more intelligible and relevant. The "information gap" between the governors and the governed has been substantially removed. But the CDO has not been as successful in its "information input" as in "information output." Despite its efforts to reach people in the street, it has thus far not been very successful in penetrating the masses in a structured way, although it has been fairly successful in securing the views and attitudes of local leaders towards government policies and action before they are put into effect. In this respect, the CDO acts as a feedback mechanism for the government to detect the acceptability of its actions, or as a political barometer for the government to detect early symptoms of any public dissatisfaction. It is in this political communication function that the CDO has been referred to as the "eyes and ears" of the government. Regarding the interest articulation function of the CDO, it is often unrecognized or underestimated. It is interesting to note that, according to the Kaifong leaders of Kwun Tong, "represent people's interest to government" was ranked as the last among all functions of the CDO. However, the CDO's self-image is very different; they have a strong sense of mission that they are not only the "eyes and ears of the government" but also the "tongues of the people." It is here that we have found tension developed between the CDO and other local organizations, especially the Kaifongs, who claim this as their foremost function.

Whatever the relationship between the CDO and other local organizations, the CDO is involving local leaders in consultation at the Monthly Meeting and other mechanisms. But that is as far as the CDO is willing to go. The CDO is not ready to accept the local leaders' views at face value; and, more often than not, views of the local leaders tend to fade into faint echoes. Probably because of this, quite a few local leaders were dismayed and frustrated; more than one of them even went as far as to say that "the CDO was a waste of money. . . . The Monthly Meetings were a child's game."

It seems to us that local leaders and non-leaders alike often fail to appreciate the fact that the CDO has only recommendatory powers. Although the CDOs can and often do apply pressure on other Government agencies for their recommendation, there is a genuine structural weakness of the CDO. A City District Officer normally spends only two to three years in the post, with the rest of his career spent in other government departments. He cannot afford to alienate himself from his home base; he cannot push too far or too hard because he is after all a bureaucrat within the same bureaucratic structure.

The grievance redressing function of the CDO is gradually becoming more appreciated by the community. This function was the Kaifong's monopoly in the past, and is now being taken over by the CDO. The kind of grievance redressing the CDO does is often no more than just giving the complainant a "human-to-human talk." Some critics point out that the CDO's power in this respect is limited in that it cannot reverse the original decision, when the individual grievance arises from a government decision. However, in spite of the limited power the CDO has, it usually enables the individual to have a "fair hearing" in a very personal way. The CDO is no dragon-slayer; he cannot afford to be. But the significance of the "human touch" in the modern imperial bureaucracy cannot be underestimated. While grievance at local government level may often be trivial, the small issues are of substantial importance to the citizens. This function of the CDO has rendered good service for the poor and inarticulate ordinary man. In no insignificant degree, this function of the CDO has served as a "safety valve" for the release of people's imaginary or real grievances.

In analyzing the last political function of the CDO, political socialization and recruitment, we must bear in mind that generating a favorable and supportive attitude and behavior toward the Government was one of the basic reasons for the inception of the CDO Scheme. The CDO, as the political agent at the district level, is not aiming at political mobilization of the populace; in fact, it is trying to depoliticize the political process. In short, the CDO Scheme is primarily concerned with social stability rather than with social change. It is our impression that the CDO has been fairly successful in absorbing and recruiting the most active political strata—local leaders and youth—by working with and through them in undertaking community-wide cultural and recreational activities. Through this kind of orderly participation, community consciousness or local identification has often been generated; a great deal of energy has been absorbed and channelled into non-political activities; and, above all, social solidarity has been enhanced.

Conclusion

The focus of this chapter was on the political side of city life. We have treated politics not as an epiphenomenon; it is not just the reflection of the socioeconomic structure. In the case of Hong Kong, we found that its particular brand of politics shapes and is shaped by the socioeconomic structure of the society.

We have attempted to provide a conceptual framework to describe and analyze the nature of the political system of Hong Kong. Basically, we are of the opinion that Hong Kong's political stability in the last hundred years could be accounted for primarily by the successful process of the administrative absorption of politics. It is a process through which the British governing elites co-opt or assimilate the non-British socioeconomic elites into the political-administrative decision-making bodies, thus attaining an elite integration on the one hand and a legitimacy of political authority on the other. We have witnessed a system of synarchy, though a lopsided one, operating in Hong Kong. However, the synarchical system is only open to a rather small sector of the population—men of wealth, established or new. The ingenuity of the British governing elites lies in their sophisticated response in timely enlarging and modifying the structure of ruling bodies, by co-opting or assimilating emerging non-British socioeconomic elites into "we" groups at critical periods. Consequently, any strong counter-elite groups are prevented. In short, Hong Kong has been governed by an elite consensus or integration in the last century or so. However, it is our contention that elite integration could constitute a sufficient condition for legitimacy of government only in a society in which the political stratum is rather small. Once a society undergoes rapid urbanization or, more specifically, social mobilization whereby the apolitical strata is politicized, it is not elite integration but elite–mass integration which becomes necessary for a stable political system. Hong Kong has in the last two decades undergone that process of social mobilization. Hong Kong today is no longer just an economic city but also a political city; more people, especially the young literates, demand ever-increasing participation in the political decision-making process. The basic problem of legitimacy in Hong Kong today lies not in elite dis-consensus but in the elite–mass gap, as exemplified by the riots of 1966 and 1967.

The Hong Kong Government's response to the political crises was not more democracy, but the creation of the City District Officer Scheme. But it should be noted that, despite the usefulness of the CDO Scheme in the district, especially as a communication facilitator the CDO Scheme has a limited function as an administrative absorber of community politics; and this will become more evident when community life becomes progressively politicized in scale. Some fundamental features of urban life in Hong Kong seem to be working in the direction that, despite the artificial administrative-political boundaries defined by the CDO Scheme, no important socioeconomic political issue is confined to any District. That is to say, all-important political issues tend to be escalated to a level which could only be solved at the center of the political system. The CDO Scheme is good at handling personal problems but not political issues. Not only the image but the actuality of the limited power of the CDO has seemingly led people in the community to believe that big and sensitive issues should not be left to the CDO. Instead, they feel the only effective way is to march to the center of powers, ultimately of course to the Governor's House which is the symbol of the authority of the city state.

The last point we would like to make is that the Government's diagnostic statement which sees Hong Kong's current problem between the Government and the people as an "information gap" is at best a half-truth. Another half-truth might be due to the incompatibility of goals or interests between the elite and the masses. Politics is not just who knows what and how, but also who gets what and how. The CDO Scheme is effective in bridging the information gap which results from misunderstanding or misperception of goals or interests between the rulers and the ruled. But, it is too much to expect it to reconcile the conflict arising from incompatibility of goals or interest between the governors and the governed; therefore, it cannot be very useful as an administrative absorber of community politics as such. All in all, the CDO Scheme can be no substitute for sound and responsive government itself, and it certainly is no panacea for urban politics.

Hong Kong today is facing a new challenge of politics which arises basically from rapid urbanization. The kinds of issues and problems of this city-state have become increasingly political. How Hong Kong can maintain a viable political system poses a question of the first order to the students of the art or the science of governing. The century-old practice of administrative absorption of politics which has contributed to the stability of the city-state up to the present is susceptible to change in form or in substance, or in both.

8 A Non-paradigmatic Search for Democracy in a Post-Confucian Culture: The Case of Taiwan

Taiwan's Democratic Transition

Over the past three decades, the phenomenal development of Taiwan's economy has caught the attention of the world.[1] Taiwan, or the Republic of China, has successfully become one of the so-called newly industrialized countries. It is praiseworthily called one of the four little dragons together with South Korea, Hong Kong, and Singapore.

The rapid socioeconomic development of Taiwan is amply demonstrated in the following statistics:[2]

- From 1953 to 1982, GNP growth rates averaged 8.7 percent; the 1982 GNP was twelve times that of 1952, and by 1990 Taiwan ranked 25th in the world with a per capita GNP of US$7,997.

- Industry grew at an average annual rate of 13.3 percent from 1953 to 1982, increasing to forty-two times its 1953 value.

- The economic structure underwent noticeable structural change. In 1952, industry accounted for only 19.7 percent of the GNP; in 1990, 42.3 percent.

Agriculture's contribution to GNP dropped from 32.2 percent to 4.2 percent over the same period. The share of the service sector increased to 53.5 percent in 1990.

- A trade surplus has occurred every year since 1970. Taiwan achieved a trade surplus of US$15.6 billion in 1986, when its two-way trade totalled US$64 billion, and by 1990 held foreign exchange reserves of over US$80 billion, one of the highest in the world.

- There have been nine years of free compulsory education since 1968, and the illiteracy rate fell to 9.2 percent in 1986 from 27.6 percent in 1966. In 1986, about 25 percent of all persons between eighteen and twenty-one years of age attended junior colleges or universities.

- Other social indicators of living standards showed a remarkable improvement between 1952 and 1986: the percentage of households with electricity rose from 45.2 percent to 99.7 percent; telephones per 1,000 persons from 3.9 to 311.9; television sets per 1,000 persons from 1.4 (in 1962) to 106.2; automobiles per 1,000 persons from 1.0 to 77.

- Between 1952 and 1990, the percentage of the population living in cities with more than 5,000 inhabitants increased from 30 percent to 90 percent.

Not surprisingly, Taiwan's success story in economic development has generated a good number of plausible explanations by economists and other social scientists, varying in degree of theoretical sophistication and empirical richness. Broadly speaking, there are two competing intellectual camps, the institutionalist and the culturalist, that try to make an issue of the relative importance of structure as against culture.[3] What is most fascinating is the culturalist's argument crystallized in the form of a post-Confucian thesis. In a nutshell, it argues that it is the Confucian ethic that has been the driving force behind the economic miracle of Japan and the four little dragons.[4] The post-Confucian thesis is in sharp contradiction to Weber's analysis of Confucianism. For Weber, Confucian rationalism was a "rationalism of order," incapable of initiating profound social or economic change. The crux of Weber's analysis is as follows:

> Completely absent in the Confucian ethic was any tension between nature and deity, between ethical demand and human shortcomings, consciousness of aim and need for salvation, conduct on earth and compensation in the beyond, religious duty and sociopolitical reality. Hence, there was no leverage for influencing conduct through inner forces freed of tradition and convention.[5]

Weber's view has long been taken by students of Chinese studies as the authoritative basis for explaining the "non-development" of capitalism in China. Now the empirical fact of Taiwan's profound economic development should naturally evoke scholars of Confucian persuasion to question the validity of Weber's verdict on Confucianism as a negative cultural system. Thomas Metzger writes:

> He [Weber] concluded that China's failure was due largely to the effects of the Confucian ethos, and his conclusion still carries weight today, even though his early analysis of this ethos was erroneous. We however live in a world where the

development of the major societies is based on a mixture
of indigenous factors and cosmopolitan influences. We
consequently are led to ask: Why in this kind of world are
some societies more effective than others in coping with their
problems and rising to the challenges of modernization?
While Weber had to explain China's failure, we have to
explain its success, but paradoxically our answer, like
Weber's, emphasizes the role of the indigenous ethos.[6]

It is not the purpose of this chapter to settle the issue of the
role of Confucianism in the economic development of Taiwan.[7]
What concerns us here is the role of Confucianism, as a political
cultural system, in Taiwan's democratic development. For some
time, Confucianism has been seen by most scholars, Western and
Chinese alike, as a value system most congruent with oriental
authoritarianism and providing legitimacy for the centuries-old
monarchical system. Despite Taiwan's miraculous economic development, its political system was generally considered as authoritarian, and students of Taiwan's modernization almost without
exception took the view that its political development has lagged
behind its economic development. Nevertheless, since the late
1970s, and particularly in the past few years, Taiwan has clearly
moved toward democratization.[8] Taiwan now has meaningful and
extensive competition for government power through regular
elections; an opposition party of real significance has come into
existence; and considerable civil and political liberties, including freedom of expression, freedom of the press, freedom to form
organizations, freedom to demonstrate and strike, and so on have
become common features of political life. Moreover, the smooth
leadership succession following the death of the charismatic leader

Chiang Ching-kuo on January 13, 1988 showed a marked maturity of constitutionality in the Republic. All these factors indicate unequivocally that Taiwan has forever bid farewell to dynastic politics and is clearly in the process of transition to democracy. Admittedly, Taiwan's destiny, especially with regard to democracy, is not without uncertainty. However, its democratic transformation is a significant phenomenon that calls for an interpretation.

Modernization Theories and Democracy

Modernization theories, which emerged as the dominant social-scientific paradigm in the 1950s and 1960s, were no longer in fashion, if not discredited, in the 1970s and 1980s. In recent years, dependency theory and world system theory have attracted a large number of theorists who are concerned with the problem of the capitalist development of "underdevelopment."[9] However, contrary to the argument of dependency theory, Asia has experienced one of the most profound records of development, not "underdevelopment," in human history over recent decades; Asian leaders and intellectuals are vigorously, purposefully striving for modernization. After the downfall of the "Gang of Four," the People's Republic of China has, since 1978, pledged to pursue "Four Modernizations" in order to move the country out of backwardness and underdevelopment. Pye is not wide of the mark in saying that "the earlier modernization theories had a close empirical fit with the experience of Asia but not with those of either Africa or Latin America."[10]

Earlier modernization theories that imply the triumph of reason, a legacy of enlightenment, do carry an optimistic tone. However, sophisticated modernization theorists were never naïve about the inevitability of democratic development. In fact, democracy is not necessarily implied in the definition of modernization.[11] Almond cautioned us, "The movement of modernization might be in a liberal democratic direction, but it might with equal probability be in an authoritarian direction." And he argues explicitly against the simple diffusionist notion of unilaterality.[12] Max Weber, the first great theorist of modernization, who was fully aware of the paradox of rationalization, is ambivalent toward, if not downright pessimistic about, the prospect of democracy and capitalism.[13]

Modernization theories, like Weber's thesis of the Protestant ethic, address primarily the problem of economic development. Peter Berger writes, "Modernization must be seen in close relation to economic growth—more specially, to the particular growth processes released by recent technology."[14] Immediately after the Second World War, as perceptively observed by Parsons, "there was an apparently world-wide consensus on the valuation of economic productivity."[15] Indeed, there was a preoccupation with economic development in the minds of modernizing elites in the "underdeveloped" countries. True enough, the students of modernization have more often than not an inclination to embrace liberal, democratic ideas, and view democracy and pluralism as something inherently good and desirable. A normative theory of political development would most probably include democracy in the definition of modernization. And more important, modernization theories, though not arguing the causal directionality of liberal democratic development, do assert an empirical correlation between economic development and political democracy. Lipset writes: "It seems clear that the factors of industrialization, urbanization, wealth and education are so closely interrelated as to form one common factor. And the factors subsumed under economic development carry with it the political correlate of democracy."[16] However, as Dankwart Rustow points out, empirical correlation between socioeconomic factors and political democracy does not imply a causal relationship, nor can the functional explanation be taken as a genetic explanation. In short, they do not tell "how a democratic system comes into being."[17]

In the case of Taiwan, the profound changes brought about by economic development has produced structural forces that seem to have affected Taiwan's democratization. Moreover, as a result of industrialization, and particularly the dramatic expansion of education, the Confucian political culture seems to have undergone significant change. A newly emerging political culture, which, as demonstrated later in the chapter, shows clearly some characteristics of what Almond and Verba termed "the civic culture," is definitely conducive to the process of Taiwan's transition to democracy. But Taiwan's democratization is not just an automatic outcome of socioeconomic development. Like Spain's, Taiwan's transition to democracy requires an analysis concentrating on the transition process itself.[18]

The Party-State and Its Legitimacy

The most salient characteristic of Taiwan's political system has been its one-party rule. The Guomindang (National People's Party or Nationalist Party) has enjoyed dominance since it moved to Taiwan in 1949, after suffering defeat at the hands of Chinese Communists on mainland China. Despite the legal existence of two small parties, the China Youth Party and the China Democratic Socialist Party, the government of the Republic of China (ROC) was run exclusively by the Guomindang (GMD). Under the GMD, both the structure and the operation of the government were basically the same in the ROC as they had been on the mainland. The Nationalists brought along their formal, national-level party and government structures and superimposed these on one small province, with only 0.37 percent of China's total land mass and only 1 percent of its population. There were parallel party and state structures at all levels—national, provincial, county, municipal, and district—to ensure firm party control.[19]

The GMD was reorganized with the aid of Soviet advisers in 1924 as a Leninist-style party. However, the GMD is Leninist only in structure. It has its own ideology, Dr. Sun Yat-sen's *sanmin zhuyi* (Three Principles of the People), which is rendered as Nationalism, Democracy, and People's Livelihood. There is no room for democracy in Leninism. But in the GMD's ideological system, Sun Yat-sen has a three-stage development theory of state-building: military rule, democratic tutelage, and constitutional democracy. The basic difference between the GMD and a Leninist party lies in the fact that, unlike a Leninist party, the GMD never intended in theory or in practice to have total control over society. The party-state in Taiwan was, to use Metzger's concept, an "inhibited" political center.[20] The ultimate aim of the GMD's state-building was to create a democratic political system. This is at least the theoretical position of the *sanmin zhuyi*, which had an abiding effect on the practice of the ruling party in Taiwan.

In keeping with Sun's ideas of tutelary democracy, a new constitution was promulgated by the GMD in 1946. However, the promulgation of a constitution did not bring China into the era of constitutionalism. The civil war between the ROC government and the Chinese Communists then accelerated to an unprecedented level. Amid the war, the first session of the first term of the National Assembly was convened in Nanjing in 1948, and elected Chiang Kai-shek as the president of the ROC. It also adopted "temporary provisions for the Duration of Mobilization to suppress the Rebellion" through the procedure for constitutional amendment. Upon establishing its rule over Taiwan, the GMD government declared martial law in 1949, and justified its restriction of political and other rights—including the right to organize new political parties— as a necessary measure arising from the subversive threat from the Communists.

The GMD government in the 1950s was preoccupied with the issue of national security since a military invasion by Communist China seemed obvious and imminent. In 1949, 1954, and 1958 there were several military confrontations between these two regimes. From the mid-1950s on, the ROC began to receive economic and military aid from the United States. Moreover, the US commitment to prevent a Communist attack gave the government a breathing spell to create an effective economic and political system. Although the Nationalists under President Chiang never lost hope of returning to the mainland, they shifted their strategy decisively to develop Taiwan into a model province for the whole of China in the early 1950s.

The GMD began its development program with land reform. The motivation was probably more political than economic.[21] The process of implementing land reform was bloodless, and its success was far-reaching, economically and politically. On the one hand, Taiwan created the most equitable rural scene in all of Asia; on the other, it definitely enhanced the sociopolitical stability of the island. The former Taiwanese landlords who had been compensated for their land with government bonds became an entrepreneurial class, using their bonds as capital for the first stages of Taiwan's industrialization. In the ensuing years, the GMD government wasted no time in establishing, outside the conservative bureaucratic system, new institutions for guided capitalist development. President Chiang Kai-shek and the premier, the late vice-president Chen Cheng, attributing their debacle on the mainland in large part to the collapse of the economy, gave greater scope over Taiwan's economy to Western-trained technocrats. Indeed, persons like K. Y. Yin, a US-trained electrical engineer, and K. T. Li were virtually given a free hand to design and implement Taiwan's economic plan.[22]

Understandably, the United States, through the Agency for International Development (AID), had a deep influence over Taiwan's economy, and Americans supported the modernizing technocrats, who were mainly US-educated, in their pursuit of economic development. It probably is no exaggeration to say that Taiwan's economic modernization was to a large extent the creation of these technocrats, who enjoyed the unflagging support of the top leaders. The more the economy developed, the more the technocrats became involved in the state's affairs. The result was the ever-increasing vitality of the economy and society, though this by no means developed at the expense of the power of the party-state. Moreover, the distinguishing characteristic of Taiwan's development was, to use Gold's expression, "the bifurcation of the economy from the polity."[23] Deliberately intended or not, the GMD's legitimacy has increasingly been based upon its capacity to deliver economic growth. Vidich writes:

In the contemporary world, both in Third World nations and in the industrialized countries, legitimacy processes include production and economic performance as a critical dimension on which legitimacy is made. The economic performance of a regime may constitute a major prop for legitimacy in the eyes of groups and classes which have accepted life style enhancement as a life goal.[24]

Vidich's observation seems to be confirmed in Taiwan. According to the results of six elections held in the 1970s and 1980s, the GMD consistently won about 70 percent of the votes, and the GMD voters tended to be better educated, higher in occupational status, and more often middle high in income than non-GMD voters. Furthermore, concerning the attitude of voters toward government policies, 78.7 percent expressed their satisfaction with the quality of life.[25] The positive response from the people to the GMD's rule reinforced the party's development-oriented policies. One point worth mentioning is that Taiwan's industrialization has not only brought about wealth but also successfully skipped the so-called Kuznets Trap, according to which inequality tends to increase in the first stage of industrial growth. Taiwan has achieved a remarkable record of equitable income distribution. The Gini coefficient of income inequality fell from 0.6206 in 1953 to 0.2955 in 1972, and further decreased to 0.2806 in 1979.[26]

Bifurcation of Polity and Economy

The bifurcation of the economy from the polity created a mixed image of the ROC. On the one hand, the ROC was widely acclaimed as a progressive state that produced one of the most dynamic economies in world history. On the other hand, the ROC was seen to be a regime that was ossified, its leaders resistant to change.[27] Neil Jacoby wrote, for example, "in contrast to its rapid social and economic development, Taiwan experienced little basic change in its political structure during 1951–65."[28] In terms of the ROC's formal structure, Jacoby's observation in 1966 was not to be disputed. However, the political change taking place below the surface was not insignificant, especially in the years after the 1960s. Nevertheless, the ossified image of Taiwan's political system persisted even up to the 1970s.

The image of non-development in Taiwan's political system can be attributed to several main reasons. First, as mentioned above, there has been little change in the structure and operation of the government. Its basic framework has not been altered since the move to Taiwan in 1949. Second, the ROC's political ideology and its official claims to be the custodian of Chinese culture, as well as its adamant anti-Communist stand remained unchanged throughout the years. Third, the death of Chiang Kai-shek (1975) produced no visible political change as he was succeeded by his son, Chiang Ching-kuo, after the fashion of succession in Imperial China.[29]

This image was too superficial to reflect the substantial changes in politics taking place in the 1960s and 1970s. Nevertheless, there was no denying the fact that the Nationalists had not yet loosened their restrictions on freedom of political activities, including freedom of speech, freedom of the press, and freedom of association. In 1960 Lei Chen, editor of the influential political journal *Free China*, who attempted to organize an opposition party, was charged with harboring a Communist agent on his staff and sentenced to ten years in prison.[30] In the 1960s, several arrests were made on charges of advocating Taiwan's independence. Among them, the arrest of Dr. Peng Mingmin, a well-known legal scholar was the most publicized.[31] In Taiwan, opposition to leadership, attempts to organize new opposition parties, or any attempt to advocate separatist ideologies were severely repressed. Taiwan's political system was indeed correctly called authoritarian in these respects. The GMD's determination to suppress challenges to its political authority could be matched only by its determination to promote economic development.

By this juncture, the bifurcation of the economy from the polity had produced an extraordinary distribution of power between the so-called mainlanders and the Taiwanese. Of Taiwan's population of twenty million, 15 percent, or about three million, are "mainlanders" who came over from the Chinese mainland since 1945 and their descendants. Though mainlanders and Taiwanese are both of Chinese origin, there are marked differences of dialect and customs between the two groups. For a long time, the primary source of tension was the dominant position of mainlanders on the island. At the national level, all the higher positions in the government, the party, and the army were initially occupied by mainlanders. In the three elective bodies in the central government—the National Assembly, the Legislation Yuan, and the Control Yuan—the mainlanders constituted the great majority because they had been elected in 1946 on the mainland to represent all the provinces of China. Because the ROC persistently asserted that it was the sole representative government for all China, and because it never officially gave up the goal of recovering the mainland, it justified its perpetuation of a national government that represented all China and therefore one that must not be dominated and staffed by Taiwanese. Being denied the road to national political power, the Taiwanese were, however, encouraged by the GMD's policies to engage in business ventures. Throughout the years, increasingly larger numbers of Taiwanese established successful business careers. For example, the 1974 edition of *Taiwan 500 Gongshen renming lu* listed 500 prominent businessmen in Taiwan, of whom 68 percent were Taiwanese. A 1973 statistical abstract of Taipei City showed that 73 percent of those who moved between 1968 and 1973 into the relatively affluent suburbs of Shilin, Beitou, and others were Taiwanese. In a real sense, the society that was represented overwhelmingly by the economic power of the Taiwanese stood strong vis-à-vis the party-state.

By the 1970s, a division of power was evident between the mainlanders and Taiwanese: the former controlled the political sector, and the latter dominated the economic sector. The great beneficiaries of Taiwan's economic development were Taiwanese economic elites, who were more than willing to give tacit support to the government's authoritarian way of achieving the national goal of growth and stability. The newly emerging capitalist classes showed no interest or inclination to translate economic muscle into political activity. This is probably one of the reasons that the ethnic difference between mainlanders and Taiwanese was not transformed into class-based conflict, which was conspicuously absent in the political arena. It was not accidental that Taiwan could enjoy continuous political tranquility from 1947 to the Zhongli incident of 1977.

Society and State in Tension

The GMD's modernization program, although placing high priority on economic development, was not entirely reluctant about democratization. Although the people were virtually denied access to the three elective bodies at the national level until the end of the 1960s, the GMD pledging to build Taiwan into a model province in conformity with the state-building goals set forth in Sun's writings, began as early as 1950 to implement local self-rule at provincial and lower levels. As with land reform, the development of local representative institutions was geared to gain the support of the local populace, thus ensuring the political stability of the island.[32]

As expected, the GMD dominated the provincial and local elections. With the exception of the elections at village and township assembly level, the GMD candidates have consistently won overwhelming majority votes, ranging from 60 percent to 85 percent at provincial, municipal, and county levels. However, the provincial and local elections showed a high degree of political competition and participation. For example, in 1984 more than 1,500 candidates (including 230 women) filed for 907 seats. Voter turnout was high: in 1964, more than 76 percent voted, and in 1977, 80 percent. A student of Taiwan's politics has the following to say on Taiwan's local democracy:

> Clearly, democracy at the grass roots is seriously limited by the authoritarian and bureaucratic political structure. But it is remarkable that vigorous competition has occurred and some legislative control of executive power has appeared in city and county governments. However, local political

competition does not mean lessening Nationalist domination. This is clear in light of the relative power of political parties.[33]

The provincial and local elections brought a number of non-GMD politicians, running independently, into the political arena, and some of them emerged as prominent political figures. A point that should be emphatically made here is that since the 1950s, elections at the local and provincial levels have become a mode of political participation of both the people and the politicians in Taiwan. From 1969 onward, important new avenues for political participation have been opened up at the national level as well. Because a sizable proportion of the members of the three national elective bodies—the National Assembly, the Legislative Yuan, and the Control Yuan—who had been elected in 1949 on mainland China had died by 1969, the government felt that new members had to be added. Consequently, supplementary elections were held in 1969, 1972, 1973, 1976, 1980, 1983, 1985, and 1989. The GMD were consistently able to get about 70 percent of the vote, but 30 percent went to the independent or opposition politicians. (This percentage continued to hold in the December 1991 elections for an entirely new National Assembly, which was characterized by formal party competition and followed sweeping institutional reforms initiated by President Lee Teng-hui.) The GMD's one-party hegemony was being seriously challenged, and it was indeed appropriate to characterize the ROC's political system from the 1970s onward as a "one-party-plus-independents" system.[34] At the same time, however, the GMD's long string of election victories, one after another, gave its elites sufficient confidence to see that the GMD's legitimacy would be built most effectively through popular elections. Equally important was the growing realization throughout these years on the part of non-GMD politicians and independents that electoral competition was a safe and viable road to political eminence and power sharing.

The so-called independents were sometimes called *dangwai* ("outside the party") figures. Because the GMD did not allow any new political parties, the opposition politicians had to become "independents." The *dangwai* was a heterogeneous group consisting of two main factions. The "Mainstream Faction" advocated gradual political reform and favored the Western model of a free market economy and pluralistic politics. The second faction, sometimes referred to as the "Action Faction," was more radical and advocated the use of mass-movement tactics. They were in favor of unqualified "Taiwanization" in the institutional life of the country and in cutting any emotional ties with the mainland.[35]

The emergence of the *dangwai* is usually traced to the 1977 Zhongli incident, a violent demonstration against alleged election tampering in Zhongli City. This was the first open challenge of the opposition forces to the GMD's political authority in thirty years. Symbolically, it can be seen as the resistance of an increasingly autonomous society against the powerful party-state. Politically and psychologically, the Zhongli incident was a watershed event in Taiwan's post-war political development. Thomas Gold writes:

> In retrospect, the Chung-li [Zhongli] Incident offers a unique key to understanding both the success and the shortcomings of Taiwan's development strategy wherein a strong authoritarian state guides and participates in rapid economic growth while suppressing the political activities of the social forces it has generated in the process.[36]

Indeed, it can well be argued, from a social and economic viewpoint, that "the Chung-li [Zhongli] Incident was inevitable as Taiwan's dynamic social forces, desirous of political participation and a say in the nation's destiny, continued to clash with an ossified political regime."[37] After the Zhongli incident, the *dangwai*, through magazines (*Formosa Magazine* was the main one), campaigns, and demonstrations, began aggressively to press their interests and claims against the party-state. On December 10, 1979, Human Rights Day, the *dangwai* staged a mass demonstration in Kaohsiung, Taiwan's second-largest city. During what became known as the Kaohsiung incident, violence broke out and 183 policemen were injured (only a few demonstrators were hurt, because the police had been instructed not to react with force). The government arrested and tried the leaders of the *dangwai* and more than sixty others, of whom eight received severe sentences, and closed the offices of *Formosa Magazine*, which was the organization—behaving like a political party—behind the demonstrations. Public opinion surveys showed a large majority of the population supported the government's action; the dissidents had to be viewed as a source of political instability that constituted a threat to public order and to the economy.[38]

However, though the GMD's role had the support of the majority of the population, "some Taiwanese voters have deep-seated feelings of having been colonized, and they respond emotionally to the martyr symbolism around such jailed leaders as the Kaohsiung Eight. In this political culture mass allies, emotional rhetoric, and confrontational demonstrations are tools of electoral survival for political moderates."[39] Pye has perceptively observed the unique character of the ethnic division between mainlanders and Taiwanese. He writes:

> Whereas in most ethnically divided societies the social
> differences are basic and politics often serves as the main
> avenue for bridging differences, in Taiwan it is the other way
> around. There is little social distance between the Taiwanese
> and the mainlanders . . . the only area of tension is politics.
> Hence measures taken to reduce political strains in the
> political realm have had dramatic payoffs in integrating
> the society.[40]

In this respect, the GMD government, far from ossified as
critics often alleged, was in fact sensitive and responsive to the rapidly changing political reality. The GMD was prepared to take an
accommodative approach toward social forces, yet was determined
to ensure that change took place within the existing constitutional
framework. As Myers writes, "Offering more pluralism but determined to control the parameters of political competition, the GMD
faces both an implacable minority and a supportive majority."[41]

Democratic Engineering from Above

Clearly, any major decision in Taiwan's politics has to come from
the leader of the Nationalist party-state. Here the late president
and party chairman Chiang Ching-kuo became crucial in Taiwan's
transition to democratization. Chiang Ching-kuo, like his father
Chiang Kai-shek, enjoyed supreme authority in the Taiwan political
system and made himself popular among the people after becoming
the premier in 1972. Chiang Ching-kuo never lost touch with the
changing spirit of the society. While vigorously pushing the modern-

ization program in the economic realm, including the ambitious Ten Major Projects, he quietly engaged in political reform by initiating a process of "Taiwanization." Taiwanese were not only appointed to the cabinet but also elected to the powerful Standing Committee of the party. As of 1983, Taiwanese representation in the policy-making bodies at cabinet, provincial, and county-city levels was 40 percent, 75 percent, and 100 percent, respectively. Thus, except at the national level, where the mainlanders still enjoyed a majority, Taiwanese had a great majority at the provincial level and monop-olized the county-city level. Moreover, since the party has become more electorally oriented, its nominated candidates for elective bod-ies at all levels have been overwhelmingly Taiwanese. As of today, the GMD has a membership of two million, 75 percent of whom are Taiwanese. The most conspicuous cases of Chiang Ching-kuo's Taiwanization were his vice-presidential appointments of Hsieh Tung-min in 1978 and Lee Teng-hui in 1984. (Lee succeeded to the presidency following Chiang's death in 1988 and was re-elected in 1990.) Indeed, the party-state of Taiwan has become substantially "Taiwanized."

Chiang Ching-kuo's Taiwanization was inseparable from his policies of liberalization and democratization. He was fully cogni-zant of the changing times. He said in early November 1986, "The time is changing and so are the environment and the trend. To fit in with these changes, the GMD must adopt new concepts and new forms according with the basic spirit of the democratic and con-stitutional system. Only by doing so can the GMD be in line with current trends and forever be together with the public."[42] In fact, as early as May 1986, the party-state, obviously with Chiang's bless-ing, agreed to enter a dialogue (*goutong*) with *dangwai* members.

This symbolized nothing short of the GMD's de facto recognition of the *dangwai* as a legitimate competitor. In fact, President Chiang's determination to democratize Taiwan's political system was fully manifested at the third plenum of the GMD's Twelfth Central Committee in March 1986. He single-handedly persuaded the group of senior party conservatives to accept his view that the time had come to implement further the party's long-standing goal of constitutional democracy. On April 9, he appointed a twelve-man task force of Standing Committee members to suggest reform measures. On October 15, Chiang, using his enormous personal power and prestige, was able to push resolutions through the GMD Central Standing Committee adopting two key reform proposals prepared by the task force. The first called for abolition of martial law. The second called for the revision of the law on civic organization to reverse the ban on the formation of new political parties. These steps signified a breakthrough in the history of Chinese democratic development. Admittedly, Chiang's democratic reform was no guarantee of full-fledged democracy in Taiwan, but it was a giant step in that direction.

At this juncture the *dangwai*, despite a warning from the GMD, went ahead to found the Democratic Progressive Party on September 28, less than a month before the GMD's reform resolutions were passed. Again, it was Chiang who decided to tolerate the newly formed opposition party. A new era was born. For the first time in modern Chinese history, one-party politics came to an end. The strong personal leadership Chiang exercised toward this eventuality is a striking instance of Larry Diamond's argument that "the most favorable development for democratization is a firm and forceful commitment to the process on the part of a country's leadership."[43] The argument is particularly relevant in Taiwan's case.

In the process of Taiwan's democratic transition, there were many personal and impersonal forces operating at different levels, and in different directions. Among them, the *dangwai*'s determination and aggressiveness in challenging political authority and in demanding the right to form an opposition party certainly created great pressure on the GMD, but no one could dispute the fact that it was the charismatic Chiang Ching-kuo who was the real architect of Taiwan's democratic engineering. He was not only pragmatic and confident enough to accommodate and respond to opposition views and demands in a conciliatory way, but was also realistic and powerful enough to overcome the resistance of the conservative forces within the party-state. Ironically, it was the leader of an authoritarian party who used nothing less than his authoritarian power to engineer and legitimize a democratic breakthrough.

Yet, despite the central importance of the role Chiang Ching-kuo played in the party-state, it would be a mistake to neglect the substantial presence in the GMD leadership stratum of reform-minded liberals, especially the young and Western-educated liberals who emerged prominently in the 1970s and 1980s. The reform-minded party elites, young and old, seemed to believe that to recognize the existence of the oppositional party was not only politically inevitable but also ideologically desirable. Chiang did not stand alone; his decisions for democratic opening had considerable support.

The Political Culture: Continuity and Change

In Taiwan, the GMD consciously saw itself as the custodian of Chinese culture, in contrast to the Chinese Communists on the mainland, who have tried systematically to replace Confucianism with Marxism-Leninism. The *sanmin zhuyi*, a creative and adaptive amalgam of both Chinese and Western values and concepts, was the official ideology of the party-state and has moved to the island. Studies of the educational process showed that schools in Taiwan were authority-group-centered and paternalistic in their methods of operation. According to Richard Wilson, there was an apparent effort to shift the children's loyalty from the family to the nation and its leaders. Submission to authority and group norms were two basic values of the Chinese children.[44] "Norms of conformity and deviance are among the most heavily sanctioned in the society. . . . There is no concept of a loyal opposition."[45] Although the degree of success in this socialization at school, except in the elementary grades, was somewhat questionable,[46] one survey conducted in the early 1970s recorded that 93 percent of the students responded that respect for elders was a "most important virtue," while only 13 percent agreed that majority rule, periodic elections, the protection of dissent, and more than one political party were important characteristics of democracy.[47]

The above findings indicate that although Confucianism has been under serious attack by various intellectual forces since the late Qing period, especially during and after the May Fourth New Cultural Movement in 1919, people's attitudes and values in Taiwan still bear a strong mark of Confucian influence.[48] These political attitudes and values can hardly be seen as democratic in nature. However, Confucianism is not totally lacking in semi-democratic or pro-democratic ideas. As is well known, Mencius flatly asserted that "the people are the most important element in a state, whereas the sovereign is the least."[49] This stream of Confucian thought was a firmly accepted part of Confucian political doctrine, which was labeled "people-centered" thought (*minben sixiang*).

Further evidence of the shallowness of democratic culture in Taiwan comes from John Lee's study of political change in Taiwan from 1949 to 1974. He concluded that Taiwan's democratization has largely involved "substantive" democracy in the sense that people-oriented government policies have benefited the population. "People in Taiwan do not have a firm belief in democracy so as to act democratically on all occasions. They believe that policies should be in the interest of the people but they seem to prefer authoritarian and informal ways of decision-making to rules of law called for by open process of political competition."[50] It was clear that the political attitudes and values of the people in Taiwan up to the early 1970s were still influenced by Confucian persuasion. To the extent these findings were valid, they imply that political values and attitudes were more congenial to and supportive of the people-oriented authoritarian power of the GMD government, at least until then.

Resistant as culture is to change, twentieth-century Taiwan no longer lives under the Confucianism that Weber analyzed. Weber's Confucianism can probably be labeled "imperial Confucianism," which was a complex and sophisticated combination of state ideology and a set of strategic institutions, including literati, the examination system, and above all, the imperial bureaucracy. In the post-Confucian era, the strategic imperial institutions of Confucianism are all deconstructed. Clearly, the most important new political institution was the constitution promulgated in 1946, the guiding principles of which were derived from western democratic ideas rather than from Confucianism. In the constitution, the concept of "popular sovereignty" was unequivocally adopted and was written into the textbooks of civic education.

Taiwan's class structure has also undergone rapid change especially since the 1970s. From 1970 to 1980, the middle class (both the new and the old) increased from 21.9 percent to 31.5 percent.[51] The number of people belonging to this class is now around six million. More significantly, several studies show consistently that more than 50 percent of the electorate in Taiwan identify themselves as "middle class." Apart from rapid industrialization, the most important reason for the emergence of the fast-growing middle class was the dramatic expansion of higher education. In 1970, there were 203,473 students enrolled in colleges and universities; by 1988, there were 442,648 students. By 1987, Taiwan had in total 1.4 million graduates of institutions of higher education. Universities and colleges are entirely different in methods of operation from primary and secondary schools. Students at the tertiary level are exposed more to liberal-democratic views than to Confucian values, because many teaching personnel at universities and colleges are Western-trained. As elsewhere, the political attitudes of the middle class ranged from moderately conservative to liberal, favoring gradual and stable change. However, a newly developed middle class shows a much higher expectation for political reform and social progress. Not surprisingly, the rise of the middle class is empirically shown to be closely related to the rise of political pluralism in Taiwan.[52]

The change in the political realm over the past ten years was quite significant. In 1978, 57.1 percent of the electorate never talked about politics; in 1985, the percentage had dropped to 32.1 percent.[53] The people have become increasingly interested in and concerned with public and political affairs since the Zhongli incident in 1977. A citywide survey on the voting motives of the Taipei electorate, conducted by Hu Fu and You Ying-long in February 1981, was exceedingly revealing of the changing political attitudes and values.[54]

As Table 8.1 indicates, the reason "to exercise civil rights" or "to perform civic duties" were each mentioned by two-thirds of the voters. More significant, "to exercise civil rights" was cited by 47.4 percent and "to perform civic duties" was cited by 43.9 percent as the most important reason for taking part in the election. From these figures, it is reasonable to assume that the people in Taiwan have formed a role concept of the citizen and a participant orientation toward the political system. This probably can partially explain the relatively high turnout in elections (about 65 to 70 percent) in recent years. The survey also showed that one-fourth of the voters felt they were capable of influencing government policies, and nearly 12 percent said this was a most important reason for exercising the vote. That one perceives oneself as able to affect government policies means that one has a sense of political efficacy. In the present case, 24 percent of the voters have what Almond and Verba would label "citizen competence."[55] Admittedly, this percentage is rather low in comparison with what Almond and Verba found in the United States (66 percent) and the United Kingdom (56 percent), but it is comparable to what they found in Italy (27 percent).[56]

Table 8.1   Reasons for Voting, Taipei Electorate, 1981

Reason for Voting	n	Mentioned (%)	Most Important (%)
To exercise civil rights	519	68.8	47.3
To perform civic duties	498	66.0	43.9
To express own views	247	32.8	15.5
To support the candidate he (she) likes	228	32.8	12.2
To influence government policies	181	24.0	11.9
Instructed by or advised by parties or other political groups	98	13.0	5.6
Urged by family members or relatives	79	10.5	5.6
Urged by neighborhood associations	49	6.5	2.7
Urged by organization he (she) belongs to	38	5.0	2.3
Candidates he (she) has acquaintance with	28	3.7	0.9
Urged by colleagues of the organization he (she) works for	14	1.9	0.5
Other	15	2.0	1.7

Source: Hu Fu and You Ying-long, "The Voting Motives of the Electorate," *Journal of Social Science* (Taipei), 33 (October 1985): 6.
Note: Each survey respondent could cite one or more reasons for voting, and one or more reasons as most important. Total *n* = 747.

According to an island-wide survey conducted in 1985 by Hu Fu,[57] people in Taiwan have a high "subject competence" but relatively low "citizen competence."[58] As many as 85 percent of the persons twenty to seventy years of age said that they had the right to appeal to the government about its officials; that they expect officials to be responsive to the needs of the people; that they would express dissenting views on government policies, and so on. But only 13 percent of the people surveyed felt that they had the right to demand and to influence government policies. These findings indicate that the political culture of Taiwan in the early 1980s was a mixture of high "subject competence" and low "citizen competence." Nevertheless, it is interesting that a sizable percentage of respondents (42.8 percent) felt that they had the right to influence the assembly in the making of the rules. Hu explains that this was probably due to the fact that assemblymen, unlike bureaucrats, were elected, and concludes that elections in Taiwan have served well as a mechanism for political socialization. Hu's observation gives additional support to Rustow's argument that there is reciprocal influence between belief and action, democratic values and democratic practice. In the case under study, the forty-year-long practice of elections in Taiwan first at the local and provincial levels, then at national level, has developed gradually and deeply among the politicians and citizens a "habitual vision" of democratic participation and democratic competition. It can well be argued that this kind of democratic "habituation" has become an important source of changes in political values and attitudes.[59]

Table 8.1 shows that the electorate's reasons for voting, apart from fulfilling their rights or duties, were mainly for some explicit purpose, that is, to express one's own views (32.8 percent), to support particular candidates he (she) likes (30.2 percent), and especially to influence government policies (24 percent). In other words, voting has been seen as an instrument to achieve political purposes. Thus, it can be said that a considerable number of the voters have an instrumental-rational orientation towards voting. Some people's voting behavior was also affected by social and environmental forces, such as pressures from parties and other political groups (13 percent), from family members and relatives (10.5 percent), and so on. Yet the latter percentages were relatively low, suggesting that in the emerging political culture of Taiwan, what Huntington and Nelson call "mobilized participation"—participation that is not "self-motivated" but pressured from other sources—is declining. Put another way, political participation in Taiwan is becoming more mature and "autonomous."[60]

Also of note is the finding of Hu and You that the instrumental-rational orientation toward voting was positively correlated with the index of socioeconomic status and level of education. We argue that this is a rather promising phenomenon because education and industrialization have continuously been upgraded and developed in Taiwan.

Based on the survey data cited above, Hu Fu has given another analysis of the voters' orientation toward political issues, which further illuminates the emerging political culture in Taiwan. The pattern of voting showed that 58.9 percent of the voters were candidate-oriented; 38.7 percent political issues–oriented; 21 percent political organizations–oriented; 17.1 percent personal relations–oriented; 10 percent social relations–oriented; and 9.8 percent were based on other factors.[61] Of all types of voters, the political issues–oriented are the most important because their attitudes inform us more about the changing political culture. It was found that about 42 percent of these voters gave their support to issues with an emphasis on national identity and national prestige; another 33.5 percent supported issues with an emphasis on political stability. Only 18 percent supported issues with an emphasis on political reform and democratization. Judging from the statistics, the great majority of the electorate in Taiwan had a strong psychological inclination to identify with the political system and to see the status quo maintained. They were not in favor of radical socio-political change of any kind. This observation is corroborated by Wei's study, which characterized Taiwan's opinion structure as a "moderate-supportive type."[62]

In light of the above analysis, we can say that the evolution of Taiwan's political culture shows a marked departure from Confucianism, but the influence of the latter is far from dead. Some characteristics of a civic culture are taking root. It probably is not too presumptuous to say that a kind of democratic culture is in the making.

A Non-paradigmatic Search

The relationship between modernization and democracy has long been one of the central interests for students of development. In the case of Taiwan, it seems that in the earlier phases of modernization, roughly up to the mid-1970s, the development-oriented, authoritarian power of the GMD did not face any serious society-wide or structurally based political protests and challenges. Its legitimacy was, in large measure, justified by its capability in producing a very successful and equitable economy. And the political values and attitudes of that period seemed to be compatible with the people-oriented authoritarianism. However, in the later phase the very success of economic development produced a number of structural forces, including especially a growing middle class, which began to affect Taiwan's liberalization and democratization. As a result of the industrialization—but not caused by it—a new political culture that is more congenial to democracy has been evolving.

Indeed, as Lucian Pye writes, "Taiwan is possibly the best working example of the theory that economic progress should bring in its wake democratic inclinations and a healthy surge of pluralism, which in time will undercut the foundations of the authoritarian rule common to developing countries."[63] In this connection, an empirical correlation does seem to exist between economic development and democracy in Taiwan, as was argued by Lipset. But Taiwan's transition to democracy would not be likely without the democratic engineering from above, particularly that of the charismatic leader President Chiang Ching-kuo. True enough, Chiang Ching-kuo himself was not immune to the structurally based democratic forces generated by the modernization he had helped to foster. It was not accidental that in December 1986, in a now-famous speech, he announced in no uncertain terms that the Chiang family members "cannot and will not" be his successors.

In his excellent study *State and Society in the Taiwan Miracle*, Thomas B. Gold concluded that "too many unique elements shaped Taiwan's experience to make it a viable model."[64] This is true insofar as Taiwan's modernization is concerned, and is particularly true with regard to Taiwan's democratization. There is no paradigm of democratic transition in the social science literature, and Taiwan's democratization, which took place in a unique social-historical context, had no paradigm to follow. It was a heroic, non-paradigmatic search for democracy. And Taiwan's case is not likely to be made a paradigm of democratic transition.[65] This of course does not mean that Taiwan's case is of no relevance to other countries in transition from authoritarianism/totalitarianism to democracy. The study of modernization is, after all, the study of both generalities and particularities.

The unique and non-duplicable elements of Taiwan's case apart, its generalizable features are of great value for the construction of a much-needed paradigm of democratic transition. To begin with, politics and the economy were intricately interrelated and interactive. The party-state, which was an "inhibited" political center, played a "big-push" role in the people-oriented economic development. The continuous success of economic development, with an equitable income distribution, generated powerful structural forces, including a sizable middle class. The newly emergent and expanding middle class had a strong identification with the political system, yet a desire for moderate and gradual democratic reform. In short, Taiwan's successful economic development fostered the emergence and development of a pluralistic society that, while harboring no animosity against the party-state, was strong enough to exert pressures upon the latter to be more responsible. And the continuing support of the people for the party-state in various elections, especially in the 1970s and 1980s, made the GMD leaders willing to commit themselves to electoral competition. In the same vein, the political challengers also found that electoral competition was a viable and effective route to power sharing. In a significant way, the political contenders have consciously and unconsciously come to the realization of the necessity of a settled respect for the rules of games, what Robert Dahl called a "system of mutual security."[66]

In Taiwan, politics was never a mere epiphenomenon. The political system, though it was demonstratively influenced by economic development, has always been an autonomous force. The steady effort toward political development in the 1970s and 1980s, especially the giant step taken in 1986, were engineered from the very political center in which President Chiang played a decisive role. The importance of the top leadership should not be theoretically submerged in the sociologistic argument of structural determinism. To fully understand Taiwan's transition to democracy, the politics of development must be autonomously assessed parallel to and together with the economics of development.

True enough, economic development did produce significant changes of political attitudes and values. These attitudes and values show some characteristics of "civic culture" that depart markedly from Confucianism. Our study shows unambiguously that there was an empirical correlation between economic development and the emergence of political democracy. But what should not be overlooked is the fact that parallel to and independent of economic development, the nearly half-century-long practice of elections at local and provincial levels have institutionalized the values and "rules of the game" of democratic participation and competition. This attests forcefully Rustow's concept of "habituation" as an important source of democratic cultural change.

9 State Confucianism and Its Transformation: The Restructuring of the State–Society Relation in Taiwan

The rise of the East Asia region, manifested first in Japan as a super economic power and subsequently in the so-called "four little dragons" as Newly Industrialized Countries (NICs), has captured the interest and imagination of scholars of different persuasions. Among the explanations accounting for this phenomenal success in economic modernization, a post-Confucian thesis emphasizing the role of Confucian cultural values has been articulated in various forms. What I address here is the challenge of democracy confronting those countries that can be broadly conceived as post-Confucian states.

No student of politics today can afford to be unaware of what Lucian Pye calls "the crisis of authoritarianism."[1] The crisis of authoritarianism, in most cases, is concomitant with the challenge of democracy. Speaking on democracy, Ernest Gellner has provided a vivid description:

> Looking at the contemporary world, two things are obvious: democracy is doing rather badly, and democracy is doing very well. . . . Democracy is doing very badly in that democratic institutions have fallen by the wayside in very many of the newly independent

"transitional" societies, and they are precarious elsewhere. Democracy, on the other hand, is doing extremely well in as far as it is almost (though not quite) universally accepted as a valid form.[2]

John Dunn perceptively points out that "democratic theory is the moral Esperanto of the present nation-state system, the language by which all nations are truly united, the public cant of the modern world, a dubious currency indeed."[3] He further suggests that "all states today profess to be democracies because a democracy is what it is virtuous for a state to be."[4] Indeed, the four little dragons (South Korea, Taiwan, Hong Kong, and Singapore) have demonstrated remarkable success in economic development, but are they able to take up the challenge of political democracy? In a broad sense, the nature of the political systems of the little dragons can be characterized as authoritarian. How can these authoritarian systems be transformed into democratic ones? I intend to analyze the transformation of Taiwan's state system, which showed a marked discontinuity with the state Confucianism of Imperial China. The theoretical focus of the analysis is on the state–society relationship and changes in it. The existence and viability of a civil society are believed to be necessary conditions for the development of a political system that is democratic in nature.

State–Society Relationships in Imperial China

The single most important factor that shaped and molded the social-political structure of traditional China was the establishment of a centralized bureaucratic state in the hands of its first emperor, Qin Shi Huang. Under the Qin empire, which grew from the collapse of the feudal substates through war, political unity was achieved for the first time in Chinese history. In the Han dynasty, which was the immediate successor of the short-lived Qin, while the basic state structure of the Qin remained relatively unchanged, Confucianism was elevated to the status of state ideology. The Confucian cultural system was then integrated with the political structure, which had a strong legalistic character. Thereafter the interpenetration of culture and politics was in a significant way the fundamental social-political reality of Imperial China. What should be noted is that the state ideology of the Han was an amalgam of Confucianism and Legalism which provided the legitimation for the imperial rulership of successive dynasties. From the Han onward, Confucianism became what can be called *institutional Confucianism* as the result of the mutual penetration of the cultural system and the political structure.

Institutional Confucianism refers to an institutional cultural complex.[5] It refers to political institutions, including imperial authority, as the keystone of the state system, the imposing bureaucracy as an instrument of the imperial state, and the literati and gentry as a status group linking the state with society. All these institutional structures were intermingled with Confucian cultural values. As the keystone of the state system, imperial authority was embodied in the concept of a cosmically based universal kingship. Benjamin Schwartz argues that "the centrality and weight of the political order" was one of the most striking characteristics of Chinese civilization.[6] He writes, "the kingship or locus of the authority which he occupies (*wei*) is an institution which comes to constitute the major link between human society and the ruling forces of the cosmos."[7]

The universal king embodies within his person the supreme authority over both the sacred and the secular realms of sociopolitical life. Max Weber showed unusual insight in noting that "secular and spiritual authority were combined in one hand, the spiritual strongly predominating."[8] The legitimacy of the universal king was based on the well-known theory of *tianming*, or the "Mandate of Heaven." The universal king was conceived as the Son of Heaven. Under the vast heaven, the universal king had, to use Schwartz's expression, "all-encompassing jurisdictional claims over the social-political life of the people."[9] Since, according to the theory of the Mandate of Heaven, imperial power was a religiously consecrated structure, it precluded the possibility of the development of a powerful priesthood or independent religious force, as Weber pointed out. The non-existence of independent religious forces in China made the Chinese monarch a "pontifex" who ruled the sociopolitical world "in the old genuine sense of charismatic authority."[10] Furthermore, according to the Confucian ideal of the sage-king, the ultimate form of politics must be a form of "ethocracy," that is, ethical politics. In Confucianism, there was no recognized autonomous realm of politics, separate from or independent of morality Confucian thinkers never intended to develop, and indeed never could envisage, institutional constraints on imperial authority. As Leon Vandermeersch points out, there was nothing in China comparable to Montesquieu's three powers.[11] And in the same vein, political pluralism was hardly conceived as a desirable state of political affairs.[12]

Bureaucracy was an indispensable institution of the imperial state. In fact, "bureaucratic power is usually thought to be the essence of state activity . . . [and] it is sometimes considered to be identical with it."[13] The Mandarins (i.e., scholar-officials) of the bureaucracy were the governing class of the Chinese state par excellence. Their status and prestige were defined in cultural terms, and qualifications for office were decided by a competitive examination based on the Confucian classics. Under institutional Confucianism the state, exemplified by the kingship institution, was entitled to make all-encompassing jurisdictional claims on the sociopolitical affairs of the empire. Xu Fuguan posits a strong thesis for the state by saying that the pivot of the Chinese autocratic system, the foundation for which was laid down in the Qin and Han dynasties, was that "outside of the imperial domination, no independent or resisting forces were allowed to exist."[14] Jacques Gernet advances a similar argument. He writes: "The only problem for the Chinese state in the course of its long history, was to prevent the development of powers other than its own, such as that of the merchants, the armies, the religious communities, and to prevent dangerous splits at the top."[15]

What should be reiterated here is that the state institutions (kingship and bureaucracy) were permeated by Confucian ethical values. The problem of the power of state Confucianism must be considered at the same time as the problem of duty. The Confucian ideal of ethocracy was based on the concept of duty or obligation instead of right or power.[16] To say that the state has an all-encompassing jurisdictional claim on the sociopolitical life of the people is tantamount to saying that the state has a comprehensive responsibility "to provide [for], to enrich, and to educate the people."[17] Seen from this perspective, it is not difficult to agree with Karl Bunger that "the Chinese emperor had no 'right' to rule, but a "Heavenly Mandate" (*tianming*), i.e., a duty to fulfill. It was his duty to keep the human society in good order (*zhi*). The guidelines for this order had to correspond to a cosmic order which was believed to include moral principles."[18]

Whether from the viewpoint of power or duty, the state had a "positive" interventionist or transformative stance toward society. In China's long imperial history, as Zhang Hao argues well, imperial power could take either a "heavy" form, in which the throne "used the machinery of state to dominate and transform society," or a "light" form, in which the political-bureaucratic center "relied mainly upon its moral and ritual influence to achieve order in society."[19] Michael Loewe's characterization of the basic attitude toward the role and duty of the government in the Western Han dynasty is also suggestive. He thinks that a more precise way to identify the government's role in economic affairs is to use the terms "modernist" and "reformist" instead of "legalist" or "Confucian."[20] Not all thinkers or scholar-officials in all dynasties would have agreed that the role or responsibility of the state (i.e., government) lies in the greatest exploitation of natural resources for the benefit of the people.[21] The crucial fact is that in the notion of universal kingship, ideologically the political system of Imperial China had the right and the duty to intervene in the socioeconomic activities of society. But empirically the level of "generalized power" of the state, as S. N. Eisenstadt argues, was rather limited,[22] and the state's penetration into society reached only to the door of the sub-county level, where "informal government," represented by traditional elite groups such as the gentry and by a variety of non-governmental social institutions, tended to dominate the scene.[23]

True enough, "the rationalism of the bureaucracy was confronted with a resolute and traditionalistic power. . . . This tremendous power of the strictly patriarchical sib was, in truth, the carrier of the much discussed 'democracy' of China, which had nothing whatsoever in common with 'modern democracy.'"[24] All these factors indicated that the power of state Confucianism in actuality was circumscribed; yet this should not lead us to think that the state was weak vis-à-vis society.

The bureaucratic domination of the state over society was most clearly manifested in the nature of Chinese cities. The Chinese city, which was "an imperial fortress, actually had fewer formal guarantees of self-government than the village. . . . [Furthermore, it] was predominantly a product of rational administration."[25] The cities in China lacked political autonomy, had no "city law," no concept of a citizenry."[26] As a result, the Chinese city was an administrative entity but not a political society or civil society. The Confucian bureaucratic state had in effect prevented the emergence of civil society in China. Therefore, in large measure the state-society relationship in Imperial China was rather unbalanced and lopsided. Admittedly, in the long imperial history there were some periods in which the omnipotence of state power was more imaginary than real.[27]

The Role of the State in Taiwan's Economic Development

For a very long time, at least up to the early 1970s, despite the fact that Taiwan had achieved considerable success in economic development, its political system was seen as an ossified one.[28] Structural features of the political system had experienced little basic change since the Guomindang (National People's Party or Nationalist

Party, hereafter GMD) moved to the island in 1949. But it would be a mistake to think that the party-state was inactive or passive while the economy was making aggressive advancement. The party-state had in fact made successful functional adaptations in coping with the problem of political modernization, that is participation, legitimation, and integration.[29] A fundamental fact, often not fully recognized until recently by students of Taiwan's modernization, is that the party-state played a vital role of guidance in Taiwan's rapid and successful economic development.[30] Roy Hofheinz, Jr., and Kent Calder argue that "East Asia has an advantage over us in the way it is organized and motivated—that its political system, broadly conceived, gives it an 'edge' in crucial areas of economic competition."[31] Talcott Parsons, in an analysis of the institutional pattern of economic development of the West and the Third World, writes: "In the case of the original development of industrialism, I have argued that it could not have occurred without the freeing of private enterprise from certain types of political control. But in the present case, I shall argue that political authority is usually a necessary agency and that under certain conditions, far from obstructing, it is likely strongly to facilitate the process."[32]

Speaking on the case of Taiwan, Alice Amsden makes the claim that to understand Taiwan's economic growth, it is necessary to understand its potent state. She convincingly demonstrates that "Taiwan is simply a particularly striking example of the positive association between state interventions and the acceleration of economic growth that is now generally accepted to prevail in cases of Third World capitalist development."[33]

At this juncture, it is worth examining the nature of the state of the Republic of China. Taiwan has been under the hegemonic rule of the GMD since 1949. Until the early 1980s, party and state were interwoven, with no clear boundaries between them. It is not inappropriate to characterize the political system as that of one-party authoritarianism, under which no independent organized political force was allowed to exist. Indeed, the party-state of Taiwan saw itself as the custodian of Chinese culture, but the relationship between Confucianism and the party-state was fundamentally different from that which existed between Confucianism and the imperial state in China. Although Confucianism is not an insignificant living force in the political life of Taiwan, institutional Confucianism was completely deconstructed. Taiwan made a marked departure from institutional Confucianism in both political institutions and political culture. It is clear that Confucianism no longer serves as a state ideology intermeshed with political authority.

The ideology of Taiwan's party-state is the *sanmin zhuyi* (Three Principles of the People) of Sun Yat-sen, which is a creative and adaptive amalgam consisting of both Chinese and Western values and concepts.[34] Though the GMD is somewhat Leninist in structure, its ideology is categorically different from Leninism. Sun's three-stage development theory of nation building (i.e., military rule, democratic tutelage, and constitutional democracy), shows unmistakably that he was firm in his commitment to political democracy. Government in Sun's proposed system would be powerful, but sovereignty would remain with the people. Indeed, Sun's concept of the political system was unequivocally democratic.[35]

What should be emphatically pointed out is that although a new constitution was promulgated in 1946, it did not bring China to the stage of constitutional democracy, as Sun's theory prescribed. Instead, the civil war between the GMD government and the Chinese communists accelerated to an unprecedented level. In an atmosphere of war, the first session of the National Assembly convened in Nanjing in 1949. The Assembly elected Chiang Kai-shek as the president of the Republic of China, and also adopted the "Temporary Provisions for the Duration of Mobilization to Suppress the Rebellion."[36]

Upon establishing its rule over Taiwan, the GMD government declared martial law in 1949. In the early years of its rule, the government was preoccupied with issues of national security, as military invasion by the Chinese communists seemed possible and imminent. Throughout the 1950s, 1960s, and the early 1970s, the GMD government, despite its vigorous development-oriented economic policies, made no serious efforts to establish constitutional democracy. Under martial law, strict control of political and other rights—including the right to organize new political parties—was imposed. The hegemonic domination of the party-state over society was never seriously challenged until the late 1970s.

The government, while making the recovery of the mainland its national policy and spending a disproportionate amount of the budget on the military, shifted its strategy decisively to precipitate economic development in the early 1950s. The GMD started first with land reform, which was ideologically sanctioned by Sun's doctrine and was considered by party-state elites a political necessity for ensuring the stability of the island. The process of land reform was peaceful and bloodless, and the results were far-reaching, economically and politically, with the creation of the most equitable rural scene in all of Asia.

Immediately after the completion of land reform, the party-state successively launched two four-year economic plans (1953–

1956 and 1957–1960) with import substitution industrialization as a development strategy. Under this strategy, the indigenous industrial sector was nourished and assisted by the state through a protectionist trade policy. In the early 1960s, the government shifted its strategy from import substitution industrialization to export-oriented industrialization, under which three successive four-year plans (1961–1964, 1965–1968, and 1969–1972) were successfully pursued, resulting in the tremendous growth of manufacturing industries in the private sector. Chu-yüan Cheng writes:

> At almost every critical turning point, the guidance from the government has proven to be vital. In the transformation of Taiwan from an inward-oriented economy to an outward-oriented economy in the 1960s, the government used tax and credit as leverage to induce private-sector activity in recent decades, the government took initiatives to upgrade Taiwan's industrial structure. In July 1979, a 2,210-hectare industrial park was created in Xinzhu to be the Silicon Valley of Taiwan. . . . More recently, the government has offered new tax incentives to attract venture capital to new enterprises in high-tech industries.[37]

The story of Taiwan's economic development has been fully analyzed elsewhere.[38] What needs to be said here is that in Taiwan's miraculous development, the party-state has, from the very beginning, played the role of guidance and control. It has not only enjoyed a highly autonomous status but has also used its power to transform the society. What were the factors making the party-state so overwhelmingly an agency for developing and transforming society in Taiwan? It has been argued that the interventionist stance of the party-state toward society may resonate directly with traditional practice in imperial days.[39] Indeed, students of Taiwan's development believe that the party-state's role in a regulated capitalist economy has much to do with the traditional Chinese cultural structure.[40] It is important to note that no less a policymaker than K. T. Li, who was one of the major architects of Taiwan's economy, attributes the state's development-oriented policy to Sun's Doctrine of the People's Welfare. He writes: "All economic activities were aimed ultimately at improving the people's living standard. This is the essential meaning of the Doctrine of People's Welfare which conceives 'to provide and to enrich the people' as the basic fundamentals."[41]

As I mentioned earlier, the Confucian idea of the state is that it has comprehensive responsibilities to provide for, to enrich, and to educate the people, and this concept is well incorporated into Sun's Doctrine of the People's Welfare. In this connection, it should be noted that as early as 1949, President Chiang Kai-shek told GMD members: "We must frankly admit that our party has done more for the political phases of our National Revolution than for the economic and social phases. Many of our members speak for social reform in theory, while in practice they rarely go into the heart of society and work for social improvement. Thus, they incurred the criticism of being 'leftists in thought but rightists in action.'"[42] This shows that the leadership of the GMD government, in the aftermath of its defeat on the mainland, had critically reflected on the inadequacy of its rule-oriented policies in the past and had consciously shifted to development-oriented policies in land reform and economic growth in Taiwan. The leaders of the GMD deliberately gave greater scope over Taiwan's economy to Western-trained techno-

crats. Indeed, K. Y. Yin, the first major architect of Taiwan's economy, who was an American-trained electrical engineer, was given a
free hand to design and implement Taiwan's economic strategies.
Moreover, the party-state even established, outside the conventional
bureaucratic structure, new institutions to guide and implement
development-oriented economic plans.

The unflagging support of the top leaders of the party-state
made it possible for the modernizing technocrats single-mindedly
to pursue economic goals.[43] As a result of economic development,
a free market economy was being developed.[44] Such a free market
economy was hardly embraced out of the convictions of the GMD
government. What Sun Yat-sen advocated was a sort of mixed
economic system under which state enterprises and private enterprise co-exist. He wrote: "All matters that can be and are better
carried out by private enterprises should be left to private hands,
which would be encouraged and fully protected by liberal laws.
All matters that cannot be taken up by private concerns and those
that possess monopolistic character should be taken up as national
undertakings. The property thus created would be state owned and
managed for the benefit of the whole nation."[45]

Under Sun's system, the state or public sector definitely has
a more prominent role than in the free market system. The shift
from state-regulated capitalism to a free market system in Taiwan
was believed to be due to the influence which the United States
exerted on the GMD government.[46] American aid agencies were of
the belief that "a shift from state to private ownership would contribute to the operating efficiency of . . . enterprises, hasten overall
economic development and decrease the [government's] financial
hurdle in subsidizing [public] activities."[47] Neil A. Jacoby, analyz-

ing the impact of US aid, wrote, "by far the most important consequence of US influence was the creation in Taiwan of a booming private enterprise system."[48] The shift of weight of the public sector vis-à-vis the private sector was unmistakably clear. According to Chu-yüan Cheng: "In the 1960s, about 48 percent of the industrial output value originated from publicly owned and managed enterprises. The share has been continuously declining. By 1986, only 14.8 percent of all production originated from the public sector, indicating that the pace of growth in the private sector has far exceeded that in the public sector."[49]

Since the 1950s, Taiwan has successfully developed into a newly industrializing country. In the process of development, the state has always played a vital role in guiding and shaping the nature of the economy. Indeed, the nature of the state is a form of authoritarianism. In Taiwan, the authoritarian form of the state seemed to contribute to economic growth as in other NICs of the East Asia region.[50] John Lee, in his study of political change in Taiwan from 1949 to 1974, observed that "people in Taiwan do not have a firm belief in democracy as to act democratically on all occasions. They believe that policies should be in the interest of the people but they seem to prefer authoritarian and informed ways of decision-making to rules of law called for by open processes of political competition."[51]

These findings show that the political attitudes and values influenced by the Confucian persuasion were more congenial to, and supportive of, the people's-interest orientation of the authoritarian party-state, at least until the early 1970s. But, intended or not, the ever-expanding market economy which was sanctioned and indeed pushed by the state was becoming more and more autonomous throughout the 1970s and 1980s, and along with it a viable civil society was coming into existence.

The Emergence of Civil Society: Reciprocal Relations between State and Economy

I have argued that the party-state enjoyed a hegemonic rule over society. It is, of course, nonsensical to regard state autonomy as the total absence of constraint. Up to the mid-1970s, the state did have a significant impact on the economy and society. Yet, along with the growing force of the economy, particularly in the private sector, the market-based society gradually asserted its status as a less dependent entity Alice Amsden argues that Taiwan's case "demonstrates the reciprocal interaction between the structure of the state apparatus and the process of economic growth."[52] Furthermore, "the Taiwan state, which appeared on its arrival from the Mainland to be an unlikely instrument for the promotion of development, proved to be a most effective one. At the same time, changes in the nature of the state itself appear to have been an important by-product of economic development. The state, in short, can be said both to have transformed Taiwan's economic structure and to have been transformed by it."[53]

The reciprocal dynamic between the power of the state and the power of society is the key to understanding the changing state–society relationship since the 1960s. Owing to the state's development strategies, the socioeconomic structures of Taiwan have undergone a fundamental change. A basically agrarian society was transformed into an industrial society. The urban working class and the urban middle class emerged as a result of industrialization

and urbanization. By 1980, only 18 percent of the working population was engaged in farming, but the work force in industry had
increased from less than 15 percent of the population in the 1960s
to more than 35 percent in 1980. What is striking is that the middle class has risen to more than 31 percent. The number of people
belonging to this class is now around 6 million. Whereas the old
middle class, which was a product of the state's development, tended
to be politically conservative, the new middle class has become more
reform-minded. Surprisingly or not, studies show consistently that
more than 50 percent of the electorate identify themselves as middle
class. Moreover, this is the class that showed the strongest identification with the GMD in elections.[54] At this juncture, it should be mentioned that Taiwan's development has produced a distinguishing
characteristic, namely, to use Thomas Gold's expression, "the bifurcation of the economy from the polity."[55]

Not only has this phenomenon of bifurcation produced
extraordinary results in the political system in terms of power distribution between the so-called mainlanders and the Taiwanese, but
also it has had an important impact on the state–society relationship. For a long time, the primary source of tension between the
mainlanders and the Taiwanese was the dominant position of the
former over the latter. At the national level, all the high positions
in the government and the army were initially occupied by mainlanders. Of the three elective bodies of the central government—
the National Assembly, the Legislative Yuan, and the Control
Yuan—the mainlanders constituted the great majority since they
were elected in 1946 on the mainland to represent all provinces of
China. Because the government of the Republic of China claimed
to be the sole legitimate representative government for all of China,

it justified its perpetuation of a national government by having all central government units staffed by mainlanders, not Taiwanese. Despite being virtually denied a road to national political power, the Taiwanese were deliberately encouraged by the GMD's policies to engage in economic ventures and activities. By the 1970s, it had become evident that a division of power had emerged between the mainlanders and the Taiwanese, with the former controlling the political sector and the latter dominating the economic sector.

Nevertheless, the more basic structural change was not the division between economic and political power along ethnic lines but the emergence of an increasingly potent civil society vis-à-vis the powerful state. In the 1970s, a growing demand for liberalization and political participation became obvious. A vigorous democratic political movement entered the political arena. One-party authoritarian rule began to be questioned. In particular, the ossified political structure of the three national representative bodies was challenged by independent politicians, who were sometimes called *dangwai* (outside the party) figures. The GMD government was not totally insensitive to these demands. Consequently, a series of supplementary elections were held in 1969, 1972, 1973, 1976, 1980, 1983, and 1985. Although the GMD was consistently able to win about 70 percent of the vote, the independent politicians took the other 30 percent. The GMD's one-party authority was being seriously challenged.

What is significant to note is that in the 1980s, apart from elections, through which anti-GMD political views were widely voiced, another totally new movement took place in Taiwan's civil society. This movement was social in nature but different from the democratic political movement. In fact, a total of seventeen social movements have been recorded and analyzed, including a consumers' movement, a nature conservation movement, a women's movement, an aborigines' human rights movement, a New Testament church protest, a teachers' rights movement, and a veterans' welfare protest. Xiao Xinhuang argues that the various movements, though with different specific objectives, "all demand a change in the existing state–society relations. The most commonly shared goal is to search for more autonomy for civil society across class boundaries. The state, rather than an adversary class, was taken as a critical target to which the participants have made strong and direct appeals."[56]

How could the democratic movements and social movements have developed so vigorously in the 1970s and 1980s? Fundamentally, as I have pointed out, they were the direct result, intended or not, of state-guided economic development. What Alfred Stepan has written about the political evolution of Latin America seems to be equally applicable to Taiwan. He writes, "The state played a central role in setting the conditions that allowed crucial developments in civil society to take place at all."[57]

Thus, one should avoid taking a sociological stance of structural determinism, treating politics as a mere epiphenomenon of the economy. The state system in Taiwan has always been an autonomous force. The political development of electoral competition in the 1970s and 1980s was, in fact, engineered from the very center of the political system in which President Chiang Ching-kuo played a decisive role. In order to understand fully Taiwan's movement toward democracy and its restructuring of the state–society relationship, the politics of growth must be autonomously assessed parallel to and together with the economics of development.

In a substantive way the GMD government, far from being

stagnant, as was often believed, was sensitive and responsive to the changing political reality. Long before the Zhongli incident of 1977, which is believed to be a watershed event in Taiwan's post-war political development,[58] the GMD government was prepared to take an accommodating approach toward the sociopolitical forces. Yet it was determined to ensure that change would take place within the existing constitutional framework, as Ramon Myers writes, "offering more pluralism but determined to control the parameters of political competition."[59] The burgeoning social movements of the 1980s are probably better interpreted as the result of the democratic transformation of the authoritarian state than that of a weakened party-state.[60]

Chiang Ching-kuo, like his father, enjoyed supreme authority and made himself popular among the people after becoming the premier in 1972. While vigorously pushing the modernization program in the economic realm, he actively engaged in political reform by initiating a process of "Taiwanization," thus bridging the gap between the state and society. Chiang was fully cognizant of the changing spirit of the society. He said in November 1986: "The times are changing and so are the environment and the trends. To fit in with these changes, the GMD must adopt new concepts and new forms according with the basic spirit of the democratic and constitutional system. Only by doing so can the GMD be in line with current trends and forever be together with the public."[61] It should be remembered that in May 1986 the party-state, obviously with Chiang's blessing, agreed to enter a dialogue with *dangwai* members. This symbolized nothing short of the GMD's de facto recognition of the *dangwai* as a legitimate competitor in the newly developing political order.

In this regard, it is worth mentioning that what changed was not only the socioeconomic structure but also people's political attitudes and values. A citywide survey on motives of the Taipei electorate by Hu Fu and You Ying-long in February 1981 revealed that 47.3 percent and 43.9 percent of the voters, respectively, answered that "to exercise civic rights" and "to perform civic duties" were the "most important reason(s) for their taking part in the election."[62] According to another island-wide survey conducted in 1985, as much as 85 percent of the population (twenty to seventy years of age) said that they had the right to appeal to the government about its officials; that they would expect officials to be more responsive to the needs of the people; and that they would express dissenting views on government policies.[63] Judging from these findings, we can see that Taiwan was evolving into a political culture that showed a marked break with Confucianism, although the influence of the latter was far from dead. The intellectual climate in Taiwan, though complicated in content and confused in expression, had long ceased to accept the idea that the state, as the guardian of the people's well-being, has an all-encompassing power over social-political life, as was conceived in Confucian political-ethical philosophy intellectuals of different persuasions share a loose consensus on "the idea of individual moral autonomy, some kind of 'democracy' and—albeit with reservations—capitalism."[64] Thomas Metzger, after examining the ideological mode of Taiwan's experience, writes: "In the ROC, however, there was an 'elective affinity' between the ideological mix that was realized and the other aspects of a political center that indeed came to focus increasingly on instrumental rationality, using this standard to revise the inherited culture and so to promote an effective program of modernization leading today even to full political pluralism."[65]

Lucian Pye makes the strong claim that:

> Taiwan, in spite of all its lingering Confucian rhetoric, has
> made a greater break with Confucian attitudes toward
> authority than has China, Korea, or Vietnam. . . . Taiwan
> has probably gone further than the other three states in
> abandoning Confucian ways—but ironically, it has been the
> most vigorous in its support of the Confucian tradition.
> The erosion of Confucianism has taken place because
> the politics of status and prestige have had to give way to
> utilitarian values of a materialistic nature. Taiwan has
> become a society so energized by economics that politics has
> yielded up its pretensions of importance. Moreover, to the
> degree that the status of officialdom has been redefined,
> Taiwan has tended toward a pluralistic polity and away
> from a dutiful, disciplined Confucian society which defers
> to government authority.[66]

Taiwan's modernization is too dynamic for us to know where
it is leading, but one thing is certain: structurally and culturally, Taiwan has made a marked departure from institutional Confucianism,
and a new more balanced state–society relation has emerged in the
process of modernization.

Confucianism, Civil Society, and Political Modernity

Daniel Bell, speaking on "American exceptionalism," writes:

> What is the distinguishing feature, then, of the United States,
> one that has been its strength throughout its history? It is

simply that the United States has been the complete civil society (to use the Hegelian term), perhaps the only one in political history. . . . In Hegel's sense, there was no "State" in the United States, no unified, rational will expressed in a political order, but only individual self-interest and a passion for liberty. In every European nation (with the partial exception of Britain), the State ruled over society, exercising a unitary or quasi-unitary power enforced by an army and a bureaucracy.[67]

In the case of China, the state ruled over society throughout its imperial history. In fact, no concept of civil society was ever articulated; in the strict sense, no counterpart of the word *society* existed in the Chinese language. Jacques Gernet is not wide of the mark when he asserts: "One could say that in China, the state is all. . . . In China, the state was an established reality from the beginning, or in any case from the time when the formula was worked out in the state of Qin, before it was extended to the whole of the Chinese realm. It was the great organizer of society and of territory."[68]

Indeed, people in Europe did not begin to apply the term state to their political entities until as late as the seventeenth century, whereas in China the concept of the state already existed in the Spring and Autumn and Warring States periods (eighth to third centuries B.C.).[69] In terms of world comparisons, what made China fundamentally different from Europe was that China, since the Qin and Han dynasties, had become a centralized unitary state with a single politico-religious order of state Confucianism, while Europe remained a multistate system with a higher degree of pluralism.[70]

As we have seen, in the imperial system politics and culture were mutually penetrating and closely interwoven. Nevertheless, the Confucian normative (ethical) paradigm of state or politics was never fully realized. What was actualized was an institutional Confucianism, under which the state was legitimized by a Confucian cultural-political ideology, and in which the state, personified by the emperor or Son of Heaven, had all-encompassing claims over the social-political order. The leadership of the state, according to the Confucian ideology of universal kingship, had comprehensive responsibilities toward the population. Imperial China, which could legitimately be called a state Confucianism, took an interventionist and transformative stance toward society. The imperial domination effectively prevented the emergence of civil society. This is a structural problem that is fundamental to the development of the modern state in China.[71]

The modernization that has taken place in Taiwan since the 1950s has resulted in the fundamental transformation of state Confucianism. A civil society has emerged owing to the development of a market economy and political pluralism. A new state–society relation has come into existence. In the process of transformation, the party-state played a dominating and guiding role in developing strategies for the economy. Probably nothing is more strikingly dialectical than the fact that the vibrant market economy, which was the very creation of the state, has in turn transformed the state. But, as I hope I have made clear, politics was never a mere epiphenomenon. The state has always enjoyed an autonomous status. No economic, deterministic argument could explain fully the transformation of the state. In point of fact, to explain Taiwan's case the self-transformation of the state is as important as, if not more important than, the impact of the market economy. The state's people-oriented developmental and transformative strategies toward the economy and society were reminiscent of the Confucian tradition, but Confucianism was no longer the state ideology.

Institutional Confucianism has been fundamentally restructured. Institutional Confucianism has become what may be called intellectual Confucianism, by which I mean Confucianism in Taiwan today is nothing more than a philosophical-cultural system, like Hegelism, liberalism, and so on. Although the GMD has been organized as a Leninist-style party, the GMD government neither intended in theory (*sanmin zhuyi*) nor tried in practice to have total control over society. The political center of the party-state in Taiwan is, to use the concept of Thomas Metzger and Ramon Myers, an "inhibited and accommodative one,"[72] which provides ample room for the development and growth of the economy and society. The story of state Confucianism and its transformation is still an unfolding process. It is part of the great drama of China's search for political modernity.

10 The Transformation of Confucianism in the Post-Confucian Era: The Emergence of Rationalistic Traditionalism in Hong Kong

The striking empirical phenomenon of success in economic development in particular, and modernization in general, of East Asian societies, namely, Japan and the four little dragons—Taiwan, South Korea, Singapore, and Hong Kong—has captured the attention of students of modernization from various disciplines. Peter Berger believes that there is a distinctively East Asian form of modernity in the making.[1] Edward Tiryakian argues that the epicenter of modernity has begun to shift from North America to East Asia.[2] The success of East Asia, which constitutes such a sharp contrast to the ineffective struggle of most of the economically backward Third World countries, calls for an explanation.

Broadly speaking, there are two theoretical tendencies in the current literature on East Asia. One, the "institutionalist" interpretation, emphasizes specific economic, legal, and political institutional arrangements within the societies at issue.[3] The other, or "culturalist" interpretation, emphasizes specific cultural factors.[4] The culturalists attribute the success of Eastern societies to their common cultural heritage, that is, Confucianism. Herman Kahn and others have put forward what may be called a post-Confucian thesis, which holds that the set of values with which the people grew up, conventionally labeled Confucian, provides them with the mentality and work ethic believed to be conducive to economic development.[5] This post-Confucian thesis, though still in a rudimentary form, can be seen as both Weberian and anti-Weberian at the same time. It is Weberian because, like Weber's Protestant thesis, it argues for the critical role of cultural factors in economic development; it is anti-Weberian because it contradicts Weber's view that the failure of capitalism to develop in traditional China was largely due to the effects of the Confucian ethos. Thomas Metzger writes: "We consequently are led to ask why in this kind of world are some societies more effective than others in coping with their problems and rising to the challenges of modernization? While Weber had to explain China's failure, we have to explain its success but paradoxically our answer, like Weber's, emphasizes the role of the indigenous ethos."[6]

This essay is not intended to join the great controversy over Weber's Protestant thesis, which has often resulted in sterile debate. One point, however, should be made clear: the post-Confucian thesis, though interestingly provocative, probably cannot fundamentally challenge Weber's original thesis. The Weberian thesis asks why the indigenous development of the West in the seventeenth and eighteenth centuries led to capitalism and the indigenous development of China did not. To Weber, the adoption of capitalism is theoretically a separate issue. As Talcott Parsons has commented: "Weber's concern was with the conditions which made it possible for 'capitalism' to develop in the West, and why this did not occur in other societies. Now it can perhaps be said that attention must be centered on the conditions of its spread from the West to other societies all over the world."[7]

The spread of capitalism from the West to other non-Western societies has been extremely uneven. And the success of non-Western societies in assimilating capitalism very much depends on their "conditions," which involve both institutional and cultural factors.[8] If we speak only of the cultural conditions involved in assimilating capitalism, we are resorting to the post-Confucian thesis, which in effect hypothesizes that Confucian values are providing the motivational drive for economic development in East Asian societies.

Ironically, from the beginning of this century, especially since the New Culture Movement of May Fourth in 1919, most intellectuals have held the view that the root of China's backwardness lay in its cultural traditions, especially its Confucian values. Not surprisingly, they vigorously attacked all aspects of Confucianism, particularly the Confucian family system. Their anti-traditionalism was total and uncompromising. What some of the leading intellectuals advocated was nothing short of wholesale Westernization. The May Fourth Cultural Revolution was aimed at a total rejection of China's past.[9]

Indeed, this view which holds that Confucianism is inimical to China's development is not totally dissimilar to that of Weber and is in opposition to the post-Confucian thesis. Students of China's development may ask, then, which view is theoretically and empirically more defensible, in light of the striking economic success of some East Asian societies. I am of the view that no definitive verdict can be given on this issue. A fundamental cultural fact must be recognized, namely, that East Asian societies no longer exist in a Confucian sociopolitical order. The May Fourth leaders' Confucianism has long since been deconstructed, if it has not totally died.

We are now living in a post-Confucian sociopolitical society, and the cultural systems of the post-Confucian societies are a mixture of indigenous values and Western influences. In this essay, I argue that insofar as Hong Kong is concerned, a kind of Confucianism which I call *rationalistic traditionalism* has come into existence. This, I believe, is an important contributing factor in making Hong Kong one of the most successful newly industrialized societies.

I am not arguing that rationalistic traditionalism (a transformed value orientation of Confucianism) is the only factor responsible for the successes of Hong Kong's modernization. No student of development of any sophistication would think that a Confucian heritage is enough to explain the successful modernization of East Asian societies.[10] There is no gainsaying that Weber was not a monocausalist. His thought is not determined by any single factor; he was as much concerned with institutional factors as with cultural ones.[11]

The suggestion by S. N. Eisenstadt that what is required for a re-examination of the Weberian thesis is "a shift of attention from the allegedly direct, causal relationship between Protestantism and capitalism (or other aspects of the modern world) to the internal transformative capacities of Protestantism and to their impact on the transformation of the modern world"[12] seems to me most appealing. He writes: "The crucial impact of Protestantism in the direction of modernity came after it could not fully realize its initial totalistic socio-religious aims. Thus the special importance of Protestantism, from a broad comparative point of view was that . . . it contained within itself the seeds of such a transformation and that in certain settings these seeds could bear fruit generously to influence the course of European civilization."[13]

Although the impact of Confucianism on the direction of modernity in Chinese societies was not quite the same as that of Protestantism in Europe, I am of the view that Confucianism does contain the seeds of transformation, and in the right institutional settings these seeds could bear fruit to influence positively the course of economic development. In the pages that follow, I discuss how the seeds of Confucianism have grown into a rationalistic traditionalism.

Hong Kong has been rapidly industrialized and modernized since the 1950s. By 1985, Hong Kong's per capita income was US$6,282. In terms of employment, 35.6 percent of the labor force was engaged in manufacturing, 54.4 percent in commerce and other service industries, and only 1.8 percent in agriculture. According to the United Nations' classification, in 1971 Hong Kong had the second highest per capita consumption of extrasomatic energy in Asia, next only to Japan. From the standpoint of energetics, Hong Kong belongs among the "ecological phase 4 societies," in which "the total use of energy by human communities, unlike in phase 1, 2, and 3 societies, is no longer running more or less parallel with population size."[14]

Hong Kong is an international city of the first order, but 98 percent of its population is ethnic Chinese, with only 2 percent non-Chinese in origin. Although Hong Kong is considerably Westernized, the Chinese population is very conscious of its ethnic and cultural identity. According to a 1982 survey of a wide cross-section of the Chinese population, with two-thirds of the sample under thirty-five years of age, the majority of the respondents (76 percent) claimed to be Chinese in terms of internal characteristics, be they values or traits. Fifty-seven percent maintained they were Chinese because they preserved values such as filial piety, frugality, and respect for teachers. Furthermore, a survey of a representative sample of students from two universities in Hong Kong showed that they perceived four main areas where differences between modern Chinese and Westerners continue to exist. The first is in family life, where the Chinese endorse filial piety and have reservations about voicing opinions different from those of their parents.[15] That the Hong Kong Chinese identify their "Chineseness" most saliently with the familistic values, particularly with filial piety, is a good indication that they have maintained the core value of Confucianism.[16]

The importance the Hong Kong Chinese have attached to the familistic ethos is also manifested behaviorally, in spite of the fact that as many as 73 percent of the households surveyed in 1974 consisted only of nuclear families. In a survey of 3,753 married men and women in 1967, R. E. Mitchell found that 32 percent of the husbands and 54 percent of the wives claimed to be ancestor worshippers. Furthermore, 65 percent of the married sons and 44 percent of the married daughters gave money to their parents, and many of these younger adults were themselves sacrificing financially in order to help their parents in this way.[17] S. K. Lau, in his 1976–1977 survey of a sample of 550 on sociopolitical behavior of Chinese residents in Hong Kong, found that at both normative and behavioral levels the Chinese manifested their primary concern with the family. Lau writes: "The significance of the family is clearly evident as 85.6 percent of the respondents rated either 'the family more important' or 'both family and society equally important' as against 13.5 percent of them who considered 'society more important' . . . The significance of the family is further indicated by the fact that 86.6 percent of the respondents stated that they spent most of their spare time with their families."[18]

The importance of the familistic ethos also extends to the economic sphere of life. The "traditional" Chinese family was a highly particularistic structure,[19] and its particularism was nowhere more evident than in economic organization where people with familial ties or kinship relationships were given preferential employment. Such a practice of preferential employment based on familistic particularism is called nepotism. How prevalent is nepotism in the Hong Kong economy? The economic structure of Hong Kong is disproportionately dominated by small industry. Among 26,149 factories surveyed in 1971, there were 23,765 small factories (90.9 percent) employing no more than fifty workers.[20] In these small factories, according to a 1978 survey, about half (47 percent) of the 415 factory owners employed relatives in their work force.[21] In another survey of 346 factories in Kwun Tong, an important industrial section of Hong Kong, Victor Mok concludes: "It is rather customary for a Chinese proprietor to put a trusted man in each department as some kind of supervisor to safeguard his own interests. Beyond direct kinsfolk and clansmen, a person who comes from the same place of origin, speaking the same dialect and probably being a remote relative would be next in line of reliability."[22] Employing relatives is not confined to small factories. A 1969 study of twenty-seven large Chinese industrial firms showed that among the twenty-three from which information was obtained, fourteen (61 percent) employed family members.[23]

All these findings suggest unequivocally that the familistic ethos is a significant force in influencing Chinese social and economic behavior in the rapidly industrialized and modernized Hong Kong.

In Weber's diagnosis, one of the essential elements of Confucianism which constitutes a great barrier to the rise of capitalism is precisely the Chinese kinship system, or the Confucian family ethos. He writes: "Family piety, resting on the belief in spirits, was by far the strongest influence on man's conduct. Ultimately family piety facilitated and controlled . . . the strong cohesion of the sib associations. . . . Chinese ethic developed its strongest motives in the circle of naturally grown, personalist associations or associations affiliated with or modelled after them."[24] Students of Chinese culture today would hardly disagree with Weber's views on the traditional Chinese family ethos. He continues: "For the economic mentality, the personalist principle was undoubtedly as great a barrier to impersonal rationalization as it was generally to impersonal matter of factness. It tended to tie the individual ever anew to his sib members and to bind him to the manner of the sib, in any case to 'persons' instead of functional tasks ('enterprises'). This barrier was intimately connected with the nature of Chinese religion."[25]

Weber's analysis of the familistic aspect of Chinese society is indeed penetrating and insightful, and has won more confirmation than refutation in the literature by contemporary social scientists. C. K. Yang writes: "Recent findings do not, in general principle, contradict Weber's interpretation of the implications of the Chinese kinship system as an inhibiting influence against capitalist development."[26]

I agree that Weber's assessment of the traditional Chinese family ethos as an impediment to economic development is basically sound, although there is an error in Weber's interpretation of Chinese civilization, namely, his denial of the existence within Confucian China of any transcendental tension.[27] What I argue is that the Chinese in Hong Kong no longer live uncritically under the traditional Confucian familistic persuasion, though they remain "modern Chinese" in the sense that they still, ideologically and behaviorally, attach importance to some Confucian familistic values. But they do not necessarily deem such values intrinsically good in the economic sphere of life. They have adopted a rationalistic, instrumental attitude toward familistic values, thus turning them into a cultural resource to achieve other purposes. Through a continuous process of cognitive selection, the Hong Kong Chinese have, whether consciously or subconsciously, transformed Confucianism into a kind of rationalistic traditionalism. By this I mean that traditions are not necessarily always treasured affectively for their intrinsic goodness but are selectively preserved mainly, though not exclusively, for their extrinsic usefulness in pursuing economic goals.

Hong Kong is often called the meeting place of East and West. Indeed, a sensitive casual visitor to the city will notice the influence of both Western and Chinese cultures. But the great Confucian tradition had never been truly developed in Hong Kong when it was ceded to the British in the late nineteenth century. Rich in Chinese folk traditions such as *fengshui*, *shen*, and *gui*, as well as in the elements of Confucian familism which I have just discussed, Hong Kong has developed a full set of institutional arrangements which are Western in nature. As Stephen Boyden and his associates point out: "The way of life of the Chinese people in Hong Kong is profoundly affected by modern Western culture. For example, their livelihood depends upon striving for material wealth and status defined by the West, and the education system is a British one."[28] Striving for material wealth, however, is nothing new or alien to traditional Chinese. Weber was in fact fully aware of the much-bewailed "crass 'materialism' of the Chinese."[29] In Hong Kong, says the anthropologist James Hayes: "The pursuit of wealth has long been a common goal. . . . It has drawn generations of business-men from the West and from China alike. The Colony has always afforded an outlet for talent for which Guangdong is famous. For centuries, its immigrants have been described by other Chinese as lovers of money, subordinating all else in its pursuit."[30]

Hayes's observation on the Chinese quest for wealth is not atypical among Chinese outside mainland China. Maurice Freed-man writes: "Shrewdness in handling money was an important part of the equipment which ordinary Chinese took with them when they went overseas in search of a livelihood. . . . The Chinese were economically successful in Southeast Asia not simply because they were energetic immigrants, but more fundamentally because in their quest for riches they knew how to handle money, and organize men in relation to money."[31] E. J. Ryan, in a study of a Chinese trad-ing community in Indonesia, discusses the "focal value of wealth," writing: "In the day-to-day course of events, it is around this value that energies are mobilized, interest centered, the very life and household organized, and in the service of which social relations are patterned."[32]

In China's great tradition, wrote Weber, "Confucius might not disdain the acquisition of riches but wealth seemed insecure and could upset the equilibrium of the genteel soul."[33] Nevertheless, the folk religions of China fully sanctioned the act of "getting rich."

The god of wealth is probably the most widely worshipped god in Chinese folk religion. In present-day Hong Kong, wealth no longer upsets the equilibrium of the genteel soul. Indeed, "most people in Hong Kong are imbued with a relatively strong sense of purpose. This sense of purpose usually centers on the desire to promote the prosperity of the family."[34] For a long time, business and industrial activities in matters relating to material wealth have been regarded as socially acceptable pursuits. The impulse to pursue material wealth is evident not only among entrepreneurs and managers but also among workers. Attitude surveys of Chinese workers regularly find that monetary rewards are high on their list of priorities.[35]

In traditional China, government officials constituted the ruling stratum. Literary education was the yardstick for measuring social prestige and the basic qualification for office. The Chinese literati were a status group with a particular mentality, the Chinese ethos, which has been characterized as the status ethic.[36] The Chinese masses believed that literary education bestowed an extraordinary power on officials. Weber observed: "High mandarins were considered magically qualified. They could always become objects of a cult, after their death as well as during their lifetime, provided that their charisma was 'proved.'"[37]

In Hong Kong, by contrast, literati never came into existence as a status group, despite the fact that the Chinese have a high level of achievement motivation.[38] In a study of child-rearing attitudes and practices in Hong Kong, David Ho finds that "the most frequently mentioned personal characteristics expected of the child when grown up were those concerned with competence and achievement, followed by those concerned with moral character, sociability and controlled temperament."[39] The most outstanding feature of the learning environment in Hong Kong is the pressure put on the student, both by parents and by teachers, to study for examinations. Education is seen by most people as a prerequisite for material wealth.[40] In Hong Kong, the cult object is not the literatus or even the high mandarin but the successful industrialist and businessman. Shipping magnates and commercial managers rank highest in the occupational status hierarchy.[41] This preference is manifested throughout the Chinese communities of Southeast Asia.[42]

In the sociopolitical context of Hong Kong, there seems not to have occurred the phenomenon that Everett Hagen calls "withdrawal of status respect,"[43] which, I suspect, has happened in other East Asian societies. The overwhelming status value accorded to industrial and business elites can be explained only by the fact that, unlike in Imperial China, the most promising route to social eminence for the Chinese in Hong Kong is not by becoming officials and scholars but through gaining wealth in the business world. A career in politics was denied to the Chinese in the colony, so that "wealth was, in fact, the only means by which a Chinese individual in Hong Kong could come to have any influence at all on community affairs, and the only means by which he could stand out in society as an important person."[44] Industrial-business elites are status groups par excellence in Hong Kong. As a consequence, the pursuit of wealth has become a powerful motivation for Hong Kong Chinese and has led them to channel their energy into economic activities.

The intense motivational drive of the Chinese for material wealth and social status has created in them a pragmatic and instrumental or rationalistic attitude toward traditional values in dealing with men and economics. As I mentioned earlier, Confucian familistic values are still alive in Hong Kong. If we look more closely, however, we find that these values have been transformed. It may well be argued that a new kind of rationalistic traditionalism has appeared in the social-cultural sphere of Hong Kong. I turn now to a discussion of this transformation.

In our study of small factories in Hong Kong in 1971, my colleague and I found that Confucian familial values still played an important role among Chinese factory owners. More often than not, however, the practice of recruiting relatives was justified on rational grounds and was not simply the result of the cultural legacy of Confucian familism. We concluded:

> It is true that the owners/managers of the small factories
> are in large measure traditionalistic, paternalistic and
> conservative, but it is far from being true that they are
> persons with an inevitable and almost built-in disposition
> for nepotistic inclination which is often the mental
> characteristic of the so-called "patrimonial manager."
> On the contrary, what strikes us most is that the Chinese
> owners/managers are pragmatic, practical and serious.
> The above-mentioned fact of hiring relatives should not be
> interpreted as an indication that kinship relationship is
> cherished as a goal value in itself; instead it is more or less
> used as an instrumental mechanism to secure one whom
> they feel they can trust. It is indeed our contention that
> the Chinese traditional familistic system has been modified
> by Western business ideology and practical necessity, or
> by the functional prerequisites, if you so wish to call it,
> of the industrial system. As such, it may have enhanced

rather than undermined the economic performance of the small factories.[45]

In a survey of 255 Hong Kong employers in 1976, S. K. Lau found that most of them (85.1 percent) considered that "aggressiveness" was either an important or a very important trait for an employee to possess. And in the eyes of employers, the "ability to do the job" was also rated very high as a characteristic of the employee; 57.3 percent considered it important, and 32.9 percent considered it very important. With regard, however, to the characteristic "related to me through kinship or other ties," more than two-thirds of the sampled employers deemed it not important (32.5 percent) or extremely unimportant (34.5 percent). Lau concluded: "Though there are still traditionalistic elements of various sorts embedded in the managerial attitudes, they can in many cases be justified on rational and pragmatic grounds, in view of the specific economic and labor conditions in Hong Kong."[46] It may be that nepotism is still widely practiced in Hong Kong mainly because it has been utilized as a cultural resource for positive economic reasons. Wong Siu-lun's distinction between passive and active nepotism with regard to Chinese businessmen and industrialists is very useful. He writes, "We can expect them to shake off passive nepotism whenever circumstances permit, while they may keep active nepotism because it can serve them positively."[47]

In view of the Chinese economic mentality and behavior discussed earlier, I can fully echo what Maurice Freedman has said: "The people of the Sino-influenced cultures are to an unusual extent pragmatic-empirical problem-solving, rather than submissive and fatalistic in a problematic situation."[48] Since Hong Kong is a place where both Western and Chinese traditions co-exist, the

Chinese can theoretically become what Robert Park calls "marginal men." The theory of social marginality has not produced convincing evidence that marginal individuals tend to make creative adjustments in situations of change, and there are some who argue that such individuals are more prone than others to anomie and thus to becoming carriers of trends leading toward social disorganization.[49] Hong Kong's modern Chinese, however, seem to have no "identity" problem. They identify themselves as Chinese and, "at the grass roots level, there is no evidence for a sense of loss or cultural disintegration among the Hong Kong Chinese."[50] On the contrary, the Chinese have shown a remarkable ability to move in and out of the two traditions. Marjorie Topley, an anthropologist who has resided in Hong Kong for many years, observes that "people do not usually turn to Western ideas because they come to believe them truer than the traditional ones. Rather, they follow some Western practices because they find them effective in some circumstances and some Chinese practices for similar reasons. People may move in and out of Chinese and Western traditions, at least at the present time. The effect is the proof—if it works, it is true."[51]

The ease with which Hong Kong Chinese move in and out of different cultural traditions is due to pragmatic-empirical considerations and, more often than not, is based on cost-benefit calculations. The process is one of cognitive selectivity in which the individuals exercise rational judgments. S. K. Lau has argued that "utilitarianistic familism" has become the dominant cultural code in Hong Kong. He writes:

> Briefly, utilitarianistic familism can be defined as a normative and behavioral tendency of an individual to place his family interest above the interest of society or any of its component

individuals and groups, and to structure his relationships with other individuals and groups in such a fashion that the furtherance of his familial interests is the primary consideration. Moreover, among the familial interests, materialistic interest takes priority over all other interests.[52]

It should be pointed out that utilitarianistic familism, unlike traditional Confucian familism, is characterized by a marked element of rationality. "As a faction-oriented entity," writes Lau, "the familial group exercises rationality in both family organization and member recruitment so as to maximize the efficiency of resource mobilization and utilization. The vagueness or fluidity of the boundary of the familial group is both the result and cause of rational consideration."[53]

Given these findings, it could be said that, though Confucianism never existed in Hong Kong as a systemic, intellectualized cultural system, the Chinese tradition of which the Confucian familial ethos constitutes the core is still operative in Hong Kong. In a large measure, modern Hong Kong Chinese ideologically identify more with Chinese traditions than with Western traditions. They are not, however, sentimentally bound by traditions in their economic behavior. Hong Kong Chinese have an active self-awareness in the sense that they are capable cognitively of assessing the practical utility of the various elements of Chinese tradition for achieving their social and economic goals. Chinese traditions are not always cherished as something intrinsically sacred or good; instead, they are more often than not treated as cultural resources to be tapped and utilized according to instrumental considerations. This does not mean that the Chinese familistic values in Hong Kong have been thoroughly changed. What I argue here is that modern Hong Kong

Chinese have been able to use the "personalist principle," which, according to Weber, was intimately concocted with Confucian ethics in a rational and selective fashion aimed at achieving personal economic goals.[54]

People follow traditions, but they are not traditionalistic; Confucian traditions are preserved and practiced mainly because they serve current rationalistic ends. I venture to argue that it is not the Confucianism Weber came to know but rationalistic traditionalism, or rationalistic Confucianism, which seems to be an important contributing factor to the economic success of Hong Kong. If there is a "post-Confucian" culture, then it is, for Hong Kong, the culture of rationalistic traditionalism.

As the foregoing discussion should have revealed, the assimilation of capitalism in Hong Kong has been facilitated by the cultural "conditions," to use Parsons's expression, provided by a transformed type of Confucianism, or by what I call rationalistic traditionalism. It is clear that the Confucianism discussed by Weber is now dead and never took root in Hong Kong at all. Weber's Confucianism can probably be identified as imperial Confucianism or institutional Confucianism, which was a complex and sophisticated combination of state ideology combined with a set of strategic institutions, including the literati, the examination system, and above all universal kingship and the imperial bureaucracy. In Hong Kong, there is only social Confucianism or the Confucianism of everyday life, which refers to a set of Confucian beliefs and values accepted widely by the man in the street.

What I wish to stress is that this social Confucianism is not a rigid belief system. It consists of a group of guiding social principles for the conduct of familial and extra-familial relationships. In the post-Confucian era, the strategic imperial Confucian institutions are all dead or deconstructed in the Chinese societies of East Asia. But Confucian social-cultural beliefs and values have found new and more dynamic expressions in non-Confucian institutional settings. Moreover, these beliefs and values, as I have suggested, can be effectively utilized as resources for modernizing purposes. That Confucianism contains the seeds of a transformative capacity is amply manifested in the newly emerging rationalistic traditionalism of the post-Confucian era. Rationalistic traditionalism is not necessarily unique to Hong Kong. It is rather, I suspect, a general cultural phenomenon of secularization in other East Asian societies also pursuing economic development. I have not attempted or intended to confirm or refute the Weberian thesis. I have, however, tried here to give substantive meaning to the "post-Confucian" thesis.

11 Max Weber and the Question of Development of the Modern State in China

State and Society in Weber's Works

In recent years, Max Weber's Protestant ethic thesis has become a hot topic of contention among the scholars and intellectuals in both mainland China and Taiwan. The main cause lies in the fact that the East Asia area which is culturally characterized as a "Post-Confucian region," has had phenomenal success in industrialization and modernization after the Second World War. That this empirical phenomenon deserves an explanation is not entirely different from what the rise of capitalism in the West had made the central theme of intellectual preoccupation of scholars like Max Weber and others. Weber's Protestant ethic thesis argues that it was Confucianism, as a value system which was basically responsible for the non-development of capitalism in China. Since East Asia is culturally influenced by Confucianism, therefore, it is not illegitimate to ask, as Thomas Metzger does:

> We consequently, are led to ask: "Why in this kind of world are some societies more effective than others in coping with their problems and rising to the challenges

of modernization?" While Weber had to explain China's failure, we have to explain its success, but paradoxically our answer, like Weber's, emphasizes the role of the indigenous ethos.[1]

A substantial literature on Confucian ethics' contribution to East Asia's industrialization and modernization has been produced in the past decade, directly or indirectly questioning Weber's verdict on Confucianism. In my account, the significance of this literature lies not in its confirmation or repudiation of Weber's Protestant ethic theses as such, but in its articulation on the relationship between cultural factors and economic development.

The most intriguing and urgent problem today on the agenda of modernization of the East Asia region is the problem of political development, particularly the problem of democracy. The four little dragons of East Asia (South Korea, Taiwan, Singapore, and Hong Kong) are facing the challenge of democracy in different manners. The challenge of democracy, in an essential sense, is one of challenging state authoritarianism.[2] Of the four little dragons, with the possible exception of Hong Kong, the authoritarian states played an important role in rapid economic development. Amsden in her analysis of Taiwan's economic development writes:

> Taiwan, then, is more a case in which the essential contribution of state intervention to economic development can be observed. It is a case that demonstrates the reciprocal interaction between the structure of the state apparatus and the process of economic growth.[3]

Interestingly enough, the democratic development in Taiwan is very much caused by a new balance of forces between state and the society and the emergence of the growing forces of society vis-à-vis state is nothing but the creation of the state itself.[4]

For some time, the role of states as actors or as society-shaping institutional structures has been rather less emphasized, if not outrightly ignored, in the dominant literature of modernization, which adopted the pluralist and structure-functionalist perspectives. These society-centered ways of explaining politics have in fact been shared by neo-Marxist writers as well. By the mid-1970s, a paradigmatic reorientation which considered states as weighty actors and probed how states affected political and social processes was adopted by social scientists. This is implied by the phrase "bringing the state back in."[5] In this new paradigmatic reorientation, scholars, Marxist or others, naturally returned to Max Weber, who, more than Marx or Durkheim, took the state as a central feature, and considered political phenomena as specific data with a logic and history of their own. In the words of Bertrand Badie and Pierre Birnbaum, once a Weberian perspective is adopted, "no longer is politics explained, as in the general models of Marx and Durkheim, by the relations of production or the division of labor. Now it contains its own determinants."[6]

Comparing Weber with Marx, it can be argued that there is in Marx no recognition of the possible existence of the state as an independent force, whereas, in contrast, much of Weber's sociology is concerned with the role of the state as an agency acting upon society. Giddens writes, "It is not a gross oversimplification to say that, whereas Marx viewed the state in terms of his presupposition about the economic infrastructure, Weber tended to view that infrastructure in terms of a paradigm derived from his analysis of the rise of the state."[7]

Weber's lifelong work is, as Wolfgang Schlucter demonstrates, concerned with the rise of Western rationalism that is manifested in the instructionally-rational modern capitalism and modern state. Weber never lived to complete his sociology of modern state.[8] Nevertheless, we can see Weber's conception of state through his available writings. To Weber, "bureaucracy is . . . the spore of the modern state," and "the great modern state is absolutely dependent on a bureaucratic basis. The larger the state . . . the more unconditionally this is the case."[9] Moreover, in Weber's view, modern states are characterized by the emergence of exclusive, legal domination. "The legitimacy of all legal domination is rational and domination with the help of a bureaucratic administration is only the purest type of legal domination."[10] It should be mentioned that Weber was fully aware that in historical reality there were not only democratic but also autocratic variants of rational domination.[11]

As sociology of religion and sociology of domination are two main theoretical domains of Weber's work, it is no accident that the central problem of Weber's China is concerned with China's "non-development" of indigenous modern capitalism and modern bureaucracy. What interests me most is how Weber views the relations between state and society in Imperial China. In trying to answer this question, Bendix's interpretative work on Weber provides us with useful clues and suggestions. While acknowledging that Weber avoided using nouns like society or polity as much as possible, Bendix considers the distinction between society and polity and their interdependence as "the fundamental theme of Weber's work as a whole."[12] He further writes:

> By emphasizing the belief in legitimacy that is shared in
> some degree by rulers and ruled, Weber retained Hegel's

idea that society and government stand in a reciprocal relationship to each other. And Weber also retained Hegel's distinction between "civil society and the state" by his emphasis on two points—that the belief in a legitimate order differs in kind from the "coalescence of material and ideal interest" in society, and that the exercise of legitimate authority depends upon an administrative organization with imperatives of its own.[13]

Weber's sociological works probably did not make the theme of interaction between society and state explicit, though his political writings did. David Beetham writes:

> It is that the significance of Weber's political writings is most apparent. They are rich in themes that are absent from his sociological work. . . . Above all, Weber's writings on the politics of Germany and Russia offer an analysis, unique in Weber, of the interaction between society and state. The importance of this can be readily shown in his treatment of bureaucracy. In *Economy and Society*, bureaucracy is presented as an abstract model, considered largely in isolation from the social and political process. In the political writings bureaucracy is set in its social and political context, and in so doing Weber developed a theory of its inherent limitations and of its interaction with other social forces and groups.[14]

I am inclined to think that in order to understand more fully the question of developing a modern state in China, it is necessary to make explicit the Weberian interactive perspective on the state–society relationship.

Value Foundations and Structural Factors

In the debate over the cause of China's failure to develop modern capitalism, there are two schools of thought: namely, institutionalist and culturalist. The former attributes to traditional China's institutional structures. The latter considers China's value system, particularly Confucianism, as the main cause.[15]

True enough, Weber has us to believe that the basic reason of China's inability to develop modern capitalism lies in the Confucian "ethos" which cannot release the "capitalist spirit" to be found in the vocational man of the modern economy.[16] Nevertheless, Weber can hardly be characterized as a "culturalist." He is far from it. In fact, Weber is as much, if not more, concerned with structural factors as with cultural factors. Bryan Turner argues:

> For Weber, therefore, the nature of capitalist relations does not emerge from the characteristics of thrifty individuals, but from a set of structures which impose rationality on the behavior of social actors. . . . Weber's description of capitalism resembles both Durkheim's view of "social facts" as external, objective and constraining and the structuralist conceptualization of capitalism as a relation which cannot be reduced to interpersonal interactions.[17]

It should be noted that Weber has discussed in detail five major structural factors in Imperial China as characterizing features relevant for the functional requirements of modern capitalism.[18] As Schluchter points out, Weber's substantive analyses of the different paths of development between the West and China demonstrates that, "it is in no way simply the ultimate value foundations and their appropriation by the respective carrier strata that separates the Chinese world from that of ascetic Protestantism. It was also the differing structural configuration; in one case, the unified state, in the other, the *standestaat* (a society organized on the basis of estates), which was one of the decisive determinants of the unique characters of respective developments."[19]

Weber classifies Imperial China as a patrimonial state characterized as a structural configuration. The reasons for the absence of modern capitalism in China, in his own words, were "mostly related to the structure of the state."[20] Weber has indeed given us an unparalleled perceptive and penetrating view, though not always a cohesive and systematic analysis of the nature of the Chinese patrimonial state, and the nature of the relationship between state and society. Weber takes the establishment of a centralized bureaucratic state in the hands of the prince of Qin as first Emperor as the most important political structural factor. Under the unified empire which arose from the collapse of the feudal substate through war, political unity was superimposed on the cultural unity already achieved during the Warring States period. Indeed, the cultural-political unity of the empire had decisive impact on the nature of the patrimonial state.

In the Han dynasty (which is the immediate successor of Qin), Confucianism was elevated to a status of state ideology, thus the Confucian cultural system was fully integrated with the political structure—one having a strong legalistic flavor. Indeed, it was the Han's amalgam of Confucianism and Legalism which constituted a cultural-structural basis for the imperial rulership for the successive dynasties. From the Han onward, in my view, Confucianism became what can be called institutional Confucianism. Institutional

Confucianism was an institutional-cultural complex including the imperial institutions, patrimonial bureaucracy, and Confucian cultural values.[21]

Weber is not wide of mark in saying that patrimonial bureaucratic power was "narrowly circumscribed" beyond the city wall, and remained, in fact, an administration of urban districts and sub-districts.[22] The village was capable of "acting as a corporate body through the temple."[23] Again, Weber is correct in his observation that the rationalism of patrimonial bureaucracy was confronted with and inhibited by a resolute and traditionalistic power represented by the uneducated sib elder of the kinship organization.[24] However, this should not lead us to think that the patrimonial state was weak vis-à-vis the society. Weber certainly did not make this claim, though he did see the tremendous power of the patriarchal sibs.[25] Max Weber was fully aware of the socio-economic implications of the unified and centralized imperial state on Chinese society.

The political competition that existed in the Warring States period was no longer contained in the imperial system. In addition, there was a conspicuous absence of "strong and independent forces" in China[26] like those existing in the West. Xu Fuguan makes it amply clear that one of the salient characteristics of the archetype of Chinese autocratic system of which the foundation was laid down in Qin and Han dynasties, was that "outside of the imperial domination no independent or resisting forces was allowed to exist."[27] Furthermore, Xu contends that under the autocratic imperial authority, which was basically armed with legalists' doctrine, together with military and penal codes as instruments, all cultural and economic activity within the state was rigidly controlled. Any deviation or non-compliance was to be destroyed. He considers this imperial domination as the ultimate source of stagnation in the Chinese society.[28] Weber's analysis of the imperial rulership of the Chinese empire was not so absolute, though he did view the rulership of Shi Huangdi of Qin as a form of oriental Sultanism.[29] To Weber, the imperial rulership was largely based on the new principle of "enlightened" patrimonialism which stipulated that personal merit and merit alone should qualify a man for office. Weber writes: "Feudal elements in the social order gradually receded and patrimonialism became the structural form fundamental to the Confucian spirit." In the last two millennia, there was "constant struggle of literati and Sultanism."[30] Indeed, there were no shortages of Confucian scholar-officials and literati who held steadfast to their conviction in Confucian people-oriented cultural values placing virtue above repressive penal code in the administration of the people.[31] They also were inclined to have an anti-statist tendency.[32] Throughout imperial history, one could not miss the fact that the bureaucracy which was represented and headed by the "prime minister" was subordinated to the emperor. The imperial authority was ultimate and absolute, whilst the bureaucratic authority was derivative, coming directly from the emperor.[33] The patrimonial bureaucracy was in large measure an instrument of the imperial authority. At this junction, it should be emphatically stated that the Chinese state system was rather based more on the legalist doctrine than on Confucian ideals. Weber obviously had not given due weight to the influences and impact of Legalism on the patrimonial state system. The Chinese state system since Qin was as much a mixed product of Confucianism and Legalism. Karl Burger has written in another context:

We can no more speak of "Confucian law" in China than we can speak of a "Confucian state." All dynasties since the Qin have retained the fundamental principle of the legalist.[34]

The Confucianism and Legalism, though different in significant degree with respect to the method of government and administration, shared a cultural orientation towards the relation between the state and the society. Benjamin Schwartz writes that the dominant shared Chinese cultural orientation is "the idea of a universal, all-embracing sociopolitical order centering on the concept of a cosmically based universal kingship."[35] He holds the view that "The Kingship or locus of authority which he occupied (*wei*) is an institution which comes to constitute the major link between human society and ruling forces of the cosmos."[36] It is here Weber showed his unusual insight in saying that "secular and spiritual authority were combined into one hand, the spiritual strongly predominating."[37] Weber saw that the Chinese monarch remained primarily a pontifex, and the Chinese emperor ruled in the genuine sense of charismatic authority.[38] The universal king embodied within his person the supreme authority over the sacred and secular realms of sociopolitical life. He had "all-encompassing jurisdictional claims," to use Schwartz's terminology, over the traditional sociopolitical order. This is well expressed in the famous line: "Under the vast heaven, there is nothing which is not the land of the King; of all the subjects of the earth, there are none who are not the servants of the King."[39] It is well known that the universal king's legitimacy is based on the theory of the "Mandate of Heaven." And the King is accordingly called "Son of Heaven." This cultural perception of the universal king as the embodiment of authority over the sacred and secular realms had tremendous ideological and structural implications for the patrimonial state.

Firstly, since this imperial power was a supreme and religiously consecrated structure, thus precluding the possibility of the development of a powerful priesthood or independent religious forces.[40] In China, never did the power of the church develop distinct from the state, as in the West, let alone to challenge the power of the state (or King) over the spiritual realms. Secondly, since the emperor was the embodiment for the Mandate of Heaven, he, therefore, by definition, was a moral (as well as religious) leader. Chinese thinkers, Confucian or otherwise, never intended, and indeed, never could envisage, institutional constraints on imperial authority. Lin argues, "The idea of moralization of politics precluded any constitutional limits of political power. To think that power may be corrupt and require institutional check and balance is a contradiction in terms."[41] Viewed in this context, it is not difficult to agree with Schwartz that to place high confidence in the power of the emperor to shape society represents the "most exuberantly optimistic interpretation of the idea of the sociopolitical order."[42] And it is here that we can appreciate more why Weber saw Confucianism as a rational system of "radical world-optimism."[43]

Theoretically speaking, there were no limits on the power of the state (personified in the universal king) in Imperial China, and there was a potential and tendency towards the unhindered, uninhibited use of power by the state to shape the social-political life of the society. Though, as Eisenstadt perceptively argues, the level of "generalized power" of the ruler was rather limited.[44] The political system of Imperial China had, to borrow Metzger's expression, an "uninhibited political center"[45] which was ever ready to intervene the socioeconomic activities of society. As was mentioned above, the imperial state did not allow independent forces to exist, it was clearly reflected in the non-development of independent religious communities, and it was even more clearly manifested in the nature of Chinese cities. In the analysis of Chinese cities, Weber not only showed the difference between Chinese cities and Western cities but also touched upon more directly, though implicitly, the relation between state and society in China. He writes:

> In contrast to the occident, the cities in China . . . lacked political autonomy. The oriental city was not a "polis" in the sense of Antiquity, and it knew nothing of the "city law" of the Middle Ages, for it was not a "commune" with political privileges of its own nor was there a citizenry in the sense of a self-equipped military estate such as existed in occidental Antiquity.[46]

Furthermore, the Chinese city, unlike the English city at that time, had no "charter" to guarantee its "liberties." The city which was "an imperial fortress, actually had fewer formal guarantees of self-government than the village."[47] Weber pointed out that the Chinese city was predominately a product of rational administration.[48] No citizenry, i.e., no burghers, ever came into existence. As a result, the city was an administrative entity, but not a political society or civil society. In this sense, Balazs was correct in saying that Imperial China was a "bureaucratic society."[49] The state had largely prevented the emergence of "civil society" in China. And this is one of structural problems fundamental to the development of the modern state in China.

At this juncture, we should be reminded, as pointed out by

Schluchter, that the central problem of Weber's China was, apart from indigenous development of modern capitalism, the indigenous development of modern bureaucracy. To Weber, Chinese patrimonialism made bureaucracy irrational, and unable to produce a truly efficient central administration.[50] He saw this as the result of both the "spirit of bureaucracy" as well as of economic and political factors. The most important of these economic and political factors was the unified Chinese state. In the unified state, several centralization measures, or "characteristic patrimonial means," to use Weber's words,[51] which included the triannual system of shift of officials, the prohibition of holding office in one's home office, were able to check the feudalization of the empire. However, the price was the weakening of the power of the central authorities and the lack of development of rational local administration,[52] since the patrimonial bureaucrats were forced to depend upon the local officials representing traditionalistic power and interests.[53] Consequently, "the empire resembled a confederation of satrapies under a pontifical head."[54] According to Weber, the "irrationality" of the patrimonial bureaucracy resulted as much from the value system of Confucianism as from political structure of the unified state. Weber analyzed Confucianism as "the status ethic of prebendaries, of men with literary education who was characterized by a secular rationalism."[55] For Weber, "Confucian rationalism meant rational adjustment to the world."[56] And the spirit bureaucracy was incarnated in the "gentleman ideal" of the mandarin whose style of life conduct did not make the world into an object "rational" transformation; instead, it inclined to elevate the perfection of the status quo to its highest goal.[57] Moreover, to Weber, the particular irrationality of the patrimonial bureaucracy lies in the Confucian mentality evinced in its particularistic "personal principle" in the conduct of the ethical way of life. Weber wrote: "Chinese ethic developed its strongest motives in the circle naturally grown, personalist associations or associations affiliated with or modelled after them. This contrasts sharply with the puritan ethic that amounts to an objectification of man's duties as a creature of God."[58] The Confucian personalistic ethos which established a "community of blood" as contrasted to the puritan "community of faith" was a barrier to the development of bureaucratic mentality indispensable not only to the operation of modern capitalism but also to the practice of modern bureaucracy.[59] The reason that the Chinese bureaucracy remained for Weber a patrimonial bureaucracy lies principally in the fact that the Chinese patrimonial state had no strict distinction between formal law and substantive justice. Weber rightly argued that Chinese statutes were "codified ethical rather than legal norms."[60] Weber's observation was fully verified by the findings of Qu Tongzu who showed that the phenomenon of "Confucianization of law" in Confucian ethical norms were fully integrated into Chinese law.[61] As a consequence, the patrimonial bureaucracy was not able to depersonalize (or rationalize) the machinery of bureaucracy, making it unable to develop the capacity for formal rationalization.[62]

Crisis of the State: In Search of New Forms of the Modern State

The imperial state of two millennia was crushed by the Republican Revolution of 1911. However, the destruction of the imperial state did not automatically guarantee the birth of a modern state. Schurmann writes, "The rise of the Chinese republic marked not triumph of a new system, but the funeral of the old."[63] Fairbank argues in the same vein that the significance of the Revolution "lay in its negative achievement—the extinction of the monarchy, which was not just a national kingship of a European type but the universal kingship of the Son of Heaven."[64] In no small measure, the Republican Revolution of 1911 created what may be called an "authority crisis." What was at stake was the fate of the Chinese state. Indeed, not only the state was in disorder, the whole of Chinese civilization was seriously challenged by the Western industrial powers. The preoccupation of the intellectuals in early years of the century was about national survival and development, overshadowing the issues of democracy and individual rights.

After the 1911 Revolution, efforts of intellectuals, reformers and revolutionaries never ceased to search for a new form of the state. The top-priority goal was state-rebuilding for both the Guomindang and the Chinese Communist Party (CCP). In that historical context, it is not surprising that Marxism-Leninism finally emerged as the triumphant ideology for the state-rebuilding. Tang Tsou writes:

> The reasons why many radical Chinese intellectuals accepted Marxism-Leninism as a solution to China's problem have been frequently discussed. Marxism is a theory of total crisis. It envisages a total transformation of society in the near future. It thus resonated with the sense of total crisis, the as yet vague and unstructured demands for total transformation, and the desire for immediate practical action among radical Chinese intellectuals. The underlying theory of power in Leninism met the needs of the Chinese radicals in their endeavor to effect a total transformation.[65]

The CCP's goal was nothing short of a total transformation of the Chinese society and to establish a modern Chinese state. Among other things, the strategy of the CCP's state-rebuilding was to establish or re-establish the legitimacy of state authority. Like other new states in the twentieth century, the Chinese Communist state had to establish, as Reinhard Bendix points out, its government "on a new basis and define 'the people' as the ultimate source of authority."[66] True enough, the CCP fully understood that to establish its "Mandate of Heaven" in the minds of Chinese people was to establish its mandate in the name of "people."[67] The erstwhile theory of the "Mandate of Heaven" had lost its appeal. The CCP's endeavor in reconstituting authority was based on Mao's famous theory of "mass line" couched in the so-called Sinification of Marxism-Leninism. And the party is supposed to be the embodiment of the will of the proletariat or the people. In a significant way, Chinese Marxism-Leninism is a total break with institutional Confucianism. Schurmann writes:

> In traditional China, the trinity of ethos, states group,
> and modal personality was represented by Confucianism,
> the gentry, and the pater familiars (*jiazhang*). By 1949,
> the revolution had destroyed all those . . . with the
> traditional trinity of authority gone, the social system
> itself has disappeared.[68]

In Schurmann's view, the traditional trinity has been replaced by ideology (Marxism-Leninism-Maoism), organizational leader of the party and the cadre.[69] As was stated above, the CCP's revolution was aiming at a total transformation of the society. In this respect, the party-state, not unlike the imperial authority, has all-encompassing jurisdictional claims over all spheres of sociopolitical life. Since 1949, the party-state has not only tried to control but to transform society. Vogel's description of the "political conquest of society" is a succinct expression of what has happened in China since the Communist takeover in 1949.[70] Tang Tsou has characterized Communist China as a form of "totalitarianism" in terms of its "unlimited extension of state function" over the civil society and economy.[71] Under the Chinese Communist rulership, the authority of the political center has successfully reached directly down to the local population. The "self-governing" of the village or the "power of the patriarchal sib" was basically shattered. The party-state bureaucracy, unlike the patrimonial bureaucracy, had, in large measure, succeeded in rationalizing administration on both the central and local levels of government. Consequently, the state system created by the Chinese Communists no longer "resembled a confederation of satrapies under a pontifical head," a description Weber had for the Chinese empire of the past. The collectivization and communization of socioeconomic life in late 1950s saw the state's unlimited expansion of power over society which led Schurmann to say:

> The Chinese Communists are the first state power in Chinese history convinced that it has the means of managerially directing all of society. What Karl A. Wittfogal attributed to "oriental despotisms" thus has been true only of the modern Communist state, and specially that of China.[72]

Schurmann's characterization of the modern Chinese Communist state is somewhat overdrawn, but it is beyond dispute that the party-state enjoyed supreme authority in the Chinese Communist sociopolitical order. As Huntington writes in another context: "The theory of party supremacy is . . . the twentieth-century counterpart to the seventeenth-century theory of absolute monarchy."[73] Moreover, the Chinese party-state established an unchallengeable hegemonic universe, under which periphery of the political system was fully mobilized by and subjected to the political center. The Leninist party-state, like the traditional imperial authority, recognized no independent status of civil society. Insofar as the relationship between state and society is concerned, there is a marked continuity between the imperial system and communist system. Although the Marxism-Leninism is fundamentally different from the Confucian cultural system, some elements of Chinese political culture in terms of pressure for ideological uniformity and of the veneration to the top leaders that remain great today resonate with the Communist political system. It could well be argued that the Chinese Communist system is one variant of state socialism or bureaucratic socialism. The Communist cadres are a new mandarinate par excellence. What emerged in the People's Republic of China after 1949 was not "dictatorship of proletariat" or "dictatorship of the people," but "dictatorship of the official," as Weber so accurately predicated for the fate of socialism.[74] Within the Chinese Communist system, again, not unlike the imperial system, there are no institutional checks. And legal authority, or rule of law, was never enshrined in contemporary China as was the case in Imperial China.

Mao's Cultural Revolution was launched in the name of anti-bureaucratism echoed with fanaticism by the millions of the masses. Mao masterfully used the extra-party mechanism (i.e., the youth) to destroy the party machine, thus creating what was proclaimed "Great Democracy." Indeed, it is not far-fetched to say that Mao's Cultural Revolution brought a charismatic breakthrough to the rigid Chinese bureaucratic system.[75] In a way, the triumph of Cultural Revolution in the 1960s was a triumph of the substantive rationality implied in the slogans of the movement, such as equality, justice and democracy, over the bureaucratic rationality. Ironically or not, the Cultural Revolution which defied all types of party norm and legal code resulted not in creating a "Great Democracy," but in what was called Revolutionary Feudalist Fascism, totally free from procedural rationality. After the Gang of Four, a new ideology of the Four Modernizations—agriculture, industry, science and technology, and national defense—was launched with great fanfare. One of the elements of this program was to re-establish party authority. An effort was painfully made to reinstitute the bureaucracy in line with the Weberian model.[76] The present leaders of the Chinese Communist party seem to believe that a modern bureaucracy of the Weberian type is indispensable to the Four Modernizations, a program in which political modernization is conspicuously absent. I am inclined to argue that the Chinese Communists' Four Modernizations program is fatally flawed since it leaves no room for the growth of democracy which is the problem China must face if she intends to become a genuine modern state.

Conclusion

This chapter is an attempt to deal with the question of the development of a modern Chinese state. I believe that Weber's works on modernization and modernity in general and on China's patrimonial state and patrimonial bureaucracy in particular, are of great significance to China's contemporary search for answers. In traditional patrimonialism, imperial authority had an all-encompassing jurisdictional claim over the socioeconomic activities of the people. Though the village had a relatively high degree of autonomy, no independent religious or economic forces were allowed to exist outside of the government. The cities had no "charter," nor "freedom" but they were the product of the administration. Society existed under the shadow of the state. Chinese Marxism-Leninism is fundamentally different from institutional Confucianism, but the Communist system has a marked continuity with the imperial system in terms of the relationship between the state and society. As a matter of fact, the Communist state, armed with a more interventionist ideology and a more powerful organization, has further subjugated the society to administrative domination.

In the previous pages, I have indicated that Weber is a sociologist who saw the state as a society shaping institutional structure. Furthermore, as shown by Bendix and others, Weber considered that society and polity stand in reciprocal relation to each other. However, Weber never lived to complete his sociology of the state, nor did he provide a comprehensive treatment of the reciprocal relation between polity and society in the modern state. Moreover, from the writings of Weber, I suspect that he seems to define the modern state more in administrative than in political terms. Weber's concern with the "means of administration" is just overwhelming as Marx's concern with the "means of production." True enough, Weber, more than any other thinker, Marx or Durkheim, takes the relationship between bureaucracy and democracy as the main issue in the modern the state.[77] Thanks to Schluchter, we know Weber had his fourth principle of legitimation,[78] in addition to the traditional, the rational legal, and the charismatic principle. And Weber's conception of "bureaucratic democracy"[79] is probably one of the most plausible solutions for the problem of legitimacy and governability facing the modern state in our time. Nevertheless, Weber's advocacy of "plebiscitarian leader–democracy" which he defines as an anti-authoritarian version of "charismatic dominations" is not without inherent problems. Mommsen writes:

> He [Weber] considered stagnation and ossification the real danger of his age, rather than charismatic breakthroughs. In his opinion, the fatal decline of dynamism and mobility in politics could be cured only by one antidote, namely "charismatic leadership." Charismatic leaders had to check the aspirations of the bureaucracy. . . . It was up to them to keep the society "open" against the inhuman forces of bureaucratization.[80]

Mommsen rightly raised the question, "Where then is the borderline between a type of charismatic rules which guarantees freedom within a democratic social order and that which may result in the emergence of a totalitarian or quasi-totalitarian regime?"[81] The Chinese experience of the Cultural Revolution demonstrates clearly that Mao's charismatic breakthrough only brought China an "institutional bankruptcy" of the sociopolitical order. The danger inherent in the plebiscitarian leader–democracy cannot be over-exaggerated. In this connection, I would like to side with Schluchter in arguing that there is a certain flaw in Weber's general pessimistic perspective on the trend of bureaucratization in modern society.[82] Furthermore, that Weber seems to assign the task of combating collectivized bureaucracy (also the state) to "autonomous individuals" cannot be, as Schluchter contends, a satisfactory answer to the main problem of our time, namely—"how can concentrated power be controlled."[83] Weber would certainly agree that China's path to modernization is impossible without bureaucracy. But I am inclined to believe that bureaucratization does not have to lead to an "iron cage."[84] However, the answer to the question "how can concentrated power be controlled" lies not in "autonomous individuals" as suggested by Weber, but rather in "autonomous society." Alvin Gouldner in his critique of Marxism, writes:

> No emancipation is possible in the modern world,
> however, without a strong civil society that can strengthen
> the public sphere and can provide a haven from and
> a center of resistance to the Behemoth state.[85]

Here, in a way, we return to Weber again, since Weber's preoccupation was precisely with the reciprocal effects of society and state. Unfortunately, Weber's sociology of state is left incomplete and some of his ideas are not the best guide for building Chinese democracy. We have to critically take up Weber's unfinished work in search of a form of modern state in which the autonomous status of society should be fully recognized.

12 Confucianism, Modernity, and Asian Democracy

New Wave of Democratization

The political revolution in 1989 in Eastern Europe and the dramatic events of August 1991 in Moscow did not only mark the end of the Cold War era, but also the beginning of a worldwide wave of democratization. Marc F. Platter hailed the arrival of democracy on the ruins of Leninist Socialism as "the democratic moment," and stated that "we may at last be entering a sustained period of peaceful democratic hegemony a land of 'Pax Democratica.'"[1] Samuel P. Huntington saw that, between 1974 and 1990, at least thirty countries made transitions to democracy doubling the number of democratic governments in the world. He called it democracy's "third wave." Although Huntington, as a political realist, cautioned that the third wave of democratization might be followed by a third reverse wave, nonetheless he pondered the question: "were these democratizations part of a continuing and ever expanding 'global democratic revolution' that will reach virtually every country in the world?"[2] Francis Fukuyama, in his now famous article entitled "The End of History," advanced a strong claim that we may be witnessing "the end point of man's ideological evolution and the universalization of Western liberal democracy as the final form of human government." He has taken the view that "the triumph of the West . . . is evident first of all in the total exhaustion of viable systematic alternatives to Western liberalism."[3] He further writes,

> What is emerging victorious, in other words, is not so much liberal practice, as the liberal idea. That is to say for a very large part of the world, there is now no ideology with pretensions to universality that is in a position to challenge liberal democracy.[4]

Fukuyama's optimism for liberal democracy though extraordinary, is not unprecedented in history. In fact, several times before in the past century, it seemed that democracy had won universal acceptance, but the acceptance was much less trustworthy than had been imagined. In 1900–1901, leading newspapers announced the good news that the twentieth century was to be the century of democracy.[5] History, with "the cunning of reason" perhaps, proved that wrong, and future events will probably do the same to Fukuyama and other like-minded prophets. There is no shortage of scholars who see the uncertainties in the "democratic age."[6] Charles S. Maier recently talked about the "moral crisis" of democracy and wrote, "on the aftermath of 1989's collapse of communism, a feeling of anticlimax has succeeded initial euphoria."[7] It is not difficult to be carried away by the sudden triumph of democracy. However, the triumph of democracy probably has less to do with the "success" of democracy than with the widespread disenchantment with communism. More than forty years ago, Louis Hartz wrote, "the competition between democracy and communism . . . is . . . a curious one, a kind of reverse competition in the process of disillusionment."[8] The central problem seems to stem from a discrepancy between ideal and practice. Democracy, as an ideal, has promised much, but the ideal of communism has promised even more. The "realities" of both liberal democracy and communism have betrayed these promises, but communism's betrayal is considerably greater, and thus it brought about its own defeat in the "competition of disillusionment." No one could fail to notice that the end of communism does not signal the end of the problems facing liberal democracy. Ken Jowitt has rightly reminded us:

> Liberal capitalist democracy has aroused a heterogeneous
> set of opponents. . . . For all the real and massive differences
> that separate these diverse oppositions, one can detect a
> shared critique. Liberal capitalist democracy is scorned for
> an inordinate emphasis on individualism, materialism,
> technical achievement, and rationality. . . . Liberal capitalism
> is indicted for undervaluing the essential collective dimension
> of human existence.[9]

Modernity and the Question of the Universalizability of Liberal Democracy

John Dun said some time ago, "we are all democrats today because we so transparently ought to be. Democratic theory is the public cant of the modern world. . . . All states today prefer to be democracies because a democracy is what [it] is virtuous for a state to be."[10] Ernest Gellner made a perceptive observation concerning democracy:

Looking at the contemporary world, two things are obvious: democracy is doing rather badly and democracy is doing very well. . . . Democracy is doing very badly in that democratic institutions have fallen by the wayside in very many of the newly independent "transitional" societies, and they are precarious elsewhere. Democracy on the other hand, is doing extremely well in so far as it is almost (though not quite) universally accepted as a valid form.[11]

Indeed, it is no exaggeration to say that democracy—the meaning of which is simply "the rule of the people"—is now so transparently a virtuous form of government that no state can afford not to be democratic. But it is one thing to say that there is no viable ideological rival to democracy in the contemporary world; it is quite another thing to say that there is no alternative to *liberal democracy*, which is a very special form of democracy. For the moment, the disintegration of communism has left the idea of liberal democracy standing alone, with no viable ideological competitor in sight. But this does not render valid the idealist, ahistorical assertion that liberal democratic civilization is the absolute end of history, the definitely final civilization. It seems to me that to ask whether there is an alternative to liberal democracy is not as pertinent as is the question: "Is liberal democracy universalizable?" As David Held rightly points out,

The celebratory view of liberal democracy neglects to explore whether there are any tensions, or even perhaps contradictions, between the "liberal" and "democratic" components of liberal democracy. . . . Furthermore, there is not simply one institutional form of liberal democracy. . . .

An uncritical affirmation of liberal democracy essentially leaves unanalyzed the whole meaning of democracy and its possible variants.[12]

It should be noted that liberal democracy is a blend of liberalism and democracy, and its two components have different historical-cultural roots. It has been well argued that

the conjunction "liberal democracy" is paradoxical, because the relationship between liberalism and democracy has been a deeply ambiguous one. Liberalism has provided not only the necessary foundation for, but also a significant constraint upon democracy in the modern world.[13]

Both democracy and liberalism are creations of the West, and the question of the universalizability of liberal democracy inevitably touches upon the issue of culture and modernity.

Since the eighteenth century, modernity, which originated in Europe, has spread progressively across the globe.[14] Today, the whole world is willy-nilly involved in modernization. The so-called Third World, voluntarily or not, is "condemned to modernization,"[15] to use the phrase of Octavio Paz, the Mexican poet and Nobel Prize winner. Clearly, the category of modernity "remains incorrigibly Western in most of its terms of reference."[16] However, the assertion that Western modernity will eventually be the universal form of modernity is, to say the least, questionable, if not downright wrong. Surprisingly or not, most modernization theories are hardly sensitive to cultural factors. Charles Taylor renders a great service to the debate by distinguishing two kinds of theories of modernity—i.e., "cultural" and "a-cultural." As he sees it, the dominant theories of modernity over the past two centuries have been of the a-cultural sort. A-cultural theory of modernity is defined by "a rational or social operation which is culture-neutral." According to this kind of theory, "modernity is conceived as a set of transformations that any and every culture can go through and that all will probably be forced to undergo." Indeed, "just relying on a cultural theory," warned Taylor, "would make us neglect certain important facets of the transformation." On the other hand, according to Taylor, it would be equally wrong to rely on a purely a-cultural theory which tends to make the mistake of "seeing everything modern as belonging to one Enlightenment Package." Fully convinced of the existence of alternatives to Western modernity, Taylor writes,

> In short, exclusive reliance on an a-cultural theory unfits us for what is perhaps the most important task of social science in our day: understanding the full gamut of alternative modernities that are in the making in different parts of the world. It locks us into an ethnocentric prison, condemned to project our own forms onto everyone else, and blissfully unaware of what we are doing.[17]

Bearing in mind this sage advice, let us look into the cultural particularities of liberal democracy that are part and parcel of Western modernity.

The Culture of Liberal Democracy

Democracy made its first appearance in the Athenian city-state. Liberal democracy by contrast, did not emerge in Europe until the seventeenth century.[18] Athenian democracy, which manifested itself in the universal device of having the people manage their own affairs, was grounded in a sense of community. The claims of the state were given a unique priority over those of the individual citizen. It was a form of collective existence case of a community ruling itself. This is probably why Gastil would like to call classical Athenian democracy "tribal" or "community" democracy.[19] Athenian democracy's legacy to posterity is the concept of "rule by the people," which has indeed become the ground of legitimacy for any kind of government called a democracy.[20] In contrast, liberal democracy, though it shared the concept of "rule by the people" with classical democracy, was grounded on the individual. The root is liberalism, "defined as that set of social and political beliefs, attitudes and values which assumes the universal and equal application of the law and the existence of basic human rights superior to those of state or community."[21] Liberalism affirms the basic worth of individuals. The heart of liberalism is that it takes the individual as the ultimate and irreducible unit of society. In other words, "the individual is conceptually and ontologically prior to society and can in principle be conceptualized and defined independently of society."[22] The true mark of liberal democracy then, is not that individual rights are cherished and respected, but that rights are not defined in "social" or "communal" terms. It is thus not accidental that liberalism is seen to be a form of "individualism." The liberal idea—derived from a variety of religious and secular tenets of the West—is culturally and historically specific. And a democracy based upon such a culturally specific principle can hardly claim to be intrinsically universal in nature.

At this juncture, it is worth noting that whether the individualism/collectivism antithesis is the central shared orientation of modernity is very much in doubt.[23] Only the extreme version of the a-cultural theory of modernity—to use Taylor's concept—would tend to presume that the individualistic principle of liberal democracy defines the only truly modern polity. Eisenstadt, while recognizing that the spread of modernity from the West to the rest of world has produced a "very strong convergence" in different modern societies, asserts,

> But while modernity has spread to most of the world, it has not given rise to a single civilization, and one pattern of ideological and institutional response but to several, or at least to many basic variants, which are constantly developing their own closely related but not identical dynamics. A great variety of modern or modernizing societies, sharing many common characteristics but also evincing great differences among themselves, developed out of these responses.[24]

True enough, democracy is now the "Moral Esperanto" of present nation-states. But the appeal of "liberal democracy" is far from universal. Bhikhu Parakh demonstrates convincingly the cultural particularity of liberal democracy and provides a useful decoupling of liberalism and democracy. He points out that "the democratic part of liberal democracy consisting of such things as free elections, free speech and the right to equality have proved far more attractive outside the West and is more universalizable than the liberal components." He makes it unmistakably clear that while non-Western societies have no difficulty in accepting democratic values, they are very uneasy with, if not downright hostile to, liberal values. He writes,

> millions in non-Western societies demand democracy albeit in suitably indigenized form, whereas they shy away from

liberalism as if they instinctively felt it to be subversive of what they most valued and cherished. This is not because it leads to capitalism, for many of them welcome the latter, but because the Third World countries feel that the liberal view of the world and way of life is at odds with their deepest aspirations and self-conceptions. As they understand it, liberalism breaks up the community, undermines the shared body of ideas and values, places the isolated individual above the community, encourages the ethos and ethic of aggressive self-assertions . . . weakens the spirit of mutual accommodation and adjustment.[25]

The problem of liberal individualism is not that it places too much weight on the rights of the individual, but that the rights of the individual are defined in "asocial" or "nonsocial" terms. In liberalism, to be an individual is almost synonymous with being an individualist. John Dun perceptively noted,

To be individual is to be distinctive, and to be an individual is simply the common fate. But to be an individualist is to embrace this fate with a suspicious alacrity to make a vice out of necessity. Being individual—in aspiration at least—is simply doing one's own thing, a private concern or a consensual pleasure. But being an individualist is well on the way towards disregarding the interests of others or denying the presence of any basic affective commitment of one human being towards another.[26]

In short, to be an individualist is to be an egocentric individual without regarding the larger society of which one is a part. America as a land of individualism was first described with acuity by Tocqueville. He saw that the Americans, though individualistic in many private pursuits, were remarkably capable of combining in voluntary associations to pursue collective interests. In a word, the independence and assertiveness of individuals were coupled with a significant level of responsibility. However, according to Riesman, a truly dramatic change has taken place in the United States in the growth of public approval of egocentric behavior.[27] It is interesting to note that in recent years certain American academics, including sociologists like Robert Bellah and Amita Etzioni, have been advocates of the social-political philosophy of communitarianism, which, loosely speaking, is intended to temper the excesses of American individualism in the light of a strong assertion of the rights of the larger society. The communitarian theorists have openly challenged the primacy of the "unfettered" individual. Amita Etrioni and his co-editors of *Quarterly Journal, The Responsive Community*, declared in their statement of purpose: "we say that the rights of individuals must be balanced with the responsibilities to the community." And, interestingly, the February 1991 issue of *Harper's* featured a Symposium on whether the United States Constitution needs a Bill of Duties to offset the Bill of Rights.[28]

America, in both contemporary and historical terms, is a liberal democracy par excellence. However, the coupling of liberalism and democracy in the United States was circumstantial rather than deliberate in nature. In the last two hundred years, liberalism and democracy in American politics have co-existed in a "creative tension" and have had a "deeply troubled relationship."[29] From a historical and developmental perspective, the communitarian "movement" represents but the latest phase of the troubled relationship between liberalism and democracy in American political culture.

Modernity, Confucianism, and Asian Democracy

The rapid ascendancy of the East Asian economy in the last two to three decades has made this region the focal point for students of development of different persuasions. Peter Berger calls it the "second case" of capitalist modernity.[30] The great German sociologist, Max Weber, in his classic entitled *The Religion of China*, asserted that Confucianism as a rationalism of adjustment was responsible for the "non-development" of capitalism in Imperial China.[31] In light of the phenomenal success in economic development of East Asia, which is, culturally speaking, a Confucian region. The Weberian thesis has been subjected to various criticisms. In my view, Weber's work on Confucianism is not without problems,[32] but these do not refute his thesis because today's Confucianism is not the Confucianism that Weber wrote about—which should be thought of as imperial Confucianism or what I call "institutional Confucianism."[33] What is pertinent to our discussion here is that the success of East Asian economic development has made it imperative to rethink the role of Confucianism as a cultural system in relation to modernization. Admittedly, the economic success of East Asia has a great deal to do with institutional factors.[34] Nevertheless, students of East Asian modernization believe that the economic features of East Asia are linked to its distinctive social and cultural features, which include "a very strong achievement-oriented work ethic, a highly developed sense of collective solidarity, and the enormous prestige of education." There should be little doubt that these social and cultural features are also part of the "East-Asian model."[35]

Whether the authoritarian system is the "cause" of economic development in East Asia is far from being agreed upon among scholars. I tend to agree with Huntington that "economic reform requires a strong authoritative government, although not necessarily authoritarian government."[36] But there is no denying the fact that Taiwan, South Korea, Singapore and, to some extent, Hong Kong all achieved their miraculous economic success under a development-oriented authoritarian system of one kind or another. What is more remarkable is that these East Asian societies, following the success of economic development and industrialization, have made a fundamental shift in their political orientation. The authoritarian systems have undergone a basic transformation toward democracy. The East Asian experience, which demonstrates unmistakably that there is a strong empirical correlation between economic factors and political democracy, confirms what Seymour Lipset asserted years ago.[37] The present study does not attempt to disentangle the causes of democracy in East Asia.[38] Suffice it to say that industrial capitalism is a necessary, though not a sufficient, condition for political democracy.[39] A fact that must be recognized is that in East Asia, after Japan, the so-called dragons, like Taiwan and South Korea, have clearly embarked on the road toward democracy. What this chapter argues is that, although East Asia's democratization is not only desirable but also feasible, East Asian democracy does not necessarily follow the Western model of liberal democracy. In short, East Asian countries are consciously or unconsciously searching for an alternative to Western liberal democracy.

Fukuyama's unbounded faith in liberal democracy does not make him entirely oblivious to the challenges liberal democracy might face. He admits that

> The most significant challenge being posed to the liberal
> universalism of the American and French revolutions today

is not coming from the communist world, whose economic failures are evident for everyone to see, but from those societies in Asia which combine liberal economics with a kind of paternalistic authoritarianism.[40]

Elsewhere he writes,

For us in the West, we have to wonder whether rather than being at a stage of evolution toward being more like us, Confucian democracies have found a route toward 21st century modernity that we really don't know about.[41]

Gilbert Rozman reminds us that the distinction between capitalist and socialist provides a useful way of perceiving our century. "Yet we see an advantage in redrawing this dichotomy somewhat so that more distinctions can be made. Above all, we propose to add a 'third dimension' to the analysis in order to capture the East Asian qualities labeled here as 'Confucian.'"[42] But what will be the nature of democracy informed by the Confucian heritage in East Asia? Huntington, speaking of the Asian democracies that are still being developed, asserts that they may meet the "formal requisite of democracy" but differ significantly from the Western democratic systems. He writes, "This type of political system offers democracy without turnover. It represents an adoption of Western democratic practices to serve not Western values of competition and change, but Asian values of consensus and stability."[43] Although Huntington believes that "in practice, Confucian or Confucian-influenced societies have been inhospitable to democracy," he deems that Confucianism, like any major cultural tradition, "has some elements that are compatible with democracy, just as both Protestantism and Catholicism have elements that are clearly undemocratic." He observes that "Confucian democracy may be a contradiction in terms, but democracy in a Confucian society need not be."[44]

The phrase "Confucian democracy" as it is used by Fukuyama and Huntington, is loose but interesting. It is worth mentioning in passing that "capitalist democracy," not unlike "Confucian democracy," is also a contradiction in terms. According to Ralph Miliband, who sees capitalist democracy as another name for liberal democracy,

> capitalist democracy is a contradiction in terms, for it encapsulates two opposed systems. On the one hand there is capitalism, a system of economic organization that demands the existence of a relatively small class of people who own and control the main means of industrial, commercial, and financial activity as well as a major part of the means of communication. . . . On the other hand there is democracy, which is based on the *denial* of such preponderance, and which requires a rough *equality of condition* that capitalism, as Fukuyama acknowledges, repudiates by its very nature. Domination and exploitation are ugly words that do not figure in Fukuyama's vocabulary but they are at the very core of capitalist democracy, and are inextricably linked to it.[45]

I am not prepared here to settle the scores between Confucian democracy and capitalist (or liberal) democracy. What is worth noting is that both Fukuyama and Huntington have shown a concern for the relationship between culture and democracy, though neither of them has provided a systematic exposition of the cultural particularities of Asian democracy.

The East Asian democratic experience shows that most countries in this region have adopted democratic institutions, but they have not followed truly liberal principles. Lipset, in a paper entitled "The Centrality of Political Culture," states that "cultural factors deriving from varying histories are extraordinarily difficult to manipulate, political institutions—including electoral systems and constitutional arrangements—are more easily changed."[46] To call East Asian democracy "Confucian democracy," as Fukuyama does, is not unreasonable, since East Asia's culture evolved through centuries within the orbit of China and the once hegemonic cultural system that was Confucianism. According to Rozman, "justification for a regional focus is not hard to find. This focus is evident in the common heritage of the region, which is customarily, although somewhat imprecisely, called the Confucian heritage."[47] Today, though institutional Confucianism is long dead, Confucian ethics and values are still a living cultural force. For East Asia, if democracy is going to be fully developed, it has to come to terms with Confucianism.

Confucianism never advocated the democratic form of government; in fact, it was not concerned with "forms" of government as such. To the great Confucians of the past, the paramount issue was how a government was to be justly administered. In a fundamental sense, Confucianism deals with the *Dao* (way) of administration but not with the *Dao* of politics.[48] While saying that Confucianism was no advocate of democracy, we cannot characterize Confucianism as simply anti-democratic. Confucianism is a complex system which cannot be interpreted unidimensionally as "for" or "against" democracy. Richard Solomon lists three tensions inherent in the Confucian tradition: (1) dependence on hierarchical authority versus self-assertion; (2) social harmony and peace versus hostility and aggression; (3) self versus group.[49] Confucianism not only contains elements or seeds of democracy, but arguably also offers a sinicized version of the "liberal tradition."[50] The most salient political component in Confucianism is the *minben*. The Confucian dictum, "The people are the basis of the state," is consistently and unequivocally articulated by great Confucians throughout Chinese history. Mencius said, "It is the people who are primary, the gods second, and the ruler last." In the words of the great Ming Confucian Huang Zongxi, people should be the "masters," the ruler the "guest." True, *minben* (people-as-the-basis) is not democracy. It contains the essence, perhaps, of what Lincoln meant by "of the people" and "for the people," but it does not extend to "by the people."[51] On balance, *minben*, which can be seen perhaps as containing the seed of democracy, has serious limitations if taken as material out of which modern democracy can be built. De Bary, who forcefully expounded that there is a liberalism in the Confucian tradition, particularly in Huang Zongxi's work, finds that there is "trouble" with Confucianism. He writes,

> even though Huang (Zongxi) went further than any other Confucian in asserting the primacy of the people—that they should be masters of the land, and the ruler the guest—he still was unable to articulate the means whereby the people as commoners (*min*) could actually assume this magisterial function.

Furthermore, he adds,

> In the end, however, what failed the Confucians repeatedly . . . was not the lack of a prophetic voice but the lack of an articulate popular audience—the absence of a political and

social infrastructure that would have given the people themselves a voice.[52]

The "trouble" with Confucianism was first revealed in China's
encounter with Western civilization in the nineteenth century. The
civilization state of the Middle Kingdom was assaulted and defeated
by the Western powers, which had already been baptized by industrialization and modernization. China was faced with a challenge
unprecedented in her long history. Reluctant at first, China had no
choice but to learn from the West. In a real sense, China was "condemned to modernization." The old moral-political order collapsed.
China was challenged with twin crises: a crisis of the political order
and an intellectual crisis or an "orientational crisis."[53] And a search
for a new moral-political order by the Chinese intellectuals ensued,
driven by the impulse to gain "wealth" and "power" for the "new"
nation of China.[54] The readiness of Chinese intellectuals to be
attracted to the idea of democracy as a new "form" of government
can only be understood within this historical context. However, for
Yan Fu and other like-minded intellectuals, democracy or liberal
ideas were treated, as Benjamin Schwartz makes clear, as a means
to an end.

> Liberty, equality (above, all, equality of opportunity) and
> democracy provide the environment within which the
> individual's "energy of faculty" is finally liberated. From
> the very outset, however, Yen Fu [Yan Fu] escapes some of
> the more rigid dogmatic antitheses of nineteenth-century
> European liberalism. Precisely because his gaze is ultimately
> focused not on the individual per se but on the presumed
> results of individualism, the sharp antitheses between the

individual and society individual initiative and social organization, and so on, do not penetrate to the heart of his perception.[55]

It is worth noting here that the idea of democracy became the dominant political aspiration of the late Qing intellectuals, and the Confucian concept of *minben* (people-as-the-basis) was integrated into the Western concept of *minzhu* (democracy).[56] To be sure, it was Dr. Sun Yat-sen who started the first "democratic revolution" in Chinese history. Significantly, though Sun's idea of democracy came from the West, he never failed to remind the Chinese people that there were many seeds of democracy in ancient China.[57] In the New Cultural Movement of 1919, "Democracy" as an emancipatory institution was presented—together with "Science"—as one of the two fundamental "symbolic resources" in constructing a new Chinese culture. In contemporary China, most, if not all, intellectuals would probably agree that democracy is a necessary part of modern political life. What is significant is that even the most representative New-Confucian scholars have reached the point of contending that the development of democracy should not be thought of as something extremely imposed upon China, but rather as the intrinsic necessity of Chinese cultural development.[58] They believe that if China is to carry forward her cherished tradition of developing a moral society, the promotion of democracy is both urgent and essential to the task.[59]

We can see, then, that there are elements in Confucianism that are compatible with democracy and Confucianism has not constituted a real obstacle to the acceptance of democracy in China. However, the relationship between Confucianism and liberalism is quite a different matter. The gap between them is more difficult to bridge. In the view of Tu Wei-ming, the Confucian ethic,

> unlike the puritanic ethic which stresses a consciousness of one's rights, entails duty-consciousness. It stresses the importance of social solidarity and finding one's niche in a particular group. This means understanding one's role in society with reference to a whole body of social conventions and practices. It is more of a harmonizing than a competitive model. It assigns great importance to the personal cultivation and discipline (especially the spiritual and psychological discipline) of the self. It stresses consensus formation, not through the imposition of a particular will upon the society at large but through the participation of a large segment of the group in a gradual process of mutual consultation. . . . It seeks to create a kind of fiduciary commitment to a larger and more lasting goal.[60]

The basic difference between Confucianism and liberalism lies in their respective views on the relationship between the individual and society. Although both liberalism and Confucianism cherish the worth of the individual, Confucianism does not see the individual and society in polar terms. As Fingarette asserts, "we would do better to think of Confucius as concerned with the nature of 'humanity' rather than with the polar terms 'individual' and 'society.' The formulation in terms of individual and society reflects western preoccupations and categories."[61]

As mentioned above, liberalism and individualism have a special relationship, and Western modernity is linked to individualism.[62] But the East Asian experience demonstrates that democracy and modernity are not necessarily inseparable from individualism. Peter Berger holds that "the development of modernity in the West suggests a reciprocal relationship with individualism" and this has made various theorists of modernization assume that individualism is inevitably and intrinsically linked to modernity. But, he argues,

> The East Asian experience, at the very least, makes this assumption less self-evident. . . . [I]t can be plausibly argued that East Asia, even in its most modernized sectors, continues to adhere to values of collective solidarity and discipline that strike the Western observer as very different indeed from his accustomed values and patterns of conduct. The recent discussion about Japanese styles of business and industrial management has brought this feature into sharp relief. Could it be that East Asia has successfully generated a non-individualistic version of capitalist modernity? If so, the linkage between modernity capitalism and individualism has not been inevitable or intrinsic; rather it would have to be reinterpreted as the outcome of contingent historical circumstances.[63]

Though the Confucian value orientation cannot be neatly characterized as collectivist, it is certainly not individualist.[64] Berger's observation that East Asia has generated a "non-individualist version of capitalist modernity" should be of considerable interest to students of modernization. In the same vein, it may be argued that the distinctive feature of Asian democracy is its "non-individualistic" character.

Given the above analysis, it is plausible to suggest that "non-individualistic" Confucianism could be made a partner of democracy. If we consider an Asian political system, it probably would not and should not be a "Confucian democracy" in the sense that Confucianism would be the dominant partner vis-à-vis democracy, but it might be and should be "democratically Confucian," in the sense that democracy would be the dominant partner and Confucianism would operate within the limits set by it. A "democratically Confucian" political system, not unlike liberal democracy, would cherish and respect individuals, and their rights, but would define them and their rights in "communal" and "social" terms.[65]

Asian democracy, by which I mean a "democratically Confucian" political system, is still in the early stages of developing and unfolding. I am aware that there might be as "troubled" a relationship between democracy and Confucianism as there is between liberalism and democracy. (Indeed, the "trouble" might be even greater.) However, I see no intrinsic reason why Confucianism, and especially its reconstructed version,[66] cannot become a genuine partner of democracy. It may not be wide of the mark to say that if East Asia is going to become politically modern, this will most plausibly be as a "democratically Confucian" society. And, if there is to be a viable alternative to liberal democracy provided by the East, it will be this form of "Asian democracy."

Notes

Chapter 1

*   Reprinted from *Individualism and Holism: Studies in Confucian and Taoist Values*, edited by Donald J. Munro, Ann Arbor: Center for Chinese Studies, The University of Michigan, Copyright © 1985 by the Lieberthal-Rogel Center for Chinese Studies, The University of Michigan.

1   Frederick W. Mote, *Intellectual Foundations of China* (New York: Knopf, 1971), 45.

2   Lin Yu-sheng, "The Evolution of the Pre-Confucian Meaning of *Jen* and the Confucian Concept of Moral Autonomy," *Monumenta Serica* 31 (1974–1975): 184.

3   Reciprocity as a moral principle has been applied to social relations of all kinds, and it provides a common ground for both gentlemen and small men. See Lien-sheng Yang, "The Concept of *Pao* as a Basis for Social Relations in China," in John K. Fairbank (ed.), *Chinese Thought and Institutions* (Chicago: University of Chicago Press, 1957), 291–309.

4   In the *Analects* (4:15), it is stated: "*Shan*. My doctrine is that of an all-pervading unity. The disciple Tsang replied "yes." The Master went out, and the other disciples asked, saying, "What do his words mean?" Tsang said, "The doctrine of our Master is loyalty and reciprocity—this and nothing more" (translation slightly adapted from James Legge [trans.], *The Chinese Classics*, 5 vols. [Hong Kong: Hong Kong University Press, 1960], 1:168–69). Also in the *Analects*: "Tsze-kung asked, saying, "Is there one word which may serve as a rule of practice for all one's life?" The Master said, "Is not reciprocity such a word? What do you not want done to yourself, do not do to others'" (15:23; translated in Legge, *Chinese Classics*, 1:301).

5   Robert J. Lifton, *Thought Reform and the Psychology of Totalism* (Middlesex, England: Penguin, 1967), 445.

6   Charles A. Moore, "Introduction: The Humanistic Chinese Mind," in Charles A. Moore (ed.), *The Chinese Mind* (Honolulu: University of Hawai'i Press, 1967), 5.

7   Hu Shi, *Zhongguo zhexue shi dagang* [An outline of the history of Chinese philosophy] (Shanghai: Commercial Press, 1919), 116.

8   Lin Yu-sheng, "The Pre-Confucian Meaning of *Jen*," 193.

9   Ruey Yeh-fu, "The Five Social Dyads as a Means of Social Control," *Journal of Sociology* 3 (April 1967): 53.

10   C. K. Yang, *Chinese Communist Society: The Family and the Village* (Cambridge: MIT Press, 1959), 7.

11   Robert N. Bellah, *Tokugawa Religion* (Boston: Beacon Press, 1970), 178.

12   Derk Bodde (ed.), *A Short History of Chinese Philosophy* (New York: MacMillan, 1964), 21.

13   Ibid.

14   Yang, *Chinese Communist Society*, v.

15   Feng Youlan has called it "the ideological basis of traditional society." See Feng, "The Philosophy as the Basis of Traditional Chinese Society," in F. S. C. Northrop (ed.), *Ideological Differences and World Order* (New Haven: Yale University Press, 1949), 18.

16   Lifton, *Thought Reform*, 419.

17   Hu Shi, *Zhongguo zhexue*, 129.

18   The difference between symmetrical and asymmetrical rule, according to Goffman, is as follows: "A symmetrical rule is one that leads an individual to have obligations or expectations regarding others that these others have in regard to him. . . . An asymmetrical rule is one that leads others to treat and be treated by an individual differently from the way he treats and is treated by them." Erving Goffman, *Interaction Ritual* (London: Allen Lane, The Penguin Press, 1972), 52–53.

19   Qu Tongzu, *Zhongguo falü yu Zhongguo shehui* [Chinese law and society] (Hong Kong: Longmen shuju, 1967).

20   John C. H. Wu, "The Status of the Individual in the Political and Legal Traditions of Old and New China," in Moore (ed.), *The Chinese Mind*, 346.

21   Chie Nakane writes: "The Japanese family system differs from that of

the Chinese system, where family ethics are always based on relationships between particular individuals, such as father and son, brothers
and sisters, parents and children, husband and wife, while in Japan they
are always based on the collective group, i.e., members of a household,
not on the relationships between individuals." Nakane, *Japanese Society*
(Middlesex, England: Penguin Books, 1973), 14.

22   K. Abbott, *Harmony and Individualism* (Taipei: The Orient Cultural Ser-
     vice, 1970), 57.

23   Richard W. Wilson, *Learning to Be Chinese* (Cambridge: MIT Press,
     1970), 20.

24   Yang, *Chinese Communist Society*, 172.

25   Liang Shuming, *Zhongguo wenhua yaoyi* [The essential features of Chi-
     nese culture] (Hong Kong: Jicheng tushu gongsi, 1974), 260.

26   Ibid., 90.

27   Kang Youwei, *Da tungshu* [The book of the grand unity] (Beijing: Guji
     chubanshe, 1956).

28   Tan Sitong, *Ren xue* [A study of *ren*] (Beijing: Zhonghua shuju, 1958).

29   H. Blumer, "Society as Symbolic Interaction," in Arnold M. Rose (ed.),
     Human Behaviour and Social Processes (Boston: Houghton-Mifflin,
     1962), 189–90.

30   Dennis H. Wrong, "The Over-socialized Conception of Man in Modern
     Sociology," *American Sociological Review* 26 (1961): 183–93.

31   Feng Youlan, *Xin shilun* [A new discussion of the issues of the practical
     world] (Taipei: Commercial Press, 1967), 78–79.

32   C. K. Yang, "Some Characteristics of Chinese Bureaucratic Behaviour,"
     in D. S. Nivison and A. F. Wright (eds.), *Confucianism in Action* (Stan-
     ford: Stanford University Press, 1959), 134–64.

33   Lin Yu-sheng, "The Pre-Confucian Meaning of *Jen*," 194.

34   Robert K. Merton and E. Barber, "Sociological Ambivalence," in E. A.
     Tiryakian (ed.), *Sociological Theory, Values and Sociocultural Change*
     (New York: Harper Torchbooks, 1967), 98.

35   "In the most extended sense, sociological ambivalence refers to incom-
     patible normative expectations of attitudes, beliefs and behaviour
     assigned to a status or to a set of statuses in a society. In its most
     restricted sense, sociological ambivalence refers to incompatible norma-
     tive expectations incorporated in a single role of a single social status."
     Ibid., 94–95.

36   "From the perspective of sociological ambivalence, we see a social role as a dynamic organization of norms and counter-norms, not as a combination of dominant attributes (such as affective neutrality or functional specificity). We propose that the major norms and minor counter-norms alternatively govern role-behaviour to produce ambivalence." Ibid., 103.

37   R. Turner, "Role-Making Process Versus Conformity," in Rose (ed.), *Human Behaviour and Social Processes*, 149.

38   Walter Buckley, *Sociology and Modern Systems Theory* (Englewood Cliffs: Prentice-Hall, 1967), 148–49.

39   Zhang Degong, *The World of the Chinese: Struggle for Human Unity* (Hong Kong: The Chinese University Press, 1980), 116.

40   Fei Xiaotong, *Xiangtu Zhongguo* [Peasant China] (Taipei: Luzhou chu-banshe, 1967), 29.

41   B. E. Ward, "Sociological Self Awareness: Some Uses of the Conscious Model," *Man* 1 (1968): 201–15.

42   Fei Xiaotong, *Xiangtu Zhongguo*, 24.

43   Benjamin Schwartz, "Some Polarities in Confucian Thought," in Nivison and Wright (eds.), *Confucianism in Action*, 50–62.

44   Fei Xiaotong, *Xiangtu Zhongguo*, 27–28.

45   Ibid. Fei's views on the Chinese are somewhat different from that of Francis Hsu. Contrasting the Chinese and American views of the individual. Hsu writes, "In the American way of life the emphasis is placed upon the predilections of the individual, a characteristic we shall call individual-centered. This is in contrast to the emphasis the Chinese put upon an individual's appropriate place and behaviour among his fellow men, a characteristic we shall term situation-centered. Being individual-centered, the American moves toward social and psychological isolation. Being more situation-centered, the Chinese is inclined to be socially and psychologically dependent on others." Francis L. K. Hsu, *American and Chinese, Two Ways of Life* (New York: Abelard-Schurman, 1953), 10.

46   *The Analects*, trans. D. C. Lau (Middlesex, England: Penguin Books, 1979), 12:1 (112).

47   Liang Shuming, *Zhongguo wenhua yaoyi*, 94.

48   Pan Guangdan, *Zhengxue zui yan* [Comments on political issues] (Shanghai: Guancha She, 1948), 133.

49   Hu Shi, *Zhongguo zhexue*, 116.

50   Surprising or not, in the People's Republic today, the personal relation-
     ship is still as crucial a factor in social communication as ever. There is
     even a newly coined term, *guanxi xue*, denoting such a social phenome-
     non. See *Renmin ribao*, September 29, 1981. For a systematic treatment
     of Chinese interpersonal relationships, see Ambrose Y. C. King, "Ren zhi
     guanxi zhong renqing zhi fenxi" [An analysis of *renqing* in interpersonal
     relationships], in *Collection of Papers of the International Conference of
     Sinology* (Taipei: Academia Sinica, 1981), 413–28.

51   The common belief in China that individuals are capable of constructing
     their own relational networks is often neglected by social scientists stud-
     ying personality in that society. For a systematic elaboration of this topic,
     see Ambrose Y. C. King and Michael H. Bond, "A Confucian Paradigm
     of Men: A Sociological View" (Paper delivered at the Conference on Chi-
     nese Culture and Mental Health held at the East-West Center, Honolulu,
     Hawai'i, March 1982), i.e., Chapter 3 of this book.

52   "What a man dislikes in his superiors, let him not display in the treat-
     ment of his inferiors. What he dislikes in his inferiors, let him not display
     in the service of his superiors; what he hates in those who are before him,
     let him not therewith precede those who are behind him. What he hates
     in those who are behind him, let him not therewith follow those who are
     before him, what he hates to receive on the right, let him not bestow on
     the left; what he hates to receive on the left, let him not bestow on the
     right. This is what is called 'The principle with which, as a measuring
     square, to regular one's conduct.'" *Daxue* [The great learning], Chapter
     10, in Legge (trans.), *Chinese Classics*, 1:373–74.

53   Hu Shi, *Zhongguo zhexue*, 112.

54   Fei Xiaotong, *Xiangtu Zhongguo*, 37.

55   Edwin O. Reischauer, *The Japanese* (Tokyo: Charles E. Tuttle, 1978),
     138–39.

56   King and Bond, "A Confucian Paradigm of Men," 15.

57   Lifton, *Thought Reform*, 453.

58   Wilfram Eberhard, *Moral and Social Values of the Chinese: Collected
     Essays* (Taipei: Zhengwen Publishing Company, 1971), 8, 11.

59   Lifton, *Thought Reform*, 435.

60   The idea of establishing a new *lun* on the relationship between the indi-
     vidual and society was first proposed in Li Guoding's lecture entitled
     "Bashi niandai shehuixuezhe miandui de tiaozhan" [The challenge facing

the sociologists of the eighties] (Paper delivered at the Annual Meeting of the Chinese Sociological Society, Taipei, March 1981). This was reported and discussed widely in Taiwan. See *United Daily News* (March 16, 1981).

Chapter 2

*   Reprinted from Ambrose Yeo-chi King and John T. Myers, "Shame as an Incomplete Conception of Chinese Culture: A Study of Face" (Occasional paper, Social Research Centre, The Chinese University of Hong Kong, 1977).

1   See A. Smith, *Chinese Characteristics* (New York: Fleming, H. Revell, 2nd ed., 1894); K. Latourette, *The Chinese: Their History and Culture* (New York: Macmillan, 3rd ed., 1947); Y. T. Lin, *My Country and My People* (New York: Harper, 1953); H. C. Hu, "The Chinese Concept of Face," *American Anthropologist* 46 (1944): 45–66; F. L. G. Hsu, "Suppression Versus Repression: A Limited Psychological Interpretation of Four Cultures," *Psychiatry* (1944): 223–42; W. Eberhard, *Guilt and Sin in Traditional China* (Berkeley: University of California Press, 1967); J. Agassi and I. Jarvie, "A Study in Westernization," in Agassi and Jarvie (eds.), *Hong Kong: A Society in Transition* (London: Routledge and Kegan Paul, 1969), 130–65; R. Wilson, *Learning to Be Chinese: The Political Socialization of Children in Taiwan* (Cambridge, MA: MIT Press, 1970); and L. Stover, *The Cultural Ecology of Chinese Civilization* (New York: New American Library, 1974), to mention only a few.

2   Yao Wenyuan, *Lu Xun—Zhongguo wenhua geming juren* [Lu Xun—The giant of Chinese Cultural Revolution] (Shanghai: Wenyi she, 1959), 100.

3   See R. Benedict, *The Chrysanthemum and the Sword* (Boston: Houghton Mifflin, 1946).

4   Hsu, "Suppression Versus Repression."

5   Eberhard, *Guilt and Sin in Traditional China*, 122.

6   J. Fairbank, *The United States and China* (New York: The Viking Press, 1962), 104.

7   H. C. Hu, "The Chinese Concept of Face," 45.

8   Agassi and Jarvie, "A Study in Westernization," 139.

9   R. A. D. Forrest, "The Southern Dialects of China," in *The Chinese in Southeast Asia* (London: Oxford University Press, 1951), 673–76.

10   *Ci Yuan* ([Dictionary) (Taipei: Commercial Press, 1947), 1230.

11   P. T. Ho, *The Ladder of Success in Imperial China: Aspects of Social Mobility 1368–1911* (New York: Columbia University Press, 1962).

12   Hsu, "Suppression Versus Repression," 234.

13   Hu Shi, *Zhongguo zhexue shi dagang* [An outline of the history of Chinese Philosophy] (Shanghai: The Commercial Press, 1919), 285.

14   Fei Xiaotong, *Xiangtu Zhongguo* [Earthbound China] (Shanghai, 1947), 88.

15   H. C. Hu, "The Chinese Concept of Face," 45.

16   Hu Shi, *Zhongguo zhexue shi dagang*, 285.

17   Ibid.

18   B. Schwartz, "Some Polarities in Confucian Thought," in D. S. Nivison and A. F. Wright (eds.), *Confucianism in Action* (Stanford: Stanford University Press, 1959).

19   Tang Junyi, *Zhongguo wenhua zhi jingshen jiazhi* [The Spiritual values of Chinese culture] (Taipei, 1953).

20   Benedict, *The Chrysanthemum and the Sword*.

21   Eberhard, *Guilt and Sin in Traditional China*, 124.

22   E. Erikson, *Childhood and Society* (New York: W. W. Norton & Co., 2nd ed., 1963), 253.

23   A. S. Chen, "The Ideal Local Party Secretary and the 'Model' Man," *China Quarterly* (1964): 229–40.

24   Yao Wenyuan, *Lu Xun*, 100–103.

25   R. Lifton, *Thought Reform and the Psychology of Totalism* (London: Penguin Books, 1967).

26   R. Solomon, *Mao's Revolution and the Chinese Political Culture* (Berkeley: University of California Press, 1971), 54.

27   G. De Vos, "The Relation of Guilt Toward Parents to Achievement and Arranged Marriage among Japanese," in R. Hunt (ed.), *Personality and Cultures* (New York: The Natural History Press, 1967), 261–90.

Chapter 3

*   Reprinted from *Chinese Culture and Mental Health*, edited by Wen-shing Tseng and David Y. H. Wu, Orlando: Academic Press, Inc., Copyright © 1985 by the Academic Press, Inc.

**   In this chapter, the term "man" is used to refer to the individual in accordance with Confucian terminology. However, it should be understood that in most cases, it refers both to man and to woman.

1   A. F. Wright, "The Formation of *Sui* Ideology," in J. K. Fairbank (ed.), *Chinese Thought and Institutions* (Chicago: University of Chicago Press, 1957), 71–104.

2   R. H. Solomon, *Mao's Revolution and the Chinese Political Culture* (Berkeley: University of California Press, 1971).

3   M. H. Bond and S. H. Wang, "Aggressive Behaviour in Chinese Society: The Problem of Maintaining Order and Harmony," in A. P. Goldstein and M. Segall (eds.), *Global Perspectives on Aggression* (New York: Pergamon, 1983).

4   D. Bodde, "Harmony and Conflict in Chinese Philosophy," in A. F. Wright (ed.), *Studies in Chinese Thought* (Chicago: University of Chicago Press, 1953), 19–80.

5   H. Fingarette, *Confucius—The Secular as Sacred* (New York: Harper Torchbooks, 1972), 53.

6   F. W. Mote, *Intellectual Foundations of China* (New York: Knopf, 1972), 49.

7   D. C. Lau, *The Analects* (New York: Penguin, 1979), Chapter 12, paragraph 11.

8   F. L. K. Hsu, "Psychosocial Homeostasis and *Jen*: Conceptual Tools for Advancing Psychological Anthropology," *American Anthropologist* 73 (1971): 23–44.

9   A. Y. C. King, "The Individual and Group in Confucianism: A Relational Perspective" (Paper presented at the Conference on Individualism and Wholism, York, Maine, June 24–29, 1981).

10   C. A. Moore, "Introduction: The Humanistic Chinese Mind," in C. A. Moore (ed.), *The Chinese Mind* (Honolulu: University of Hawai'i Press, 1967), 5.

11   Hu Shi, *Zhongguo zhexue shi dagang* [An outline of the history of Chinese philosophy] (Shanghai: The Commercial Press, 1919), 283.

12   Z. Bauman, *Toward a Critical Sociology* (London: Routledge Kegan Paul, 1976), 26–57.

13   Lin Yusheng, "The Evolution of the Pre-Confucian Meaning of *Ren* and Confucian Concept of Moral Autonomy," *Monumenta Sinica* 31 (1974–1975): 193.

14   Fingarette, *Confucius*, 72–73.

15   Liang Shuming, *Zhongguo wenhua yaoyi* [The essential features of Chinese culture] (Hong Kong: Jicheng tushu gongsi, 1974), 94.

16   Ibid.

17   See also Solomon, *Mao's Revolution and the Chinese Political Culture.*

18   King, "The Individual and Group in Confucianism," 19–24.

19   W. T. de Bary, "Individualism and Humanitarianism in Late Ming Thought," in de Bary (ed.), *Self and Society in Ming Thought* (New York: Columbia University Press, 1970), 149.

20   James Legge, *Chinese Classic, Vol. 1: Confucian Analects* (Hong Kong: Hong Kong University Press, 1960), 324.

21   Ibid.

22   The relationship between the sovereign and the subject is in terms of father (i.e., *zhunfu*) and son (i.e., *zimin*), and the relationship between friend and friend in terms of elder brother (i.e., *wuxiong)* and younger brother (i.e., *wudi*).

23   Y. P. Mei, "The Status of the Individual in Chinese Social Thought and Practice," in C. A. Moore (ed.), *The Chinese Mind* (Honolulu: University of Hawai'i Press, 1967), 331.

24   Feng Youlan, *A Short History of Chinese Philosophy*, trans. D. Bodde (New York: MacMillan, 1948), 21.

25   C. K. Yang, *Chinese Communist Society: The Family and the Village* (Cambridge, MA: MIT Press, 1959), 5.

26   In such a symmetrical relationship, if the father or elder brother failed to perform his required role, then the rebellion of the son or younger brother would be accorded a certain degree of legitimacy. See Solomon, *Mao's Revolution and the Chinese Political Culture*, 56.

27   Hu Shi, *Zhongguo zhexue shi dagang*, 128.

28   Ibid., 126.

29   Feng Youlan, "The Philosophy at the Basis of Traditional Chinese Society," in F. S. C. Northrop (ed.), *Ideological Differences and World Order* (New Haven: Yale University Press, 1949), 18.

30   Solomon, *Mao's Revolution and the Chinese Political Culture*, 78.

31   R. J. Lifton, *Thought Reform and Psychology of Totalism* (Harmondsworth, England: Penguin, 1967), 419.

32   Yang, *Chinese Communist Society*, 89.

33   K. A. Abbott, *Harmony and Individualism* (Taipei: The Orient Culture Service, 1970).

34   D. Y. F. Ho, "Chinese Patterns of Socialization" (Unpublished manuscript, Psychology Department, University of Hong Kong, 1980).

35 Solomon, *Mao's Revolution and the Chinese Political Culture*, 49–52.

36 Bond and Wang, "Aggressive Behaviour in Chinese Society."

37 Abbott, *Harmony and Individualism*; R. W. Wilson, *Learning to Be Chinese* (Cambridge, MA: MIT Press, 1970).

38 W. S. Tseng, "The Concept of Personality in Confucian Thought," *Psychiatry* 36 (1973): 191–202.

39 Lifton, *Thought Reform and Psychology of Totalism*, 453.

40 Solomon, *Mao's Revolution and the Chinese Political Culture*, 69.

41 H. Wilhelm, "Chinese Confucianism on the Eve of the Great Encounter," in M. B. Jansen (ed.), *Changing Japanese Attitudes Towards Modernization* (Princeton, NJ: Princeton University Press, 19650, 293.

42 V. A. Rubin, "Individual and State in Ancient China," trans. S. I. Levine (New York: Columbia University Press, 1976), 20–27.

43 K. C. Hsiao, *Zongguo zhengzhi sixiang shi* [A history of Chinese political thought] (Taipei: Zhonghua wenhua chubanshe, 1954), 1:90.

44 T. A. Metzger, *Escape from Predicament* (New York: Columbia University Press, 1977), 42.

45 Yang, *Chinese Communist Society*, 158.

46 H. Kelman, "Processes of Opinion Change," *Public Opinion Quarterly* 25 (1961): 57–78.

47 P. J. Hiniker, "Chinese Reactions to Forced Compliance: Dissonance Reduction or National Character," *Journal of Social Psychology* 11 (1969): 157–76.

48 F. L. K. Hsu, *Americans and Chinese: Two Ways of Life* (New York: Abelard-Schuman, 1953).

49 See also T. Doi, "Some Psychological Themes in Japanese Human Relationships," in J. C. Condon and M. Saito (eds.), *Intercultural Encounters with Japan* (Tokyo: Simul Press, 1974).

50 Wilson, *Learning to Be Chinese*, 20.

51 M. H. Bond, "How Does Cultural Collectivism Operate? The Impact of Task and Maintenance Contributions on Reward Distribution," *Journal of Cross-Cultural Psychology* 14 (1983): 41–63; M. H. Bond, K. Leung, and K. C. Wan, "The Social Impact of Self-Effecting Attributions: The Chinese Case," *Journal of Social Psychology* 118 (1982): 157–66; G. Hofstede, *Culture's Consequences: International Differences in Work-Related Values* (London: Sage, 1980).

52 C. Nakane, *Japanese Society* (Harmondsworth, England: Penguin, 1973), 14.

53 D. Bodde, *China's Cultural Tradition* (New York: Holt, Rinehart and Winston, 1957), 66.

54 R. F. Johnson wrote, "Nothing is more important for an understanding of the wonderfully table and long-lived social system of China than this fact: that the social and the political unit are one and the same, and that this unit is not the individual but the family." See Johnson, *Lion and Dragon in Northern China* (New York: Dutton, 1910), 135.

55 Yang, *Chinese Communist Society*, 172.

56 D. Y. F. Ho, "Psychological Implications of Collectivism: With Special Reference to the Chinese and Maoist Dialects," in L. H. Eckensberger, W. J. Lonner, and Y. Poortinga (eds.), *Cross-Cultural Contributions to Psychology* (Lisse: Swets and Zeitlinger, 1979).

57 M. H. Bond and P. W. H. Lee, "Face Saving in Chinese Culture: A Discussion and Experimental Study of Hong Kong Students," in A. Y. C. King and R. P. L. Lee (eds.), *Social Life and Development in Hong Kong* (Hong Kong: The Chinese University Press, 1981).

58 D. Y. F. Ho, "On the Concept of Face," *American Journal of Sociology* 81 (1976): 867–84.

59 A. Y. C. King and J. T. Myers, "Shame as an Incomplete Conception of Chinese Culture: A Study of Face" (Occasional paper, Social Research Centre, The Chinese University of Hong Kong, 1977); see Chapter 2 of this book.

60 E. R. Hughes, *The Individual in East and West* (London: Oxford University Press, 1937).

61 Liang Shuming, *Zhongguo wenhua yaoyi*, 260.

62 B. Schwartz, "Some Polarities in Confucian Thought," in D. S. Nivison and A. F. Wright (eds.), *Confucianism in Action* (Stanford: Stanford University Press, 1959).

63 According to Solomon, the three contradictions inherent in the Confucian tradition are: (1) dependency on hierarchical authority versus self-assertion; (2) social harmony and peace versus hostility and aggression; and (3) self versus group. See Solomon, *Mao's Revolution and the Chinese Political Culture*, 78–80.

64 T. Y. Lin, "A Study of the Incidence of Mental Disorder in Chinese and Other Cultures," *Psychiatry* 16 (1953): 313–36.

65 Yang, *Chinese Communist Society*, 11, 168.

66 F. M. Wong, "Modern Ideology, Industrialization, and Conjugalism: The

Hong Kong Case," *International Journal of Sociology of the Family* 2 (1972): 139–52; "Industrialization and Family Structure in Hong Kong." *Journal of Marriage and the Family* 37 (1975): 985–1000.

67 M. Fried, *Fabric of Chinese Society: A Study of the Social Life of a Chinese Seat* (New York: Octagon Books, 1953), 218–32.

68 Abbott, *Harmony and Individualism*, 304.

69 L. S. Yang, "The Concept of *Pao* as a Basis for Social Relations in China," in Fairbank (ed.), *Chinese Thought and Institutions*.

70 Solomon, *Mao's Revolution and the Chinese Political Culture*, 128.

71 Ibid., 126.

72 J. K. Fairbank, "How to Deal with the Chinese Revolution," *The New York Review of Books* 6.2 (1966): 12.

73 Fei Xiaotong, *Xiangtu Zhongguo* [Peasant China] (Taipei: Luzhou Chubanshe, 1967), 22–37.

74 Yang, *Chinese Communist Society*, 89.

75 Fei Xiaotong, *Xiangtu Zhongguo*, 27.

76 W. Eberhard, *Moral and Social Values of the Chinese: Collected Essays* (Taipei: Zhengwen Publishing Company, 1971), 8, 11.

77 Fei Xiaotong, *Xiangtu Zhongguo*, 27–30.

78 Lifton, *Thought Reform and Psychology of Totalism*, 435.

79 Fei Xiaotong goes so far as to suggest that *ziwo zhuyi* (egoism) lies at the very heart of Chinese social thought, including Confucianism. See Fei Xiaotong, *Xiangtu Zhongguo*, 27.

80 W. La Barre, "Some Observations on Character Structure in the Orient: II," *Psychiatry* 9 (1946): 215.

81 Fei Xiaotong, *Xiangtu Zhongguo*, 26.

82 D. Bodde and C. Morris, *Law in Imperial China* (Cambridge: Harvard University Press, 1967); A. F. P. Hulsewe, *Remnants of Han Law* (Leiden: Mouton, 1955).

83 C. C. Lau and R. P. L. Lee, "Bureaucratic Corruption and Political Instability in Nineteenth-Century China," in R. P. L. Lee (ed.), *Corruption and Its Control in Hong Kong* (Hong Kong: The Chinese University Press, 1981).

84 A. H. Bloom, "A Cognitive Dimension of Social Control: The Hong Kong Chinese in Cross-Cultural Comparison," in A. A. Wilson, S. L. Greenblatt, and R. W. Wilson (eds.), *Deviance and Social Control in Chinese Society* (New York: Praeger, 1977).

85   This salient social phenomenon was officially recognized and criticized. See the speech given by Premier Zhao to the annual session of The Fifth National People's Congress (*People's Daily News*, 1978).

86   *Beijing Daily News*, 1981.

87   A. Y. C. King and D. Leung, "The Chinese Touch in Small Industrial Organizations" (Occasional paper, Social Research Centre, The Chinese University of Hong Kong, 1975).

88   S. K. Lau, "Utilitarianistic Familism: The Basis of Political Stability," in King and Lee (eds.), *Social Life and Development in Hong Kong*.

89   L. Y. K. Fung, "Strategies for Occupational Mobility in Hong Kong: A Biographical Approach" (Unpublished Master's thesis, The Chinese University of Hong Kong, 1981).

90   A. Y. C. King, "Ren zhi guanxi zhong renqing zhi fenxi" [An analysis of *renqing* in interpersonal relationships] (Paper presented at the International Conference of Sinology, Taipei, 1980); Yang, "The Concept of *Pao* as a Basis for Social Relations in China."

Chapter 4

*   Reprinted from Ambrose Yeo-chi King, "*Kuan-hsi* and Network Building: A Sociological Interpretation," *Daedalus* 120:2 (Summer 1991): 63–84. © 1991 by the American Academy of Arts and Sciences, published by the MIT Press.

1   The concepts of *mianzi* and *renqing* are dealt with in my two papers: Ambrose Y. C. King, "Renji guanxi zhong renxing zhi fenxi" [An analysis of *renqing* in interpersonal relationships], in *Collected Papers of the First International Sinological Conference* (Taipei: Academic Sinica, 1980), 413–42; and "Mian, chi yu Zhongguo ren xingwei zhi fenxi" [*Mien, chi* and the Chinese social behavior], in *Collected Papers of the Second International Sinological Conference* (Taipei, Academic Sinica, 1986), 39–54.

2   The concept is originally developed by Alfred Schutz. See Schutz and Thomas Luckmann, *The Structure of the Life-World*, trans. R. M. Zarner and H. T. Engelhardt, Jr. (Evanston, IL: Northwestern University Press, 1973), 99–182.

3   Liu Binyan, "Ren yao zhijian" [Between human and demon], *People's Literature* (September 1976): 34–35.

4   Fox Butterfield, *China: Alive in Bitter Sea* (London: Coronet Books, 1983), 74–75.

5   J. Bruce Jacobs, "A Preliminary Model of Particularistic Ties in Chinese Political Alliance: *Kang-ch'ing* and *Kuan-hsi* in a Rural Taiwanese Township," *China Quarterly* 78 (June 1979): 237–73.

6   Charles A. Moore, "Introduction: The Humanistic Chinese Mind," in C. A. Moore (ed.), *The Chinese Mind* (Honolulu: University of Hawai'i Press, 1967).

7   Hu Shi, *Zhongguo zhexue shi dagang* [An outline of the history of Chinese philosophy] (Shanghai: Commercial Press, 1919), 116.

8   Tu Wei-ming, "Confucian Humanism in a Modern Perspective," in Joseph P. L. Jiang (ed.), *Confucianism and Modernization: A Symposium* (Taipei: Freedom Council, 1987), 71.

9   Francis L. K. Hsu, "Psychosocial Homeostasis and *Jen*: Conceptual Tools for Advancing Psychological Anthropology," in Laura Bohannan (ed.), *American Anthropologist* 73.1 (1971).

10   Liang Shuming, *Zhongguo wenhua yaoyi* [The essential features of Chinese culture] (Hong Kong: Jicheng tushu gongsi, 1974), 94.

11   Ambrose Y. C. King, "The Individual and Group in Confucianism: A Relational Perspective," in Donald J. Munro (ed.), *Individualism and Holism: Studies in Confucian and Taoist Values* (Ann Arbor, MI: University of Michigan Press, 1985), 57–72.

12   Yu Ying-shih, *Cong jiazhi xitong kan Zhongguo wenhua de xiandai yiyi* [The modern meaning of the Chinese culture as viewed from its value systems] (Taipei: Time Publishing Company, 1984), 62.

13   Pan Guangdan, *Zhengxue zui yan* [Comments on political issues] (Shanghai: Guancha she, 1948), 133.

14   Robert H. Silin, *Leadership and Values* (Cambridge: Harvard University Press, 1970), 36.

15   Fei Xiaotong, *Xiangtu Zhongguo* [Peasant China] (Taipei: Luzhou chubanshe, 1967), 20–22.

16   Hu Shi, *Zhongguo zhexue shi dagang*, 116.

17   Richard H. Solomon, *Mao's Revolution and the Chinese Political Culture* (Berkeley: University of California Press, 1971).

18   Ambrose Y. C. King and Michael Bond, "The Confucian Paradigm of Man: A Sociological View," in Wen-shing Tseng and David Wu (eds.), *Chinese and Mental Health* (New York: Academic Press, 1985), 29–46.

19   William T. de Bary, "Individualism and Humanitarianism in Late Ming Thought," in de Bary (ed.), *Self and Society in Ming Thought* (New York: Columbia University Press, 1970), 149.

20   Fei Xiaotong, *Xiangtu Zhongguo*, 26–27.

21   Ibid.

22   Barbara E. Ward, "Sociological Self-Awareness: Some Uses of the Conscious Model," *Man* 1 (1968): 201–15.

23   Steve Duck and Daniel Perlman, *Understanding Personal Relationship: An Interdisciplinary Approach* (London: Sage, 1985).

24   John Clyde Mitchell (ed.), *Social Networks in Urban Situation* (Manchester: Manchester University Press, 1969), 13.

25   Chien Chiao, *Guanxi chuyi* [The preliminary discussion on *guanxi*], Special Bulletin No. 10, Taipei Institute of Ethnology, Academic Sinica (April 1982), 345–50. This is one of the pioneering works on *guanxi*. I have benefited greatly from this paper and from discussing it with the author.

26   W. La Barre, "Some Observations on Character Structure in the Orient: II," *Psychiatry* 9: 215.

27   Chie Nakane, *Japanese Society* (New York: Penguin, 1970), 1.

28   Ibid., 14.

29   Chuang Ying-chang and Chen Chi-nan, "Xian jieduan Zhong Ri shehui jiegou yanjiu de jiantao: Taiwan yanjiu de yixie qishi" [A review on the present stage's studies on the social structure of China and Japan], in *The Sinicization of Research in Social and Behaviour Science*, Special Bulletin No. 10, Institute of Ethnology, Academic Sinica, Taipei (April 1982), 281–310.

30   Wang Sung-hsing, *Han ren de jiazu zhi: shilun yu "guanxi, wu zu zhi" de shehui* [The lineage of the Han people] (Unpublished).

31   Jacobs, "A Preliminary Model of Particularistic Ties in Chinese Political Alliance."

32   Ibid.

33   *People's Daily* (May 8, 1979), 4.

34   Butterfield, *China: Alive in Bitter Sea*, 141.

35   Godwin Chu and Ju Yanan, *The Great Wall in Ruins: Cultural Change in China* (Honolulu: East-West Center, 1990). Chu and Ju's study drew a stratified probability sample of 2,000 respondents, including 1,199 from metropolitan Shanghai, 304 from two towns in Qingpu and 497 from twenty villages in four of the twenty rural districts. The findings of the

survey give us an overall picture of what contemporary Chinese culture looks like.

36   Ibid., 66.

37   Ibid.

38   Ibid., 132.

39   Ezra F. Vogel, "From Friendship to Comradeship," *China Quarterly* 21 (1965): 46–60.

40   Franz Schurmann, *Ideology and Organization in Communist China* (Berkeley: University of California Press, 2nd ed., 1970), iii.

41   Luk Tak-Chuen, "Guanxi: dangdai zhongguo de shehui xingtai" [*Guanxi*: The social mode of behaviour in contemporary China] (Master's thesis, The Chinese University of Hong Kong, 1988); and King K. Tsao, "Microfoundation of Structural and Historical Macroanalysis: The Prolegomenon to the Study of Chinese Human Relationship (*Guanxi*)" (Qualifying paper for PhD program, University of Chicago, 1988), 43–56.

42   Andrew G. Walder, *Communist Neo-Traditionalism: Work and Authority in Chinese Industry* (Berkeley: University of California Press, 1986); and "Organized Dependency and Culture of Authority in Chinese Industry," *Journal of Asian Studies* (1983): 51–76.

43   Tang Tsou, *The Cultural Revolution and Post-Mao Reforms* (Chicago: University of Chicago Press, 1986), 86–88.

44   Ibid., 220.

45   Thomas B. Gold, "After Comradeship: Personal Relations in China Since the Cultural Revolution," *China Quarterly* 104 (1985): 673.

46   Ezra F. Vogel, *One Step Ahead in China* (Cambridge: Harvard University Press, 1989), 407.

47   Ibid., 405.

48   Ibid., 409.

49   See King, "Renji guanxi zhong renxing zhi fenxi."

50   L. S. Yang, "The Concept of *Pao* as a Basis for Social Relations in China," in J. K. Fairbank (ed.), *Chinese Thought and Institutions* (Chicago: University of Chicago Press, 1957), 292.

51   Silin, *Leadership and Values*, 43.

52   Ibid., 162.

53   John H. Weakland, "The Organization of Action in Chinese Culture," *Psychiatry* 13 (1950): 361–70.

54 Silin, *Leadership and Values*, 43.

55 Chu and Ju, *The Great Wall in Ruins*, 37.

56 Ibid., 55.

57 D. R. De Glopper, "Doing Business in Lukang," in Arthur P. Wolf (ed.), *Studies in Chinese Society* (Stanford: Stanford University Press, 1978), 314–15.

58 Talcott Parsons, *The Structure of Social Action* (New York: Free Press, 1949), 550–51.

59 Max Weber, *The Religion of China*, trans. H. H. Gerth (New York: Free Press, 1951), 48.

60 Ibid.

61 See William Skinner, "Chinese Peasants and Closed Community: An Open and Shut Case," *Comparative Studies in Society and History* 13 (July 1971): 277.

62 Fei Xiaotong, *Xiangtu Zhongguo*, 82.

63 De Glopper, "Doing Business in Lukang," 306, 317.

64 K. K. Hwang, "Face and Favor: The Chinese Power Game," *American Journal of Sociology* 92.4 (1987).

65 Chu and Ju, *The Great Wall in Ruins*, 58.

66 Ibid., 37, 67.

Chapter 5

* Reprinted from Ambrose Y. C. King, "The Role of Intellectuals in Chinese State Confucianism" (Paper presented at the Conference on Intellectuals as Cultural Carriers during Transformation in Chinese History, World Journal Cultural Foundation, New York, October 31–November 1, 1992).

1 Consult Benjamin Schwartz, *In Search of Wealth and Power: Yen Fu and the West* (Cambridge, MA: Harvard University Press, 1964).

2 Frauz Schurmann, "Chinese Society," *International Encyclopaedia of Social Sciences* (MacMillan) 2 (1968): 414.

3 Tang Tsou, *The Cultural Revolution and Post-Mao Reforms* (Chicago: University of Chicago Press 1986), 82, 301.

4 Maurice Meisner, *Mao's China* (New York: The Free Press, 1977), 19.

5 According to Mao, before the October Revolution Chinese knew neither Lenin, Stalin, nor Marx and Engels. It was the October Revolution that brought Marxism-Leninism to China. See Zhonggong zhongyang Mao

Zedong zhuxi zhuzuo bianshi chuban weiyuanhui (ed.), *Mao Zedong geming waijiao yulu* (Beijing: Renmin chubanshe, 1977), 9.

6   *Li Zehou, Zhongguo xiandai sixiang shilun* [On the Chinese modern intellectual history] *(Taipei: Fengyun shidai chuban gongsi, 1980).*

7   Sima Lu (ed.), *Zhonggong dang shi ziliao zaocui* (Hong Kong: Union Press, 1974).

8   Tu Wei-ming, "Intellectuals Effervescence in China," *Daedalus* (Spring 1992): 264.

9   B. D. Wolfe, *An Ideology in Power: Reflections on the Russian Revolution* (London: George Allen & Unwin, 1969).

10 The concept of "total state" is developed by Bertran D. Wolfe. He writes, "The essence of the total state is not tyranny nor terror but the fact that the state aspires to be 'total.'" He argued that "The Chief problem of the twentieth century . . . was not socialism versus capitalism . . . was limited state or total state." Ibid., 154–55. Tang Tsou has talked about the problem of "totalism" (*quannengzhuji*) in twentieth-century Chinese politics. He defined "totalism" as the unrestrained intervention of political power to control every level and every domain of society. See S. R. Schram (ed.), *Foundations and Limits of State Power in China* (Hong Kong: The Chinese University Press, 1987), 253–54.

11 Benjamin I. Schwartz, "The Primacy of the Political Order in East Asian Societies: Some Preliminary Generalizations," in Schram, *Foundations and Limits of State Power in China*, 3.

12 Jerome B. Grieda, *Intellectuals and State in Modern China* (New York: Free Press 1981), 353.

13 Marie-Claire Bergère, *The Golden Age of the Chinese Bourgeoisie, 1911–1937* (Cambridge: Cambridge University Press, 1989), 240.

14 Timothy Cheek, "A Literature of Protest, A Literature of Changes: On the Role of Directed Culture in Chinese Literatures," in Bih-jaw Lin and James T. Meyers (eds.), *Forces for Change in Contemporary China* (Taipei: Institute of International Relations, National Chengchi University, 1992), 143.

15 Timothy Cheek, *Chinese Establishment Intellectuals* (Armonk, NY: M. E. Sharpe,1986).

16 The nature of power relations in China's basic work unit (*danwei*) is dealt with in Andrew Walder, *Communist Neo-Traditionalism: Work and Authority in Chinese Industry* (Berkeley: University of California Press, 1986).

17   Robert K. Nerton, *Social Theory and Social Structure* (New York: Free Press, 1968), 265ff.

18   Mao Tse-tung, "Have Firm Faith in the Majority of the People," *Selected Works of Mao Tse-tung*, Vol. V (Beijing: Foreign Languages Press, 1977), 507.

19   "Beat Back the Attacks of the Bourgeois Rightist," *Selected Works of Mao Tse-tung*, Vol. V, 469.

20   Hsu Cho-yun, *Zhongguo wenhua de fazhan guocheng* [The development of Chinese culture] (Hong Kong: The Chinese University Press, 1992), 11–21.

21   Leszek Kolakowski, *Marxism and Beyond*, trans. Jane Zielonko Peel (London: Paladin, 1971), 192.

22   Stuart Schram, *The Political Thought of Mao Tse-tung* (London: Pelican Books,1969), 331.

23   Stuart Schram, *Mao Tse-tung* (London: Penguin Books, 1967), 250.

24   Mao Tse-tung, "On New Democracy," *Selected Works of Mao Tse-tung* (Beijing: Foreign Languages Press, 1965), Vol. II, 339.

25   Benjamin I. Schwartz, "Thought of the Late Mao—Between Total Redemption and Utter Frustration," in R. MacFarquhar, T. Cheek, and E. Wu (eds.), *The Secret Speeches of Chairman Mao* (Cambridge: The Council on East Asian Studies, Harvard University, 1989), 32.

26   Mao Tse-tung, *Selected Works of Mao Tse-tung*, Vol. V, 425.

27   Ibid., 506.

28   Zhang Zuo, *Mao Zedong ping zhuan* [Commentaries on Mao Zedong] (Taiwan: Dongxi wenhua ye chuban gongsi, 1988), Chapter 6.

29   Mao Tse-tung, *Selected Works of Mao Tse-tung*, Vol. V, 468.

30   Ibid., 470.

31   Ibid., 41.

32   Robert Lifton, *Thought Reform and the Psychology of Totalism: A Study of "Brainwashing" in China* (London: Penguin Books, 1967), 440.

33   Ibid., 525.

34   Feng wrote, "To travel the road to socialism, one must accept Marxism as the guiding ideology. To expound and disseminate Marxism is the sole function of one devoted to philosophy . . . I am determined to . . . lay down my arms and surrender, and be once more a 'common soldier' in the ranks of Marxist-Leninist philosophers under the banner of the party and Marxism." Quoted in C. K. Yang, *Religion in Chinese Society* (Berkeley: University of California Press, 1967), 384–85.

35   See J. P. McGough, *Fei Hsiao-tung: The Dilemma of a Chinese Intellec-tual* (New York: M. E. Sharpe, 1979); and Fei Xiaotong, *Xingxing chong xingxing* (Ningxia renmin chubanshe, 1992), Foreword.

36   Kam Louie, *Critiques of Confucius in Contemporary China* (Hong Kong: The Chinese University Press, 1980), 147.

37   Ibid., 21.

38   Ibid.

39   Joseph K. Levenson, *Confucian China and Its Modern Fate: A Trilogy*, Vol. III (Berkeley: University of California Press, 1968), 76–82.

40   Liu Shaoqi's *How to Be a Good Communist* was attacked in the Anti-Confucius Movement as a book influenced directly by Confucian's ethical principle of "self-cultivation." Kam Louie, *Critiques of Confu-cius in Contemporary China* (Hong Kong: The Chinese University Press, 1980), 125.

41   Stuart Schram, *Mao Tse-tung* (London: Penguin Books, 1967), 220.

42   Ibid., 335.

43   Ibid., 336.

44   Liu Shaoqi, *On the Party* (Beijing: Foreign Language Press, 1950), 35.

45   See S. Schram, "Social Revolution and Cultural Revolution in China," in A. Dyson and B. Towers (eds.), *China and the West: Mankind Evolving* (London: Garnstone Press, 1970), 65–81.

46   See Martin K. Whyte, *Small Groups and Political Rituals in China* (Berkeley: University of California Press), 1974.

47   Derk Bodde, "Harmony and Conflict in Chinese Philosophy," in A. F. Wright (ed.), *Studies in Chinese Thought* (Chicago: University of Chi-cago Press, 1953).

48   Richard H. Solomon, *Mao's Revolution and the Chinese Political Cul-ture* (Berkeley: University of California, 1971), 6.

49   C. K. Yang, *Religion in Chinese Society*, 383.

50   Ibid., 385.

51   Ibid., 381.

52   James L. Waston, "Standardizing the Gods: The promotion of *Tien Hou* (Empress of Heaven) along the South China Coast 960–1960," in John-son, Nathan, and Rawski (eds.), *Popular Culture in Late Imperial China* (Berkeley: University of California Press, 1985), 292–324.

53   James L. Waston, "The renegotiation of Chinese cultural identity in the post-Mao Era" (Occasional paper 4, Social Sciences Research Centre and Department of Sociology, University of Hong Kong, 1991), 16, 18.

54 M. Goldman, *Literary Dissents in Communist China* (New York: Atheneum, 1971), 276.

55 Ibid., 8.

56 Merle Goldman, *China's Intellectuals: Advise and Dissent* (Cambridge: Harvard University Press, 1981), 16.

57 Godwin Chu and Ju Yanan, *The Great Wall in Ruins: Cultural Change in China* (Honolulu: East-West Center Publication, 1990).

58 Myron L. Cohen, "Being Chinese," *Daedalus* (Spring 1991): 130.

59 Helen F. Siu and Zelda Stern, *Mao's Harvest: Voices Prom China's New Generation* (New York: Oxford University Press, 1983), xiv.

60 Ambrose Y. C. King, "In Defense of Bureaucracy: The Deradicalization of Maoism," in J. F. Jones (ed.), *Building China* (Hong Kong: The Chinese University Press, 1980), 113–26.

61 See *Time Magazine* (January 6, 1986), 10–11.

62 Peter R. Moody, Jr., "Some Non-Official Trends in Political Thought During Mainland China's Decade of Reform," in Lin and Meyers (eds.), *Forces for Change in Contemporary China* (Taipei: Institute of International Relations, National Chengchi University, 1992), 175.

63 Tang Tsou, *The Cultural Revolution and Post-Mao Reforms* (Chicago: University of Chicago Press 1986), 59.

64 Merle Goldman, "Hu Yaobang's Intellectual Network and the Theory Conference of 1979," *China Quarterly* 126 (June 1991): 219–42.

65 S. R. Schram, *Mao Tse-tung: A Preliminary Reassessment* (Hong Kong: The Chinese University Press, 1983), 75.

66 Tsou, *The Cultural Revolution and Post-Mao Reforms*, 58–59.

67 Ibid., 65.

68 Vivianne Shue, *The Reach of the State: Sketches of the Chinese Body Politics* (Stanford, CA: Stanford University Press, 1988), 75, 120.

69 Robert F. Ash, "The Peasant and the States," *China Quarterly* 127 (September 1991): 518.

70 He Baogang and David Kelly, "China's Civil Society and the Intellectuals," in Robert Milles (ed.), *The Development of Civil Society in Communist Systems* (London: Allen and Unwin, 1992), 7.

71 Michel Bonnin and Yves Chevrier, "The Intellectual and the State: Social Dynamics of Intellectual Autonomy During the Post-Mao Era," *China Quarterly* 127 (September 1991): 587.

72 Perry Link, "The Limits of Cultural Reform Deng Xiaoping's China," *Modern China* 13 (April 1987): 115–76.

73   Bonnin and Chevrier, "The Intellectual and the State," 590.

74   Richard C. Kraus, "Four Trends in the Politics of Chinese Culture," *Forces for Change in Contemporary China*, 214.

75   Gerrit W. Gong, "Information, Secularization, and the 'Crisis of Belief': Fundamental Dynamics of Change in Mainland China," *Forces for Change in Contemporary China*, 193.

76   Moody, "Some Non-Official Trends in Political Thought," 174.

77   Ibid., 170–88; also Tu Wei-ming, "Intellectuals Effervescence in China," 281.

78   Richard Madsen, "The Spiritual Crisis of China's Intellectuals," *Chinese Society on the Eve of Tiananmen* (Cambridge: Council on East Asian Studies Publication, Harvard University, 1990), 252.

79   Andrew J. Nathan, "Tiananmen and the Cosmos," *The New Republic* (July 29, 1991), 34.

80   Wu Xiuyi, *Zhongguo wenhua re* [Chinese cultural heat] (Shanghai: Shanghai renmin chubanshe, 1988).

81   Kraus, "Four Trends in the Politics of Chinese Culture," 224.

82   Wu Xiuyi, *Zhongguo wenhua re*, 129–46.

83   Xue-Liang Ding, "The Disparity Between Idealistic and Instrumental Chinese Reformers," *Asian Survey* 28.11 (November 1988): 1121–26.

84   Ibid., 1124.

85   See Ivan Szelenyi, "The Intellectuals on the Road to Class Power," *A Sociological Study of the Role of the Intelligentsia in Socialism* (New York: Harcourt Brace Jovanovich, 1979).

86   He and Kelly, "China's Civil Society and the Intellectuals," 19.

87   Bonnin and Chevrier, "The Intellectual and the State," 582.

Chapter 6

*   This article is translated and adapted by Tam Kwok-kan and Eric K. W. Yu from the Chinese version previously published in *Peking University Journal* 1 (January 1996): 20–27.

1   Benjamin I. Schwartz, "The Primacy of the Political Order in East Asian Societies: Some Preliminary Generalizations," in S. R. Schram (ed.), *Foundations and Limits of State Power in China* (Hong Kong: The Chinese University Press, 1987), 2–3.

2   Schwartz: "One of the most striking characteristics of Chinese civili-

zation is what might be called the centrality and weight of the political order." See ibid., 1.

3   John K. Fairbank, *The United States and China* (Cambridge, MA: Harvard University Press, 4th ed., 1976), 220.

4   Cited in Chow Tse-tsung et al., *Wusi yu Zhongguo* [The May-Fourth Movement and China] (Taipei: China Times Publications, 1979), 196.

5   Ambrose Y. C. King, *Cong chuantong dao xiandai* [From tradition to modernity] (Taipei: China Times Publications, 1979), 236–37.

6   Roland Robertson, "After Nostalgia? Willful Nostalgia and the Phase of Globalization," in B. S. Turner (ed.), *Theories of Modernity and Post-Modernity* (London: Sage Publications, 1995), 45–61.

7   For details, see Immanuel Wallerstein, *The Capitalist World Economy* (Cambridge: Cambridge University Press, 1979).

8   Anthony Giddens, *The Consequences of Modernity* (Stanford: Stanford University Press, 1990), 55–56.

9   Ambrose Y. C. King, *Zhongguo shehui yu wenhua* [Chinese society and culture] (Hong Kong: Oxford University Press, 1993), 152–69.

10   Peter Berger, "An East Asian Development Model," in P. L. Berger and Michael Hsin-Huang Hsiao (eds.), *In Search of An East Asian Development Model* (New York: Brunswick, 1988), 4.

11   See P. L. Berger and H. Kellner, *The Homeless Mind* (London: Penguin, 1973).

12   R. J. Bernstein, *Habermas and Modernity* (Cambridge: Polity Press, 1985), 1–32.

13   Jürgen Habermas, *The Theory of Communicative Action*, trans. T. McCarthy (New York: Beacon Press, 1987), 391–403.

14   See Berger and Kellner, *The Homeless Mind.*

15   Charles Taylor, *Sources of the Self: The Modern Identity* (Cambridge, MA: Harvard University Press, 1989).

16   Octavio Paz, "The Search for Values in Mexico's Modernization," *Asian Wall Street Journal* (June 1, 1994), 8.

17   Ambrose Y. C. King, *Zhongguo xiandaihua yu zhishi fenzi* [China's modernization and Chinese intellectuals] (Taipei: China Times Publications, 1977), 24–54.

18   M. Berman, *All that is Solid Melts into Air* (London: Penguin, 1988), 90–129.

19   T. Parsons, *The System of Modern Societies* (New York: Prentice Hall, 1971), 138–43.

20   See S. N. Eisenstadt, "Cultural Tradition, Historical Experience and Social Change: The Limits of Convergence," The Tanner Lecture on Human Values, delivered at University of California, Berkeley (May 1–3, 1989).

21   Many scholars have pointed out that "theories of modernization" are still supported by the experiences of development in East Asia. See Lucian W. Pye, Asian Power and Politics (Cambridge, MA: Harvard University Press, 1985), 10; Francis Fukuyama, "Confucianism and Democracy," Journal of Democracy 6.2 (1995): 20–33.

22   See "Asian Values" and "The State of Asian Families," The Economist (May 28–June 3, 1994), 9–10, 23–24.

23   James Walsh, "Asia's Different Drum," Time 23 (June 14, 1993): 16–19.

24   T. Parsons, Societies: Evolutionary and Comparative Perspectives (New York: Prentice Hall, 1966), 113.

25   King, Zhongguo shehui yu wenhua, 152–69.

26   This is the thesis of Tanase Takao's essay "The Modern as a Regulative Ideal," presented at the World Conference on Legal Sociology held at Tokyo University (August 1–4, 1995).

27   Eisenstadt, "Cultural Tradition, Historical Experience and Social Change."

28   Robertson, "After Nostalgia?," 51.

Chapter 7

*   Reprinted from Ambrose Yeo-chi King, "Administrative Absorption of Politics in Hong Kong: Emphasis on the Grass Roots Level," Asian Survey 15:5 (May 1975): 422–39. © 1975 by the University of California Press.

**   This chapter is one of a series of reports produced for the Kwun Tong Industrial Community Research Programme which was financially supported by the Harvard Yenching Institute and was under the auspices of the Social Research Centre, The Chinese university of Hong Kong. I would like to thank the people at Harvard Yenching Institute, particularly Professor John Pelzel, for their generous and unfailing support of the above-mentioned research programme of which I was the coordinator and the principal investigator. Also, I want to thank my able research assistant, Kong King-leung, who worked with me closely in my City District Officer Scheme study in 1972.

1   Robert Redfield and Milton Singer, "The Cultural Roles of Cities," *Economic Development and Cultural Change* 3 (1954–1955): 53–73; and T. G. McGee, *The South-East Asian City* (London, 1967), Chapters 3 and 4.

2   Max Weber, *Central Economic History* (Glencoe, IL: Free Press, 1950), 315–18.

3   Harold Laski, "Democracy," in *Encyclopedia of the Social Sciences* (New York: Macmillan, 1973), in S. M. Lipset, *Political Man* (Garden City, NY: Doubleday Anchor Book, 1963), 34–38.

4   Brigitte Berger, *Societies in Change* (New York: Basic Books, 1971), 160.

5   Karl Deutsch, "Social Mobilization and Political Development," *American Political Science Review* 55 (September 1961): 493–514.

6   S. P. Huntington, *Political Order in Changing Societies* (New Haven, CT: Yale University Press, 1969), 4, 77.

7   G. B. Endacott, *Government and People in Hong Kong: 1841–1962* (Hong Kong: Hong Kong University Press, 1964), 229.

8   John K. Fairbank, "Synarchy Under the Treaties," in Fairbank (ed.), *Chinese Thought and Institutions* (Chicago: University of Chicago Press, 1957), 163–203.

9   Endacott, *Government and People in Hong Kong*, 231.

10   Data compiled from *Hong Kong Who's Who* (1970–73), Joseph Walker (ed.).

11   T. C. Cheng, "Chinese Unofficial Members of the Legislative and Executive Councils in Hong Kong up to 1941," *Journal of the Royal Asiatic Society Hong Kong Branch* (1971), 7–30.

12   Aline K. Wong, "Political Apathy and the Political System in Hong Kong," *United College Journal* 8 (1970–71): 1–20.

13   Ambrose Y. C. King, "The Political Culture of Kwun Tong: A Chinese Community in Hong Kong" (Research paper, Social Research Centre, The Chinese University of Hong Kong, June 1972); and J. S. Hoadley, "'Hong Kong is the Lifeboat': Notes on Political Culture and Socialization," *Journal of Oriental Studies* 8.1 (January 1970): 206–18.

14   J. S. Hoadley, "Political Participation of Hong Kong Chinese: Patterns and Trends," *Asian Surrey* XIII.6 (June 1973): 616.

15   *Hong Kong: Report for the Year 1972* (Hong Kong: Government Press, 1973), 209.

16   G. A. Almond, "Introduction: A Functional Approach to Comparative Politics," in G. A. Almond and James Coleman (eds.), *The Politics of the Developing Areas* (Princeton: Princeton University Press, 1960), 3–64.

17   *Hong Kong: Report for the Year 1972*, 209.
18   David Podmore, "Room at the Top," *Far Eastern Economic Review* 65.29 (1969): 180–82.
19   Since 1964, the Chinese "established rich" (old families) has decreased its weight in the Legislative Council, while the Chinese "new rich" (industrial elite) has increased its weight rapidly. The percentage distribution of the Chinese "established rich" and "new rich" in the composition of the Unofficials of the Legislative Council from 1964 to 1971 is as follows:

	1964	1965	1966–1967	1968–1969	1970–1971
"established rich"	66%	41%	46%	38.5%	30.8%
"new rich"	18.5%	25%	23%	38.5%	53.7%

For the composition of the Legislative Council, see Stephen Tang's senior thesis entitled: "The Power Structure in a Colonial Society—Sociological Study of the Legislative Council in Hong Kong (1948–1971)" (Unpublished, Department of Sociology, The Chinese University of Hong Kong, May 1973).

20   *Report of the Working Party on Local Administration (Hong Kong: Government Press, 1966)*, 11, 12.
21   *Kowloon Disturbances 1966—Report of the Commission of Inquiry* (Hong Kong: Government Press, *1967)*, 110–11.
22   Edward Shils, "Political Development in the New States," *Comparative Studies in Society and History* 2.3 (April 1960): 265–92; and 2.4 (July 1960): 397–411.
23   *The City District Officer Scheme*. Report by the Secretary for Chinese Affairs, Hong Kong Government (January 24, 1969), 12, 18, 21.
24   *Official Proceedings*, The Urban Council, XII.5 (March 1969): 473–74.
25   *The City District Officer Scheme*, 3.

Chapter 8

*   Reprinted from *Political Culture and Democracy in Developing Countries*, edited by Larry Diamond. Copyright © 1993 by Lynne Rienner Publishers, Inc. Used with permission of the publisher.
1   This revised essay has benefited greatly from the comments of Dr. Ramon Myers and Dr. Larry Diamond. I am particularly indebted to the latter for his ingenious suggestions.

2 *Economic Development: Taiwan, Republic of China* (Taipei: Council for Planning and Development, 1987); and Myers, Ramon, "The Republic of China on Taiwan: The Political Center, Economic Development, and Democracy" (Paper presented to the Hoover Institution conference, Economy, Society, and Democracy, May 7–10, 1992, Washington DC), 11–13.

3 Peter Berger, "Secularity—West and East" (Paper prepared for the Kokugakuin University Centennial Symposium on Culture Identity and Modernization in Asian Countries, September 11–13, 1983).

4 Herman Kahn, *World Economic Development: 1979 and Beyond* (London: Groom Helm, 1979).

5 Max Weber, *The Religion of China*, trans. and ed. H. H. Gerth (New York: Free Press, 1964).

6 Thomas A. Metzger, *Escape from Predicament: Neo-Confucianism and China's Evolving Political Culture* (New York: Columbia University Press, 1977), 234–35.

7 I have discussed this topic in "The Transformation of Confucianism in the Post-Confucian Era: The Emergence of Rationalistic Traditionalism in Hong Kong" (Paper prepared for the Conference on Confucian Ethics and the Modernization of Industrial Asia, The Institute of East-Asia Philosophies, Singapore, January 5–9, 1987), i.e., Chapter 10 of this book.

8 Alexander Lu and Ya-li Lu, "Future Domestic Developments in the Republic of China on Taiwan," *Asian Survey* 25 (October 1985): 1075, 1095; Yang-sun Chou and Andrew J. Nathan, "Democratizing Transition in Taiwan," *Asian Survey* 27 (March 1987): 277–99.

9 Ronald H. Chilcote, *Theories of Development and Underdevelopment* (Boulder: Westview Press, 1984), 79–109.

10 Lucian W. Pye, *Asian Power and Politics: The Cultural Dimension of Authority* (Cambridge: Harvard University Press, 1985), 3.

11 Robert E. Ward and Dankwart Rustow (eds.), *Political Development in Japan and Turkey* (Princeton: Princeton University Press, 1964), 5.

12 Gabriel L. Almond, *Political Development: Essays in Heuristic Theory* (Boston: Little, Brown, 1970), Chapters 5, 6. See also Almond, "The Development of Political Development," in M. Weiner and S. R. Huntington (eds.), *Understanding Political Development* (Boston: Little, Brown, 1987), 449.

13 Wolfgang J. Mommsen, *The Age of Bureaucracy: Perspectives on the*

Political Sociology of Max Welter (Oxford: Basil Blackwell, 1974), Chapter 5. The pessimistic view of Weber on modernization is particularly discussed and criticized in Richard J. Bernstein (ed.), *Habermas and Modernity* (Cambridge: Polity Press, 1985), 1–66.

14   Peter Berger, Brigitte Berger, and Hansfried Kellner, *The Homeless Mind* (New York: Penguin Books, 1973), 15.

15   Talcott Parsons, *Structure and Process in Modern Societies* (New York: Free Press, 1960), 116.

16   Seymour M. Lipset, "Some Social Requisites of Democracy: Economic Development and Political Legitimacy," *American Political Science Review* 53 (March1959): 80.

17   Dankwart E. Rustow, "Transition to Democracy: Toward a Dynamic Model," *Comparative Politics* 2 (April 1970): 337–64.

18   Jose Casanova, "Modernization and Democratization: Reflections on Spain's Transition to Democracy," *Social Research* 50 (Winter 1983): 929–73.

19   Thomas B. Gold, *State and Society in the Taiwan Miracle* (New York: M. E. Sharpe, 1986), 59.

20   The concept of "inhibited political center," which was originally developed by Thomas Metzger and later jointly elaborated by him and Ramon Myers, refers to a form of state–society relationship in which a highly differentiated, privatized society checks that center's power. The "inhibited" political center stands in contrast to the fully "subordinated" political center on the one hand and the "uninhibited" political center on the other. See Ramon A. Myers, "Political Theory and Recent Political Development in the Republic of China," *Asian Survey* 27 (September 1987): 1003–22.

21   Michael Hsin-huang Xiao, *Government Agricultural Strategies in Taiwan and South Korea* (Taipei: Institute of Ethnology, Academia Sinica, 1981), 101–64.

22   Gold, *State and Society in the Taiwan Miracle*, 67–68.

23   Ibid., 90.

24   Arthur J. Vidich, "Legitimation of Regimes in World Perspective," in A. J. Vidich and R. M. Glassman (eds.), *Conflict and Control* (London: Sage, 1979), 299.

25   Wei Yong, "March Towards a Stable, Harmonious and Innovative Society: An Analysis of the Trend of Political Development Based on the

Results of Six Public Opinion Surveys" (Taiwan: R.O.C. publication, May 5, 1986; in Chinese).

26   Michael Hsin-huang Xiao, "The Development Experience of Taiwan Society: From Colonialism to Capitalism" (Paper prepared for the Conference on the Development Experience of Modern Chinese Areas and the Future of China, Taipei, National Chengchi University, December 24–26, 1987; in Chinese), 11–12. For countries with highly unequal income distributions, the Gini coefficient typically lies between 0.50 and 0.70. A coefficient between 0.20 and 0.35 indicates a relatively equitable distribution. (Zero is perfect equality and one perfect inequality.)

27   John F. Cooper, "Political Development in Taiwan," in Hungdah Chiun (ed.), *China and the Taiwan Issue* (New York: Praeger, 1979), 37–73.

28   Neil H. Jacoby, *Aid to Taiwan: A Study of Foreign Aid, Self-Help and Development* (New York: Praeger, 1966), 11.

29   Cooper, "Political Development in Taiwan."

30   Douglas Mendel, *The Politics of Formosan Nationalism* (Berkeley: University of California Press, 1970), 114–217.

31   Ming-min Peng, *A Taste of Freedom* (New York: Holt, Rinehart & Winston, 1972).

32   Mingsien Lee, "Political Change in Taiwan, 1949–1974: A Study of the Processes of Democratic and Integrative Change with Focus on the Role of Government" (PhD diss., University of Tennessee, 1975), 87–92.

33   Ibid., 112.

34   Cooper, "Political Development in Taiwan," 37–73.

35   Lu, "Future Domestic Developments in the Republic of China on Taiwan," 1089–1091.

36   Gold, *State and Society in the Taiwan Miracle*, 3.

37   Ibid., 130, Gold's characterization of Taiwan's Political system as "ossified" is not quite accurate from my viewpoint, which will be made clear later in this chapter.

38   John F. Cooper, "Taiwan's Recent Election: Progress Toward a Democratic System," *Asian Survey* 21 (October 1981).

39   Chou and Nathan, "Democratizing Transition in Taiwan," 278

40   Pye, *Asian Power and Politics*, 223.

41   Myers, "Political Theory and Recent Political Development in the Republic of China," 1018.

42   *Chung-yang jik-pao* (November 12, 1986), 2. The translation is by Myers, ibid., 1007.

43 Larry Diamond, "Beyond Authoritarianism and Totalitarianism: Strategies for Democratization," *Washington Quarterly* (Winter 1989): 151.

44 R. W. Wilson, *Learning to Be Chinese: The Political Socialization of Children in Taiwan* (Cambridge: MIT Press, 1970), 106.

45 R. W. Wilson, "A Comparison of Political Attitudes of Taiwanese Children and Mainlander Children in Taiwan," *Asian Survey* 8 (December 1968): 992–98.

46 Sheldon Appleton, "The Social and Political Impact of Education in Taiwan," *Asian Survey* 16 (August 1976): 704–16.

47 Cooper, "Political Development in Taiwan."

48 Consult Tu Wei-ming, "Confucianism: Symbols and Substance in Recent Time," in R. W. Wilson, A. A. Wilson, and S. L. Greenblatt (eds.), *Values Change in Chinese Society* (New York: Praeger, 1979), 21–51.

49 *Mencius*, VIIb. 14.

50 Lee, "Political Change in Taiwan," 148, 211.

51 Yow-suen Sun, "A Preliminary Analysis of the Class Structure in Taiwan" (Research paper, Sociology Department, University of Hawai'i, 1986); quoted in Xiao, "The Development Experience of Taiwan," 5. "Middle class" refers to self-employed entrepreneurs and managers as well as professionals in the industrial and commercialsectors.

52 Lang-li Wen, "Structural Correlates of Emerging Political Pluralism in Taiwan" (Paper prepared for the International Conference on Taiwan, R.O.C.; A Newly Industrialized Society, September 3–5, 1987).

53 Wei, "March Towards a Stable, Harmonious and Innovative Society."

54 F. Hu and Ying-long You, "The Voting Motives of the Electorate" (in Chinese), *Journal of Social Science* (National Taiwan University, Taipei) 33 (October 1985): 34. My analysis of the changing political culture in Taiwan is mainly based on their study. I am grateful to Professor Hu Fu for his generosity in providing me with many of his works.

55 Gabriel A. Almond and Sidney Verba, *The Civic Culture* (Boston: Little, Brown, 1965), 168–85.

56 Ibid., 173.

57 Hu Fu, "The People's Attitudes Towards Political Participation" (in Chinese) (Paper prepared for Symposium on Basic Research on Taiwan's Social Change, National Taiwan University, Academia Sinica, August 28–30, 1987).

58 Almond and Verba define "subject competence" as follows: "The competence of the subject is more a matter of being aware of his rights under

the rules than of participating the making of the rules." *The Civic Culture*, 169.

59   Rustow, "Transition to Democracy: Toward a Dynamic Model," 344–45, 358–61.

60   S. P. Huntington and J. M. Nelson, *No Easy Choice: Political Participation in Developing Countries* (Cambridge: Harvard University Press, 1976).

61   The sum of these figures exceeds 100 percent because voters could give more than one answer to the question, "Why did you vote for him (her)?" See Hu Fu, "Voters' Orientation Towards Political Issues: An Analysis of Structure, Type and Practice" (in Chinese), *Journal of Social Science* (National Taiwan University, Taipei) 34 (June 1986).

62   Wei, "March Towards a Stable, Harmonious and Innovative Society."

63   Pye, *Asian Power and Politics*, 233.

64   Gold, *State and Society in the Taiwan Miracle*, 132.

65   Samuel Huntington suggested that the particular conjunctions of circumstances that created the world's democracies are not likely to be repeated. See his "Will More Countries Become Democratic?," *Political Quarterly* 99 (September 1984): 193–218.

66   Robert Dahl, *Polyarchy: Participation and Opposition* (New Haven: Yale University Press, 1971), 36.

Chapter 9

*   Reprinted from *Confucian Traditions in East Asian Modernity: Moral Education and Economic Culture in Japan and the Four Mini-Dragons*, edited by Tu Wei-Ming, Cambridge, Mass.: Harvard University Press, Copyright © 1996 by the American Academy of Arts & Sciences.

1   Pye writes: "This new challenge is that of analyzing and explaining the crisis of authoritarianism that during the last decade has been sweeping the world, bringing into question both the legitimacy and the competence of all manner of authoritarian systems." Lucian W. Pye, "Political Science and the Crisis of Authoritarianism," *American Political Science Review* 84.1 (March 1990): 3.

2   Ernest Gellner, "Democracy and Industrialization," in S. N. Eisenstadt (ed.), *Readings in Social Evolution and Development* (New York: Pergamon Press, 1970), 247.

3   John Dunn, *Western Political Theory in the Face of the Future* (Cambridge: Cambridge University Press, 1979), 2.

4   Ibid., 11.

5   For a detailed analysis of institutional Confucianism, see Ambrose Y. C. King, "The Role of Political Tradition in the Evolution of Democracy in China: Continuity and Change" (Paper presented at the International Conference on the Evolution of Democracy in China, jointly sponsored by the Pacific Cultural Foundation and the Carnegie Council on Ethics and International Affairs, New York, December 13–15, 1989).

6   Benjamin I. Schwartz, "The Primacy of Political Order in East Asian Societies: Some Preliminary Generalizations," in Stuart R. Schram (ed.), *Foundations and Limits of State Power in China* (Hong Kong: The Chinese University Press, 1987), 1.

7   Ibid., 2.

8   Max Weber, *The Religion of China*, trans. H. H. Gerth (New York: Free Press, 1964), 31.

9   Schwartz, "The Primacy of Political Order," 3.

10   Weber, *The Religion of China*, 31.

11   See Leon Vandermeesch, "An Enquiry into the Chinese Conception of the Law," in Stuart R. Schram (ed.), *The Scope of State Power in China* (Hong Kong: The Chinese University Press, 1985), 3–25.

12   Lucian Pye, *Asian Power and Politics: The Cultural Dynamics of Authority* (Cambridge, MA: Harvard University Press, 1985), 27.

13   Tilemann Grimm, "State and Power in Juxtaposition: An Assessment of Ming Despotism," in Schram, *The Scope of State Power in China*, 39.

14   Xu Fuguan, *Liang Han sixiang shi* [The thought of two Han dynasties] (Taipei: Xuesheng shuju, 1978), 257–58.

15   Jacques Gernet, "Introduction," in Schram, *The Scope of State Power in China*, xxxii.

16   Ch'ien Mu, *Guoshi xin lun* [New treatise on Chinese history] (Hong Kong: privately printed, 1953), 34.

17   Tu Wei-ming, "A Confucian Perspective on the Rise of Industrial East Asia," *Bulletin of the American Academy of Arts and Sciences* 43.6 (March 1990): 41.

18   Karl Bunger, "Concluding Remarks on Two Aspects of the Chinese Unitary State as Compared with the European State System," in Schram, *Foundations and Limits of State Power in China*, 316.

19   Chang Hao, "Neo-Confucian Moral Thought and Its Modern Legacy," *Journal of Asian Studies* 39.2 (February 1980): 260.

20 See Michael Loewe, "Attempts at Economic Co-ordination during the Western Han Dynasty," in Schram, *The Scope of State Power in China*, 239–42.

21 Ibid.

22 See S. N. Eisenstadt, *The Political System of Empires* (New York: Free Press, 1969), 365–68, 370.

23 See A. Doak Barnett, *Cadres, Bureaucracy, and Political Power in Communist China* (New York: Columbia University Press, 1967), 428–29.

24 Weber, *The Religion of China*, 95–96.

25 Ibid., 16.

26 Ibid., 13.

27 Thomas Metzger argues that the "political center" in imperial China was rather an "inhibited" one. See Thomas A. Metzger, "The Ideological Context of Modernization in the Republic of China" (Paper presented at the Eighteenth Sino-American Conference, Hoover Institution, Stanford University, June 8–11, 1989).

28 *Neil H. Jacoby, U.S. Aid to Taiwan: A Study of Foreign Aid, Self-Help, and Development (New York: Frederick A. Praeger, 1966), 11.*

29 See Hung-chao Tai, "The Kuomintang and Modernization in Taiwan," in S. P. Huntington and C. H. Moore (eds.), *Authoritarian Politics in Modern Society: The Dynamics of Established One-Party Systems* (New York: Basic Books, 1970), 424–33.

30 See Ambrose Y. C. King, *Zhongguo minzhu de kunjing yu fazhan* [The predicament and development of Chinese democracy] (Taipei: China Times Publishing Company, 1984), 206.

31 Roy Hofheinz, Jr., and Kent E. Calder, *The Eastasia Edge* (New York: Basic Books, 1982), viii.

32 Talcott Parsons, *Structure and Process in Modern Societies* (New York: Free Press, 1960), 116.

33 Alice H. Amsden, "The State and Taiwan's Economic Development," in Peter B. Evans, Dietrich Rueschemeyer, and Theda Skocpol (eds.), *Bringing the State Back In* (Cambridge: Cambridge University Press, 1985), 99.

34 See Ying-shih Yu, "Sun Yat-sen's Doctrine and Traditional Chinese Culture," in Chu-yüan Cheng (ed.), *Sun Yat-sen's Doctrine in the Modern World* (Boulder, CO: Westview Press, 1989), 79–102.

35 See A. James Gregor and Maria Hsia Chang, "The Thought of Sun Yat-

sen in Comparative Perspective," in Cheng, *Sun Yat-sen's Doctrine in the Modern World*, 130–31.

36 See Herbert H. Ma, "Republic of China," in L. W. Beer (ed.), *Constitutionalism in Asia* (Berkeley: University of California Press, 1979), 39–49.

37 Chu-yüan Cheng, "The Doctrine of People's Welfare: The Taiwan Experiment and Its Implications for the Third World," in Cheng, *Sun Yat-sen's Doctrine in the Modern World*, 253.

38 See John C. H. Fei, Gustor Ranis, and Shirley Guo, *Growth with Equity: The Taiwan Case* (New York: Oxford University Press, 1979).

39 Schwartz, "The Primacy of Political Order," 7.

40 Lo Fang-chi, *Lun si xiaolong* [On the Four Mini-Dragons] (Hong Kong: Wide Angle Press, 1988), 32.

41 K. T. Li and M. C. Chen, *Zhonghua minguo zhengzhi fazhan celue de quan mian fenxi* [A complete analysis of the developmental strategies of the economy of the Republic of China] (Taipei: Lianjing chuban shiye gongsi, 1987), 156.

42 Chiang Kai-shek, *Statement to All Members of the Kuomintang, September 1949* (Taipei: Chinese Cultural Services, 1954), 22–23.

43 The development policies of the modernizing technocrats have been criticized for being based on instrumental rationality and neglecting other normative value issues. See C. S. Chen, *Guojia zhengce ji qi pipan de gonglun* [Public discourse on national policies and its critique] (Taipei: Center of National Policy Studies, 1988).

44 See Samuel P. S. Ho, *Economic Development of Taiwan* (New Haven: Yale University Press, 1978), 116–20.

45 *Guofu zhuanji* [The collected works of Sun Yat-sen], rev. ed. (Taipei: Kuomintang Central Executive Committee, 1981), 1:517.

46 Hung-chao Tai, "The Kuomintang and Modernization in Taiwan," 431.

47 U.S. Comptroller General, "Report to the Congress of the United States: Examination of Economic and Technical Assistance Program for the Government of Republic of China (Taiwan), Fiscal Years 1955–1957," mimeographed (August 1958), 22; quoted ibid.

48 Jacoby, *U.S. Aid to Taiwan*, 137–38.

49 Chu-yüan Cheng, "The Doctrine of People's Welfare," 252.

50 The relationship between type of political system and economic growth is discussed in Stephan Haggard, *Pathways from the Periphery: The Politics of Growth in the Newly Industrializing Countries* (Ithaca, NY: Cornell University Press, 1990), 254–70.

51   John Minxien Lee, "Political Change in Taiwan, 1949–1974: A Study of the Processes of Democratic and Integrative Change with Focus on the Role of Government" (PhD diss., University of Tennessee, 1975), 211.

52   Amsden, "The State and Taiwan's Economic Development," 101.

53   Ibid.

54   See Wei Yung, *Xiang wending hexie ji chuangjian de shehui maijin* [March toward a stable, harmonious, and innovative society: an analysis of the trend of political development based on the results of six public opinion surveys]. Republic of China, government publication (May 5, 1986).

55   Thomas Gold, *State and Society in the Taiwan Miracle* (New York: M. E. Sharpe, 1986), 90.

56   Hsiao Hsin-huang, "Development, Class Transformation, Social Movements and the Changing State-Society Relations in Taiwan" (Paper presented at the Eighteenth Sino-American Conference, Hoover Institute, Stanford University, June 8–11, 1989).

57   Alfred Stepan, "State Power and the Strength of Civil Society in the Southern Cone of Latin America," in Evans, Rueschemeyer, and Skocpol, *Bringing the State Back In*, 337.

58   Thomas Gold writes: "In retrospect, the Chung-li Incident offers a unique key to understanding both the success and the shortcomings of Taiwan's development strategy wherein a strong authoritarian state guides and participates in rapid economic growth while suppressing the political activities of the social forces it has generated in the process." Gold, *State and Society in the Taiwan Miracle*, 3.

59   Ramon H. Myers, "Political Theory and Recent Political Developments in the Republic of China," *Asian Survey* 27.9 (1987): 1003–22.

60   A comprehensive discussion of the reasons for these social movements can be found in Mau-kuai Michael Chang, *Shehui yundong ji zhengzhi zhuanhua* [Social movements and political transformation] (Taipei: Center of National Policy Studies, 1989), 20–45.

61   *Zhongyang ribao* [The Central Daily] (November 12, 1986), 2; translated in Myers, "Political Theory," 1007.

62   Hu Fu and You Ying-long, "Xuanmin de toupiao dongji" [The voting motives of the electorate], *Journal of Social Science* (Taipei) 33 (October 1985): 1–34.

63   Hu Fu, "Minzhong zhengzhi canyu de taidu" [The people's attitudes toward political participation] (Paper presented at the Symposium on

Basic Research on Taiwan's Social Change, organized by Academia Sinica and National Taiwan University, Taipei, August 28–30, 1987).

64   Metzger, "The Ideological Context of Modernization," 15.

65   Ibid. Also consult Thomas Metzger, "The Chinese Reconciliation of Moral-Sacred Values with Modern Pluralism: Political Discourse in the ROC, 1949–1989," in Ramon H. Myers (ed.), *Two Societies in Opposition: The Republic of China and the People's Republic of China after Forty Years* (Stanford: Hoover Institution Press, 1991), 10.

66   Pye, *Asian Power and Politics*, 245–46.

67   Daniel Bell, "American Exceptionalism Revisited: The Role of a Civil Society," *Dialogue* 1 (1990): 9–14. Bertrand Badie and Pierre Birnbaum consider the United States together with Great Britain as prime examples of "government by civil society," characterized by "the relative weakness of the state and the relatively low level of state autonomy." Bertrand Badie and Pierre Birnbaum, *The Sociology of the State*, trans. A. Goldhammer (Chicago: University of Chicago Press, 1983), 129.

68   Gernet, "Introduction," xxxii.

69   Bunger, "Concluding Remarks on Two Aspects of the Chinese Unitary State," 319.

70   Schram, *Foundations and Limits of State Power in China*, 322–23.

71   See Ambrose Y. C. King, "Max Weber and the Question of Development of the Modern State in China" (Paper presented at the International Conference on Max Weber and the Modernization of China, sponsored by the Institut fur Soziologie der Universität Heidelberg, Bad Homburg, Germany, July 23–27, 1990), i.e., Chapter 11 of this book.

72   Metzger and Myers, *Two Societies*, xxiv.

Chapter 10

*   Reprinted from *Confucian Traditions in East Asian Modernity: Moral Education and Economic Culture in Japan and the Four Mini-Dragons*, edited by Tu Wei-Ming, Cambridge, Mass.: Harvard University Press, Copyright © 1996 by the American Academy of Arts & Sciences.

1   See Peter L. Berger, "Secularity—West and East" (Paper presented at the Kokugakuin University Centennial Symposium on Cultural Identity and Modernization in Asian Countries, September 11–13, 1983).

2   See Edward A. Tiryakian (ed.), *The Global Crisis: Sociological Analyses and Responses* (Leiden: E.J. Brill, 1984).

3   See Ezra Vogel, *Japan as Number One* (Cambridge, MA: Harvard University Press, 1979); Roy Hofbeinz, Jr., and Kent E. Calder, *The Eastasia Edge* (New York: Basic Books, 1982).

4   Vogel, *Japan as Number One*; Hofheinz and Calder, *The East Asia Edge*.

5   See Herman Kahn, *World Economic Development: 1979 and Beyond* (London: Croom Helm, 1979); S. G. Redding and G. L. Hicks, "The Story of the East-Asia Economic Miracle: Part II: The Culture Connection," *Euro-Asia Business Review* 2.4 (1983): 18–22; S. G. Redding and G. L. Hicks, *Culture, Causation, and Chinese Management* (Hong Kong: Department of Management Studies, University of Hong Kong, 1983).

6   Thomas A. Metzger, *Escape from Predicament* (New York: Columbia University Press, 1977), 235.

7   Talcott Parsons, "Some Reflections on the Institutional Framework of Economic Development," in Talcott Parsons (ed.), *Structure and Process in Modern Societies* (New York: Free Press, 1960), 99.

8   Ibid., 102ff.; Robert Bellah, "Reflection on the Protestant Ethic and Modernization," in S. N. Eisenstadt (ed.), *The Protestant Ethic and Modernization: A Comparative View* (New York: Basic Books, 1968), 245–47.

9   See Yu-sheng Lin, *The Crisis of Chinese Consciousness: Radical Anti-Traditionalism in the May Fourth Era* (Madison: University of Wisconsin Press, 1979).

10 Lucian W. Pye, *Asian Power and Politics: The Cultural Dimension of Authority* (Cambridge, MA: Harvard University Press, 1985), 56.

11 See C. K. Yang, "Introduction," in Max Weber, *The Religion of China: Confucianism and Taoism* (New York: Free Press, 1968), xiii–xliii.

12 See S. N. Eisenstadt, "The Protestant Ethic Thesis in an Analytical and Comparative Framework," in Eisenstadt, *The Protestant Ethic and Modernization*, 7–8.

13 Ibid., 8.

14 Stephen Boyden et al., *The Ecology of a City and Its People* (Canberra: Australian National University Press, 1981), 123–25.

15 See M. H. Bond and A. Y. C. King, "Coping with the Threat of Westernization in Hong Kong," *International Journal of Intercultural Relations* 9 (1986): 351–64.

16 See Robert J. Lifton, "Cultural Perspectives: The Fate of Filial Piety," in *Thought Reform and the Psychology of Totalism* (New York: Penguin Books, 1961), Chapter 19, 410–22.

17   See R. E. Mitchell, *Family Life in Urban Hong Kong*, 2 vols. (Taipei: Orient Cultural Service, 1972).

18   S. K. Lau, "Utilitarianistic Familism: The Basis of Political Stability," in Y. C. King and Rance P. L. Lee (eds.), *Social Life and Development in Hong Kong* (Hong Kong: The Chinese University Press, 1981), 204.

19   Marion J. Levy, *The Family Revolution in Modern China* (Cambridge, MA: Harvard University Press, 1949), 345.

20   Ambrose Y. C. King and Peter J. Man, "The Role of Small Factory in Economic Development," in Tzong-biau Lin, Rance P. L. Lee, and Udo-Ernst Simonis (eds.), *Hong Kong: Economic, Social, and Political Studies in Development* (White Plains, NY: M. E. Sharpe, 1979), 31–63.

21   V. F. S. Sit, S. L. Wong, and T. S. Kiang, *Small Industry in a Laissez-Faire Economy: A Hong Kong Case Study* (Hong Kong: Centre of Asian Studies, University of Hong Kong, 1979), 353.

22   Victor Mok, *The Organization and Management in Kwun Tong* (Hong Kong: Social Research Centre, Chinese University Press, 1974), 48.

23   J. L. Espy, "The Strategy of Chinese Industrial Enterprise in Hong Kong" (B.A. thesis, Harvard University, 1970), 174.

24   *Weber, The Religion of China, 236.*

25   Ibid., 236–37.

26   C. K. Yang, "Introduction," in Weber, *The Religion of China*, xxvi.

27   S. N. Eisenstadt, "This Worldly Transcendentalism and the Structuring of the World: Weber's 'Religion of China' and the Format of Chinese History and Civilization," in Andreas E. Buss (ed.), *Max Weber in Asian Studies* (Leiden: E.J. Brill, 1985), 48.

28   *Boyden et al., The Ecology of a City and Its People, 47.*

29   *Weber, The Religion of China, 242.*

30   James Hayes, "Hong Kong: Tale of Two Cities," in Marjorie Topley (ed.), *Hong Kong: The Interaction of Tradition and Life in the Towns* (Hong Kong: Hong Kong Branch of the Royal Asiatic Society, 1975), 3.

31   Maurice Freedman, "The Family in China, Past and Present," in G. W. Skinner (ed.), *The Study of Chinese Society: Essays by Maurice Freedman* (Stanford: Stanford University Press, 1979), 250.

32   E. J. Ryan, "The Value System of a Chinese Community in Java" (PhD diss., Harvard University, 1961); quoted in Gordon Redding and Gilbert Y. Y. Wong, "The Psychology of Chinese Organizational Behaviour," in Michael H. Bond (ed.), *The Psychology of the Chinese People* (Hong Kong: Oxford University Press, 1986), 267–95.

33   Weber, *The Religion of China*, 245–46.

34   Boyden et al., *The Ecology of a City and Its People*, 284.

35   See W. L. Chau and W. K. Chan, "A Study of Job Satisfaction of Workers in Local Factories of Chinese, Western, and Japanese Ownership," *Hong Kong Manager* 20 (1984): 9–14.

36   Reinhard Bendix, *Max Weber: An Intellectual Portrait* (New York: Anchor Books, 1962), 116–19.

37   Weber, *The Religion of China*, 135.

38   See D. C. McClelland, "Motivational Patterns in Southeast Asia with Special Reference to the Chinese Case," *Journal of Social Issues* 19 (1963): 6–19.

39   David Y. F. Ho, "Chinese Patterns of Socialization: A Critical Review," in Bond, *The Psychology of the Chinese People*, 25.

40   Boyden et al., *The Ecology of a City and Its People*, 295.

41   In his small-scale study of occupational prestige in Hong Kong, R. L. Moore finds that "shipping magnate" and "commercial manager" top the list, ahead of "colonial secretary" and "professor." See R. L. Moore, "Modernization and Westernization in Hong Kong: Patterns of Cultural Change in an Urban Setting" (PhD diss., University of California, Riverside, 1981); quoted in Wong Siu-lun, "Modernization and Sinic Tradition: Reflections on the Case of Hong Kong" (Paper presented at the Twenty-fifth Annual Meeting of the American Association for Chinese Studies, Santa Barbara, November 4–6, 1983).

42   S. L. Alatas, "Religion and Modernization in Southeast Asia," in Hans-Dieter Evers (ed.), *Modernization in South-East Asia* (London: Oxford University Press, 1973), 163.

43   By "withdrawal of status respect" Hagen means that in a transition from a traditional state to one of continuing economic development, an important factor initiating change is a historical shift that causes some groups that previously had a respected place in the social hierarchy to feel that they are no longer valued. See Everett E. Hagen, *On the Theory of Social Change* (Homewood, IL: Dorsey Press, 1962).

44   *Boyden et al., The Ecology of a City and Its People*, 57.

45   King and Man, "The Role of Small Factory in Economic Development," 54.

46   S. K. Lau, "Employment Relations in Hong Kong: Traditional Modern?," in Lin et al., *Hong Kong: Economic, Social, and Political Studies in Development*, 77.

47   Wong Siu-lun, "Modernization and Sinic Tradition," 5–15.

48   Freedman, "The Family in China, Past and Present," 242.

49   B. F. Hoselitz, "Economic Growth and Development: Non-Economic Factors in Economic Development," in Jason L. Findle and Richard W. Goble (eds.), *Political Development and Social Change* (New York: John Wiley and Sons, 1966), 190–91.

50   See Bond and King, "Coping with the Threat of Westernization in Hong Kong," 362.

51   Marjorie Topley, "Some Basic Conceptions and Their Traditional Relationship to Society," in Marjorie Topley (ed.), *Some Traditional Chinese Ideas and Conceptions in Hong Kong Social Life Today* (Hong Kong: Hong Kong Branch of the Royal Asiatic Society, 1966), 19.

52   Lau, "Utilitarianistic Familism," 201.

53   S. K. Lau, "Chinese Familism in an Urban-Industrial Setting: The Case of Hong Kong," *Journal of Marriage and the Family* 43.4 (November 1981): 990.

54   The new familial utilitarian values presented in this chapter existed mainly among distant relatives. The relationships among close family members are based more on affective bonds than on instrumental considerations.

Chapter 11

*   Reprinted from Ambrose Y. C. King, "Max Weber and the Question of Development of the Modern State in China" (Paper presented at the International Conference on Max Weber and the Modernization of China, sponsored by the Institut fur Soziologie, Der Universität Heidelberg, Bad Homburg, Germany, July 23–27, 1990).

1   Thomas A. Metzger, *Escape from Predicament* (New York: Columbia University Press, 1977), 235.

2   Lucian W. Pye writes: "We are today confronted with a unifying challenge in the crisis of authoritarianism that is undermining the legitimacy of all types of authoritarian systems throughout the world, including the Marxist-Leninist regimes. See his "Political Science and the Crisis of Authoritarianism," *American Political Science Review* 84.1 (March 1990): 3–19.

3   Alice H. Amsden, "The State and Taiwan's Economic Development," in P. B. Evans, O. Rueschemeyer, and T. Skocpol (eds.), *Bring the State Back In* (Cambridge: Cambridge University Press, 1985), 101.

4   Ambrose Y. C. King, "A Non-paradigmatic Search for Democracy in a
     Post-Confucian Culture: The Case of Taiwan, R.O.C." (Paper presented
     at the Conference on Political Culture and Democracy in Developing
     Countries, Hoover Institution, Stanford University, September 14–17,
     1988).

5   Theda Skocpol, "Bring the State Back In: Strategies of Analysis in Cur-
     rent Research," *Bring the State Back In*, 3–43.

6   Bertrand Badie and Pierre Birnbaum, *The Sociology of the State*, trans. A.
     Goldhammer (Chicago: The University of Chicago Press, 1983), 17.

7   Anthony Giddens, *The Class Structure of the Advanced Societies* (Lon-
     don: Hutchinson University Library, 1973), 125.

8   Wolfgang Schluchter, *Rationalism, Religion and Domination: A Webe-
     rian Perspective*, trans. N. Solomon (Berkeley: University of California
     Press, 1989),439.

9   Badie and Birnbaum, *The Sociology of the State*, 20.

10   Wolfgang Schluchter, *The Rise by Western Rationalism: Max Weber's
     Developmental History*, trans. G. Roth (Berkeley: University of Califor-
     nia Press, 1981), 109.

11   Ibid., 110.

12   Reinhard Bendix, *An Intellectual Portrait* (New York: Doubleday & Co.
     Anchor Books, 1962), 478.

13   Ibid., 494.

14   David Beetham, *Max Weber and the Theory of Modern Politics* (Cam-
     bridge: Polity Press, 1985), 15–16.

15   Peter L. Berger, "Secularity—West and East," Kokugakuin University
     Centennial Symposium on Cultural Identity and Modernization in Asian
     Countries (September 11–13, 1983).

16   Max Weber, *The Religion of China*, trans. H. H. Gerth (New York: The
     Free Press, 1964), 104, 238, 247.

17   Byran Turner, *For Weber* (London: Routledge and Kegan Paul, 1978),
     54.

18   C. K. Yang's Introduction to Max Weber's, *The Religion of China*, xx.

19   Wolfgang Schluchter, *Rationalism, Religion and Domination: A Webe-
     rian Perspective*, trans. N. Solomon (Berkeley: University of California
     Press, 1989), 110.

20   Weber, *The Religion of China*, 100.

21   The concept of "Institutional Confucianism" was elaborated at length in
     my paper, "The Role of Political Tradition in the Evolution of Democ-

racy in China: Continuity and Change in Institutional Confucianism" (Paper presented at the International Conference on Evolution of Democracy in China, jointly sponsored by the Pacific Cultural Foundation R.O.C. and The Carnegie Council on Ethics and International Affairs, USA, December 13–15, 1989, New York).

22   Weber, *The Religion of China*, 91.

23   Ibid., 93.

24   Ibid., 95.

25   Ibid., 96.

26   Ibid., 62.

27   Xu Fuguan, *The Thought of Two Han Dynasties* (in Chinese) (Taipei: Hseuch Shen Publishers, 1978), 142, 152.

28   Ibid., 154.

29   Weber, *The Religion of China*, 44–45.

30   Ibid., 138.

31   Yu Ying-shih, *The Modern Interpretation of the Chinese Intellectual Tradition* (in Chinese) (Taipei: Lien-Ching Publishers, 1987), 267–68.

32   H. G. Creel, *Confucius and the Chinese Way* (New York: Harper & Brother, Harper Torchbooks, 1960), 236–48.

33   Yu Ying-shih, *History and Thought* (in Chinese) (Taipei: Lien-Ching Publishers, 1976), 50.

34   Quoted in S. R. Schram, "Party Leaders or True Ruler? Foundations and Significance of Mao Zedong's Personal Power," in S. R. Schram (ed.), *Foundations and Limits of State Power in China* (Hong Kong: The Chinese University Press, 1987), 227.

35   Benjamin I. Schwartz, *The World of Thought in Ancient China* (Cambridge, MA: Harvard University Press, 1985), 413.

36   Benjamin I. Schwartz, "The Primacy of Political Order in East Asian Societies: Some Preliminary Generalizations," in S. R. Schram (ed.), *Foundations and Limits of State Power in China* (Hong Kong: The Chinese University Press, 1987), 2.

37   Weber, *The Religion of China*, 39.

38   Ibid., 31.

39   Quoted in Anthony Hulsewe: "The Influence of the "Legalist Government of Qin on the Economy as Reflected in the Texts Discovered in Yunmang Country," in S. R. Schram (ed.), *The Scope of State Power in China* (Hong Kong: The Chinese University Press, 1985), 216–17.

40   Weber, *The Religion of China*, 142–43.

41 Lin Yu-Sheng, "Reluctance to Modernize: The Influence of Confucianism on China's Search for Political Modernity," in Joseph P. L. Jiang (ed.), *Confucianism and Modernization: A Symposium* (Taipei: Freedom House, 1987), 25.

42 Schwartz, *The World of Thought in Ancient China*, 414.

43 Weber, *The Religion of China*, 235.

44 S. N. Eisenstadt, *The Political System of Empires* (New York: Free Press, 1969), 365–68, 370.

45 Thomas A. Metzger, "The Ideological Context of Modernization in the Republic of China" (Paper presented at the 18th Sino-American Conference, June 8–11, 1989, Hoover Institution, Stanford University), 12–13.

46 Weber, *The Religion of China*, 13.

47 Ibid., 15.

48 Ibid., 16.

49 Etienne Balazs, *Chinese Civilization and Bureaucracy*, trans. H. M. Wright (New Haven: Yale University Press, 1964), 13–27.

50 Weber, *The Religion of China*, xxiii, 100, 103; Wolfgang Schluchter, *Rationalism, Religion and Domination: A Weberian Perspective*, 356.

51 Weber, *The Religion of China*, 48.

52 Ibid., C. K. Yang's "Introduction," xxiii; Schluchter, *Rationalism, Religion and Domination*, 356.

53 Weber, *The Religion of China*, 95.

54 Ibid., 48.

55 Schluchter, *Rationalism, Religion and Domination*, 354.

56 Weber, *The Religion of China*, 248.

57 Schluchter, *Rationalism, Religion and Domination*, 360.

58 Weber, *The Religion of China*, 236.

59 Ibid., C. K. Yang's "Introduction," xxi.

60 Ibid., 102.

61 Tung-Tsu Chu [Tongzu Qu], *Law and Society in Traditional China* (Mouton: The Hague, Netherlands, 1961).

62 Schluchter, *Rationalism, Religion and Domination*, 111, 361.

63 Franz Schurmann, "Chinese Society," *International Encyclopedia of Social Sciences* (MacMillan, 1968), 2:414.

64 John K. Fairbank, *The United States and China* (Cambridge, MA: Harvard University Press, 4th ed., 1976), 220.

65 Tang Tsou, "Marxism, the Leninist Party, the Masses, and the Citizens in the Rebuilding of the Chinese State," in S. R. Schram (ed.), *Foundations*

and Limits of State Power in China (Hong Kong: The Chinese University Press, 1987), 259.

66   Reinhard Bendix, *Kings or People* (Berkeley: University of California Press, 1978), 602.

67   Bendix argues that the French Revolution has made the people or the nation the basis of all authority. Ibid., 596.

68   Franz Schurmann, *Ideology of Organization in Communist China* (Berkeley: University of California Press, 1970 [enlarged edition 1970]), 7.

69   Ibid., 8.

70   Ezra Vogel, *Canton Under Communism 1949–1968* (New York: Harper Torchbook, 1969), 350–56.

71   Tang Tsou, *The Cultural Revolution and Post-Mao Reforms* (Chicago: University of Chicago Press, 1986), xxii, 54.

72   Schurmann, *Ideology of Organization in Communist China*, 496.

73   Samuel P. Huntington, *Political Order in Changing Societies* (New Haven: Yale University Press, 1968), 342.

74   Consult Wolfgang J. Mommsen, *The Age of Bureaucracy* (Oxford: Basil Blackwell, 1974), 59.

75   Ambrose Y. C. King, "A Voluntarist Model of Organization," *The British Journal of Sociology* 28.3 (September 1977): 363–74.

76   Ambrose Y. C. King, "In Defense of Bureaucracy: The De-radicalization of Taoism," in J. F. Jones (ed.), *Building China* (Hong Kong: The Chinese University Press, 1980), 113–26.

77   Schluchter, *Rationalism, Religion and Domination*, 111, 365.

78   Ibid., 234.

79   Ibid., 373, 385.

80   Mommsen, *The Age of Bureaucracy*, 93–94.

81   Ibid., 91.

82   Consult Schluchter, *Rationalism, Religion and Domination*, 390–91.

83   Ibid., 391.

84   Among the contemporary social theorists, Habermas probably has given the most powerful defense of the "project of modernity." He takes a position that what has been happening in the modern society, is a "selective" process of rationalization, in other words, there are alternative possibilities. Hebermas's complex arguments can be found in two volumes of his *The Theory of Communicative Action*, trans. Thomas McCarthy

(Boston: Beacon Press, 1987). Also consult Richard J. Bernstein (ed.), *Habermas and Modernity* (Oxford: Basil Blackwell, 1985).

85   Alvin Gouldner, *The Two Marxisms* (New York: Oxford University Press, 1980), 371.

Chapter 12

*   Reprinted from *Justice and Democracy: Cross-Cultural Perspectives*, edited by Ron Bontekoe and Marietta Stepaniants, Honolulu, HI: University of Hawai'i Press, Copyright © 1997 by the University of Hawai'i Press.

1   Marc F. Plattner, "The Democratic Moment," *Journal of Democracy* (Fall 1991):40.

2   Samuel Huntington, "Democracy's Third Wave," *Journal of Democracy* (Spring1991): 12.

3   Francis Fukuyama, "The End of History?," *The National Interest* (Summer 1989): 3–18.

4   Francis Fukuyama, *The End of History and the Last Man* (New York: Free Press, 1992), 45.

5   Raymond D. Gastil, "What Kind of Democracy," *Dialogue* 1 (1991): 10.

6   Leszek Kolakowski, "Uncertainties of a Democratic Age," in Larry Diamond and Marc F. Platter (eds.), *The Global Resurgence of Democracy* (Baltimore: Johns Hopkins University Press, 1993), 321–24.

7   Charles S. Maier, "Democracy and Its Discontents," *Foreign Affairs* (July 1984): 54.

8   Louis Hartz, "Democracy: Image and Reality," in N. N. Chambers and R. H. Salisbury (eds.), *Democracy Today* (New York: Collins Books, 1962), 42.

9   Ken Jowitt, "The New World Disorder," *Journal of Democracy* (July 1992): 1617.

10   John Dun, *Western Political Theory in the Face of the Future* (Cambridge: Cambridge University Press, 1979), 11.

11   E. Gellner, "Democracy and Industrialization," in S. N. Eisenstadt (ed.), *Readings in Social Evolution and Future* (Cambridge: Cambridge University Press, 1979), 2.

12   David Held (ed.), *Prospects for Democracy: North, South, East, West* (Cambridge: Polity Press, 1993), 14.

13 David Beetham, "Liberal Democracy and the Limits of Democratization," in Held (ed.), *Prospects for Democracy*, 60.

14 See Roland Robertson, "After Nostalgia: Willful Nostalgia and the Phases of Globalization," in B. S. Turner (ed.), *Theories of Modernity and Post-Modernity* (London: Sage Publications, 1990), 45–61.

15 *Asian Wall Street Journal (June 1, 1994).*

16 B. I. Schwartz, "Culture, Modernity and Nationalism—Further Reflections," *Daedalus* (Summer 1993): 207.

17 Charles Taylor, "Inwardness and the Culture of Modernity," in Alex Honneth, Thomas MaCarthy, Claus Offe, and Albrecht Wellmer (eds.), *Philosophical Interventions in the Unfinished Project of Enlightenment* trans. William Rehg (Cambridge: MIT Press, 1992), 88–110.

18 Consult G. P. Macpherson, *The Life and Times of Liberal Democracy* (Oxford: Oxford University Press, 1977).

19 Gastil, "What Kind of Democracy,"13.

20 Consult Reinhard Bendix, *Kings or People* (Berkeley: University of California Press, 1978). Karl Popper saw Athenian democracy as the classical form of democracy, in which one encounters the rule of the people as such, though he by no means endorsed it. See "Popper on Democracy: The Open Society and its Enemies Revisited," *The Economist* (April 23, 1988), 23–26.

21 Gastil, "What Kind of Democracy," 12.

22 Bhikhu Parekh, "Cultural Particularity of Liberal Democracy," in Held (ed.), *Prospects for Democracy*, 157.

23 Schwartz, "Culture, Modernity and Nationalism," 215.

24 S. N. Eisenstadt, "Cultural Tradition, Historical Experience, and Social Change: The Limits of Convergence," in *The Tanner Lectures on Human Values*, Vol. XI (Salt Lake City: University of Utah Press, 1990), 503.

25 Parekh, "Cultural Particularity of Liberal Democracy," 172.

26 J. Dun, *Western Political Theory in the Face of the Future*, 33.

27 David Riesman, "Egocentrism: Is the American Character Changing?," *Encounter* (August 1980): 21.

28 "A Whole Greater than Its Parts?," *Time* (February 25, 1991).

29 See Stanley Vittoz, "The Unresolved Partnership of Liberalism and Democracy in the American Political Tradition," in Department of History, The Chinese University of Hong Kong (ed.), *10 IOTOPIA* (Hong Kong: 1993), 282, 299.

30 Peter Berger, "An East Asian Development Model," in Peter L. Berger

and Michael Hsin-Huang Xiao (eds.), *In Search of an East Asian Development Model* (New Brunswick: Transaction Books, 1988), 4.

31   Max Weber, *The Religion of China: Confucianism and Taoism*, trans. H. H. Gerth (New York: Free Press, 1951).

32   A pertinent critique of Weber's work on Confucianism can be found in Thomas Metzger, *Escape from Predicament* (New York: Columbia University Press, 1977), 235ff.

33   I have argued elsewhere that Confucianism in traditional China should be conceptualized as "institutional Confucianism" in that Confucianism provided the ideological and institutional infrastructure of the imperial system. See Ambrose Y. C. King, *Zhongguo shehui yu wenhua* [Chinese society and culture] (Oxford: Oxford University Press, 1992), 110ff.

34   Roy Hofheinz, Jr., and Kent E. Calder, *The Eastasia Edge* (New York: Basic Books, 1982).

35   Peter Berger, "An East Asian Development Model," 5.

36   S. P. Huntington, "What Price Freedom?," *Harvard International Review* (Winter 1992–1993).

37   Seymour M. Lipset, "Some Social Requisites of Democracy: Economic Development and Political Legitimacy," *American Political Science Review* 53 (March1959): 80.

38   I have explored and analyzed elsewhere the plausible causes of democratization in Taiwan in a paper entitled "A Non-paradigmatic Search for Democracy in a Post-Confucian Culture: The Case of Taiwan, R.O.C." (i.e., Chapter 8 of this book), in Larry Diamond (ed.), *Political Culture and Democracy in Developing Countries* (Boulder: Lynne Rienner, 1993).

39   Milton Friedman writes: "History suggests only that capitalism is a necessary condition for political freedom," and he adds: "clearly it is not a sufficient condition." Milton Friedman, *Capitalism and Democracy* (Chicago: University of Chicago Press, 1962), 10.

40   F. Fukuyama, *The End of History and the Last Man*, 238.

41   *Time* (June 14, 1993), 17.

42   Gilbert Rozman, "The East Asian Region in Comparative Perspective," in G. Rozman (ed.), *The East Asian Region: Confucian Heritage and Its Modern Adaptation* (Princeton: Princeton University Press, 1991), 12.

43   Huntington, "Democracy's Third Wave,"18.

44   Ibid., 15, 21.

45   Ralph Miliband, "The Socialist Alternative," *Journal of Democracy* (July

1992): 119. For C. P. Macpherson, liberal democracy has two meanings: first, "the democracy of a capitalist market society," and second, "a society striving to ensure that all its members ate equally free to realize their capabilities." However, Macpherson was of the view that up until the 1970s "the market view has prevailed: 'liberal' has consciously or unconsciously been assumed to mean 'capitalist.'" Macpherson, *The Life and Times of Liberal Democracy* (Oxford: Oxford University Press, 1977), 1–2.

46   Seymour Martin Lipset, "The Centrality of Political Culture," in Larry Diamond and Marc F. Platter (eds.), *The Global Resurgence of Democracy* (Baltimore: Johns Hopkins University Press, 1993), 137.

47   Consult Rozman (ed.), *The East Asian Region*, 6.

48   Mou Zongsan, *Sheng dao yu zhi dao* (Taipei: Guangwen shuju, 1974).

49   Richard Solomon, *Mao's Revolution and the Chinese Political Culture* (Berkeley: University of California Press, 1971), 78–81.

50   Wm. Theodore de Bary, *The Liberal Tradition in China* (Hong Kong: The Chinese University Press, 1983).

51   Ambrose Y. C. King, *Zhongguo minben sixiang shi* (Taipei: Commercial Press, 1993). A somewhat negative version on *minben* can also be found in J. Nathan, *Chinese Democracy* (New York: Alfred A. Knopf, 1985), 127ff.

52   "A Roundtable Discussion of The Trouble with Confucianism by Wm. Theodore de Bary," *China Review International* (Spring 1994): 36–52.

53   Chang Hao, "Intellectual Crisis of Contemporary China in Historical Perspective," in Tu Wei-ming (ed.), *The Triadic Chord: Confucian Ethics, Industrial East Asia and Max Weber* (Singapore: The Institute of East Asian Philosophies, 1991), 325–50.

54   A brilliant and representative case study has been done by Benjamin Schwartz, *In Search of Wealth and Power: Yen Fu and the West* (New York: Hatper Torchbooks, 1964).

55   Ibid., 239–40.

56   Wang Ermin, *Wan Qing sheng zhi sixiang shi lun* (Taipei: Huashi chubanshe, 1969), 220–76.

57   King, *Zhongguo minben sixiang shi*.

58   Mou Zongsan, Xu Fuguan, Zhang Junli, and Tang Junyi, *Zhongguo wenhua yu shijie: wo dui zhongguo xueshu yanjiu ji Zhongguo wenhua yu shijie wenhua qiantu zhi gongtong renshi* (1958).

59   Chang Hao, "Intellectual Crisis of Contemporary China in Historical Perspective," 338.

60   Tu Wei-ming, *Confucian Ethics Today: The Singapore Challenge* (Singapore: Curriculum Development Institute of Singapore, 1984), 110–11.

61   Herbert Fingarette, *Confucius: The Secular as Sacred* (New York: Harper Torchbooks, 1972), 72–73.

62   Talcott Parsons defined modernity in terms of three inseparable dimensions: the market economy, democratic polity, and individualism, See Parsons, *The System of Modern Societies* (Englewood Cliffs: Prentice Hall, 1971), 14ff.

63   P. L. Berger, "An East Asian Development Model?," 6.

64   I have argued elsewhere that neither individualism nor collectivism can characterize the Confucian relationship between the individual and the group. I have instead advanced a view that the Confucian social theory adopts neither an individualistic nor a collectivistic but "relational" perspective. I wrote, "for good or bad, the Confucian relational perspective did provide the Chinese with a way of creating a long-standing social system in which the individual who is a relational being endowed with a self-centered autonomy, finds himself in a complicated and humanly rich relational web he could hardly afford to escape." See Ambrose Y. C. King, "The Individual and Group in Confucianism: A Relational Perspective" (i.e., Chapter 1 of this book), in Donald J. Munro (ed.), *Individualism and Holism: Studies in Confucian and Taoist Values* (Ann Arbor: University of Michigan Press, 1985), 65–66.

65   I am inspired here by the writings of Bhikhu Parekh, who argues for a political system that is "democratically liberal" rather than a liberal democracy. See his article cited above.

66   Tu Wei-ming points out that the mew Confucian ethic "does not oppose western ideas of rights, individual dignity, autonomy, or competitiveness in the healthy and dynamic sense." See Tu Wei-ming, *Confucian Ethics Today*, 111. One important task of the neo-Confucians' project is to assimilate the Confucian concept of self as having a Heaven-endowed inner nature to the German concept of freedom as focused on the idea of the moral development of the self and also to the Kantian idea of treating every individual person as an end. It is argued that "implied in these ideas of freedom are not so much the May Fourth's motion of democracy as an emancipatory institution as the conception of democracy as a participatory community of morally autonomous individuals." See Chang Hao, "Intellectual Crisis of Contemporary China in Historical Perspective," 339.

Index

MAJOR PUBLICATIONS IN CHINESE
BY AMBROSE YEO-CHI KING (金耀基)

《從傳統到現代》

《中國現代化的終極願景》

《中國的現代轉向》

《中國文明的現代轉型》

《中國社會與文化》

《中國政治與文化》

《社會學與中國研究》

《大學之理念》

《再思大學之道》

《劍橋語絲》

《海德堡語絲》

《敦煌語絲》